T0331074

# Sustainability Teaching for Impact

*Sustainability Teaching for Impact* is an essential step-by-step, practical guide for those wanting to inspire and engage higher education students in the areas of sustainability.

This book encourages new and experienced university teachers across disciplines to adopt and adapt dramatic methods, with a view to develop their teaching. It introduces applied drama and performance arts methods that have been tried-and-tested across disciplines to deepen and broaden sustainability knowledge, skills, mindsets, and practices. *Sustainability Teaching for Impact* assumes no previous experience of the methods, as university teachers – with and without experience in drama – carefully walk you through some of the teaching practices they have used to create an impact in their teaching.

This book is for higher and further education tutors who wish to build on their experience and deliver exciting and accessible classroom techniques and practices that are highly interactive, creative, and engaging to help further the teaching of sustainability.

**Tony Wall** is professor at Liverpool Business School, UK, National Teaching Fellow, and holds visiting professor positions at Stockholm University in Sweden and Phu Xuan University in Vietnam. His research is ranked #1 globally in 'management development' (Google Scholar) and his impact was independently judged as 'world leading' (REF, 2021).

**Eva Österlind** is professor in applied drama at Stockholm University, Sweden. She teaches drama in teacher education, leads a master's programme in drama and applied theatre, and supervises PhD students. Her current research focuses on the potential of drama for learning, especially in connection to Higher Education for Sustainable Development.

**Eva Hallgren**'s research focuses on process drama and role taking applied across different settings including preschools, schools, psychiatric wards, and teacher education. Questions about sustainability and power are always of interest to her. Eva also teaches Drama in Education at Stockholm University on different levels and supervises PhD students.

# Sustainability Teaching for Impact

## How to Inspire and Engage Students Using Drama

# Edited by Tony Wall, Eva Österlind and Eva Hallgren

Routledge
Taylor & Francis Group
LONDON AND NEW YORK

Designed cover image: Thanumporn Thongkongkaew / iStock / Getty Images Plus

First published 2025
by Routledge
4 Park Square, Milton Park, Abingdon, Oxon, OX14 4RN

and by Routledge
605 Third Avenue, New York, NY 10158

*Routledge is an imprint of the Taylor & Francis Group, an informa business*

This publication was supported by Liverpool Business School, Liverpool John Moores University, as part of its commitment to making sustainability learning accessible for all.

*British Library Cataloguing-in-Publication Data*
A catalogue record for this book is available from the British Library

*Library of Congress Cataloging-in-Publication Data*
Names: Wall, Tony, 1979– editor. | Österlind, Eva, editor. | Hallgren, Eva, editor.
Title: Sustainability teaching for impact : how to inspire and engage students using drama / edited by Tony Wall, Eva Österlind and Eva Hallgren.
Description: Abingdon, Oxon; New York, NY: Routledge, 2025. | Includes bibliographical references.
Identifiers: LCCN 2024035913 (print) | LCCN 2024035914 (ebook) |
ISBN 9781032803050 (hardback) | ISBN 9781032769301 (paperback) | ISBN 9781003496359 (ebook)
Subjects: LCSH: Drama in environmental education. | Environmental education. |
Sustainability—Study and teaching (Higher)
Classification: LCC GE70 .S878 2025 (print) | LCC GE70 (ebook) |
DDC 304.2071/1—dc23/eng/20241213
LC record available at https://lccn.loc.gov/2024035913
LC ebook record available at https://lccn.loc.gov/2024035914

ISBN: 978-1-032-80305-0 (hbk)
ISBN: 978-1-032-76930-1 (pbk)
ISBN: 978-1-003-49635-9 (ebk)

DOI: 10.4324/9781003496359

Typeset in Adobe Garamond
by codeMantra

# Contents

## PART 3

## PART 4

## PART 5

# Contributors

**Maribel Blasco** is an associate professor at Copenhagen Business School (CBS), Denmark. She teaches cultural awareness and conducts research on management education. She co-coordinates CBS Permahaven, a lifelong sustainability learning hub, inspired by permaculture thinking, where students and staff can learn about sustainability in practice, side by side with local residents.

**Kerstin Bragby.** For Kerstin, two decades of professional theatre and performance artistry have seamlessly transitioned into over 20 years of teaching and researching applied theatre and drama in academia and beyond. This is accompanied by a PhD in applied theatre and drama and a master's in biology.

**Leif Dahlberg** is a professor in communication at KTH Royal Institute of Technology, Sweden. He has previously served as the director of master's and doctoral programmes (at KTH) and has held visiting positions at Beijing Daxue (Peking University), Birkbeck College London, and Södertörn University. Dahlberg teaches media studies, intercultural communication, and critical theory.

**Kerstin Danckwardt-Lillieström** is a PhD student in Science Education at the Department of Teaching and Learning, Stockholm University, Sweden. Her research focuses on the use of drama in upper-secondary chemistry education.

**Tim Daw** is an associate professor in sustainability science at Stockholm University, Sweden. Tim is interested in innovative methodologies and has used interactive workshops, participatory scenarios, gaming, and modelling to collaboratively analyse coastal resource systems with a range of stakeholders from artisanal fishers and citizens to government decision-makers.

**Laura Dixon** is a principal lecturer at Liverpool Business School, UK. She trained as a social anthropologist with a focus on identitarian narratives within destination marketing and has most recently begun to use visual research methods to explore end-of-life care. She also specialises in block-teaching and intensive modes of delivery.

**Michelle Dyer** is an anthropologist focused on social and gender equity and the intersections of culture, power, and decision-making. She works with role play to give students an experiential cross-cultural learning experience without leaving the classroom, based on an event she participated in during research in Solomon Islands.

**Julia Fries** is a PhD student in applied drama at the Department of Teaching and Learning, Stockholm University, Sweden. Her research explores how drama can support learners to stretch their thinking beyond the current economic paradigm and imagine truly sustainable futures.

**Charlotte Gottfries** is a lecturer in drama in education/applied theatre in teacher training at Uppsala University, Sweden. She is a course leader of aesthetic courses in preschool teacher training, a drama teacher, an actor, and a director. She is also part-time touring as an actor in two theatre plays with Teater Essence.

**Viola Hakkarainen** is a sustainability scientist working with inter- and transdisciplinary knowledge processes, sustainability education, and biodiversity conservation. Her research interests centre on cultivating collaboration and advancing inclusivity within sustainability science and ecosystem governance. She adopts a critical approach with a focus on catalysing radical and just sustainability transformations.

**Kenneth Kang** is a senior lecturer at Liverpool John Moores University. Kenneth is interested in social theory and its application to current issues, in particular, international law's regulation of transboundary rivers and oceans.

**Mary Ann Kernan** is an emeritus professor in the School of Communication and Creativity, City St George's, University of London, UK. She serves on the Board of the Centre for Creativity in Professional Practice in the Bayes Business School.

**Oleksandra Khalaim** teaches various courses related to sustainability as well as supervising master's students at Uppsala University, Sweden. Her research includes sustainability initiatives and university outreach, eco-emotions (climate anxiety), and education for teachers on how to use applied drama and gaming techniques in sustainability teaching.

**Aysel Korkmaz** earned her bachelor's degree in Early Childhood Education from Hacettepe University in 2009. Beginning her academic career in 2011 as a research assistant at Yozgat Bozok University, she later served at Hacettepe University until 2020. Now an assistant professor at Yozgat Bozok University, her research focuses on education for sustainability and creative drama.

**Anna Lehtonen** is an educational scientist working with creative approaches to sustainability education and developed applied drama practices to address climate change education challenges in her PhD. Currently, she works on the ECF4CLIM (a European Competence Framework for a Low Carbon Society and Sustainability through Education) project promoting sustainability competences.

**Alison Lui** is a reader in Corporate and Financial Law and associate dean for Global Engagement at Liverpool John Moores University. Recognised with awards for both research and teaching, she is a strategic leader in higher education. She has published extensively on financial regulation, financial crime, and the role of AI in the financial sector.

**Katja Malmborg** has a PhD in sustainability science. She teaches sustainability in production landscapes, social-ecological resilience, and transdisciplinarity. In her research, she collaborates with UNESCO Biosphere Reserves to explore people's connection to place and how to design multi-actor processes to increase sustainability and collaboration in agriculture, forestry, and nature protection.

**Radhika Mittal** is an evidence-informed strategic communication and engagement expert with over 20 years of experience in leading projects, managing narratives, training teams, developing partnerships, and enabling stakeholder engagement towards actionable results. She currently manages the research program *Ethics of Socially Disruptive Technologies* supported by the Dutch Ministry of Education, Culture, and Science and the Netherlands Organization for Scientific Research.

**Marianne Ødegaard** is a professor of science education at the University of Oslo, Norway. Her research areas are video-based classroom studies, inquiry-based science education, and the use of drama and role play in socio-scientific and sustainability issues. She works with teacher education and has a background in teaching science, biology, and drama.

**Shelley Piasecka** is an associate professor of theatre and applied drama in the Division of Communication, Screen and Performance at the University of Chester, UK. Shelley supports her teaching and research with performance practice and has a special interest in stage adaptation, applied drama, and writing for theatre.

**Richard Ridyard** is a senior lecturer at Liverpool John Moores University. His principal research interests include financial regulation, financial crime, and climate policy while also extending to other areas of corporate law. Having received awards for both teaching and research, Richard focuses on developing innovative pedagogies, such as games-based learning.

**Dave Soehren** is an experienced director in organisational behaviour and learning and development. He is a senior lecturer in human resource management at Liverpool Business School, UK, and is focused on making learning engaging and enjoyable through the real-life application of skills.

**Lenneke Vaandrager** is an associate professor Health & Society at Wageningen University and Research, The Netherlands. She teaches about inclusive healthy living environments and her research is inspired by systems thinking and salutogenesis. She is the coordinator of the European Training Consortium in Public Health and Health Promotion and an active member of the IUHPE Global Working Group on Salutogenesis.

**Sarah Jayne Williams** is a senior lecturer at Liverpool Business School, UK, with a focus on sustainable human resource management (HRM), diversity and inclusion, and ethical practice. Her doctoral research explores the emergence of sustainable HRM through the UN's Principles of Responsible Management Education initiative.

# Foreword

Vi har inte alltid varit överens men trots våra
olikheter har vi, med information och utbildning,
kommit till insikt att det krävs förändring av oss
nu, så att nästkommande generationer kan känna
hopp.
Det är tydligt att samarbete och samordning
är nyckeln.

We have not always agreed but despite our
differences we have, with information and education,
came to the realization that change is required of us
now, so that future generations can feel
hope.
It is clear that cooperation and coordination
is the key.

A collective statement of the
Swedish Citizens' Climate Assembly
*(Medborgarråd om Klimatet) 2024*

# FRAMING

1

## Chapter 1

# Teaching which makes an impact on sustainability... and how to use this book

Eva Österlind, Tony Wall, and Tim Daw

## The nature of the sustainability challenge

'The Anthropocene' is a term that captures the distinctly novel period in our Earth's long history in which the cumulative impacts of human activity are transforming our planet. The scale of human endeavours and their environmental consequences accelerated rapidly from the mid-20th century and now fundamentally impact 'earth systems' such as climate, biodiversity, nutrient and water cycles, and ocean chemistry (Steffen et al., 2015). These changes threaten to undermine the conditions for human prosperity on planet Earth, the only place in the Universe where we know that human life is possible (Richardson et al., 2023).

Global assessments of climate change (IPCC, 2023) and biodiversity loss (IPBES, 2019) set out in stark terms the seriousness of the situation and the perilous nature of current trajectories. Yet, to date, no nation has managed to meet the basic needs of citizens within sustainable limits (Fanning et al., 2021). We are faced simultaneously with over-consumption, extraction, and pollution by the wealthiest, while the poorest suffer deprivation, hunger, and exposure to the worst effects of environmental disruption (Filho et al., 2023).

In 2015, the United Nations set out a vision for a sustainable future in terms of 17 Sustainable Development Goals (SDGs) and the landmark Paris Agreement,

DOI: 10.4324/9781003496359-2

3

aiming to limit global warming to 1.5°C by the end of the century. In the early 2020s, political will and on-the-ground progress towards these targets have been insufficient and further endangered by the additional pressures of pandemic, war, and economic stagnation (UNDP, 2022a). It is increasingly apparent that sustainability requires dramatic, deep, and unprecedented transformative change in the organisation of societies (IPBES, 2019).

The failure to take sufficient action to 'bend the curve' towards a sustainable future belies some of the complexities and challenges baked into the sustainability challenge (Stoddard et al., 2021). Although often framed as a challenge of biophysical limits and environmental damage (as above), at its heart, sustainability is widely recognised as a socially complex, wicked, and deeply human problem. Complexity is characterised by the non-linearity of impacts, with time lags, intersectoral interactions, emergence, and surprise and complicated by the 'wickedness' of ambiguity, conflicting values, tradeoffs, asymmetrical power and agency, vested interests, growth imperatives, and short-termism. Even information is now tainted with populism, polarisation, and post-truth-fake-news dynamics.

If there ever was a time for imagination to transform futures and generate hope, that time is now.

## How higher education builds capability to address sustainability challenges

The central role of education, and higher education specifically, in tackling these emerging issues and now crises, has been promoted through various international initiatives, culminating in The United Nations' Decade of Education for Sustainable Development initiative (covering 2005–2014). A review of the achievements of that decade highlighted the urgent need for more research and case study work to help promote *actionable* solutions towards transformation – and a call for greater attention to the cultural, political, and spiritual pillars of action, and more specifically, competence (see Leal Filho et al., 2015).

Since then, Education for Sustainable Development (often referred to as ESD) is recognised as linking directly to building the capacities to deal with the UN 17 SDGs such as quality education (SDG4), and climate change (SDG 13), and doing so through partnership working (SDG 17). There are many frameworks which articulate sustainability competences to help drive transformation through higher education. By 2022, there were 20 studies which proposed sustainability competences in higher education (Annelin and Boström, 2022).

In terms of frameworks for practice, UNESCO developed an international framework (Rieckmann, 2018) and the European Commission (2022) created the Green-Comp (Green Competences) to be implemented across European countries. This book adopts a synthesised version of the UNESCO and GreenComp frameworks given their focus on practice and implementation and structured by the high-level categories of GreenComp: embodying sustainability values, embracing complexity in sustainability, envisioning sustainable futures, and acting for sustainability. A summary of the competences is provided below, to help you navigate the chapters of this book.

| Education for sustainable development competence framework used in this book |
| --- |
| **Embodying sustainability values** |
| **Valuing sustainability/self-awareness and normative competencies:** Reflecting on own and others' values, how they change, and consider alignment and impacts on sustainability. |
| **Supporting fairness:** Promoting equality, diversity, inclusion, and justice in relation to existing and future generations and learning about sustainability from/with previous generations. |
| **Promoting nature:** Respecting that humans are a part of nature alongside other species and nature itself, and to consider the needs and rights of others in building resilient ecosystems. |
| **Embracing complexity in sustainability** |
| **Systems thinking:** Addressing sustainability challenges with complexity in mind – from different perspectives, over time, interactions between and amongst different natural and social systems. |
| **Critical thinking:** Considering information, arguments, assumptions, and historical and cultural backgrounds and perspectives, to question and explore the current situation. |
| **Problem framing/integrated problem-solving competence:** Finding ways to formulate sustainable challenges to help anticipate, mitigate, or prevent current and future problems. |
| **Envisioning sustainable futures** |
| **Futures literacy/anticipatory competence:** Imagining alternative futures through exploring scenarios and their relative impacts and then using them to realise sustainable futures. |
| **Adaptability:** Managing sustainable transitions through taking effective decisions under the circumstances of complexity, uncertainty, ambiguity, and risk. |
| **Exploratory thinking:** Using imagination, creativity, and experimentation to explore new ideas, methods, and linkages between different disciplines. |
| **Acting for sustainability** |
| **Political agency:** Understanding political systems to be able to hold political entities to account for unsustainable behaviours and promote the adoption of effective policies for sustainability. |

| |
|---|
| **Collective action/strategic and collaboration competence:** Acting for change and sustainable futures through collaborating effectively with others. |
| **Individual initiative:** Acting to improve own contributions to sustainability initiatives and activity and understanding own potential for further contribution to enhance sustainability outcomes. |

*Source:* Adapted from GreenComp (European Commission, 2022) and UNESCO (Rieckmann, 2018).

## Particular challenges in higher education teaching

There is now evidence that teaching *methods* generate variable learning and competence outcomes (Lozano et al., 2022) and wider societal outcomes (Wall et al., 2024). This is partly because of the complexity of addressing sustainability, which involves considerations and actions including individual choices as well as global threats (see Chapter 29). The assumption that more knowledge of scientific facts will lead to more sustainable behaviour still guides many environmental educational programmes, even though its relevance has been questioned for over a decade (see Chen and Martin, 2015). ESD can be described as transdisciplinary and, to some extent, quite controversial. For example, facts and values cannot always be separated, and it is argued that 'we have to attend to the value judgements before we can attend to the facts' (Lundegård and Wickman, 2007, p. 14). Similarly, Læssøe (2010) emphasises the need to work with dilemmas and deliberative communication and points out the risk that ESD is carried out as unproblematic and consensus-oriented, which he describes as 'societal self-deception' (p. 51).

Recent empirical work suggests that ESD remains limited and often relies on disciplinary content rather than deeper pedagogical experiences which directly influence emotion, values, and beliefs (Leal Filho et al., 2019). In order to tackle sustainability issues, adequate teaching methods must be developed, but according to Leal Filho and Pace (2016) 'the preparation of university teachers has not received the same meticulous attention that is given to [school] teachers' (p. 5). Leal Filho and Pace also proposed that the transmission of knowledge is not enough, and instead, we need '*spaces for pedagogical transformation* that support transformative and transdisciplinary teaching' (2016, p. 3 original emphasis).

Here, there may be other, emotional barriers to sustainability learning. Stoknes (2014) describes the 'climate paradox' in which better knowledge of climate science does not lead to action (see Mezirow, 2000) and explains it in terms of psychological barriers and negative emotions that allow dissonance between knowledge and action. Learning about climate change may also cause anxiety among students which may activate psychological defences like reluctance to act or change (Ojala, 2012). To avoid this, it is crucial to not only focus on possible disasters but also encourage students to visualise potential solutions.

As the topic of sustainability is challenging in the ways described above, there are several initiatives to find solutions. One trend is to put forward *science education for activism* (e.g. Mueller and Tippins, 2015), but this approach might be problematic as there is a clash between fostering activism and the tradition of academic teaching as based on non-political evidence. *Outdoor education*, like field courses and investigations, is a second approach that might be suitable for ESD (e.g. Cruickshank and Fenner, 2012). Such initiatives may improve student learning but can be difficult to arrange.

A third approach is to *embrace the arts*. Clark and Button (2011) developed a model for sustainability education, which integrates community, science, and the arts. Working with the arts implies open-ended, experiential learning that encompasses contradiction and ambiguity (van Boeckel, 2013; Wall et al., 2018). Here, role playing and other forms of applied theatre, drama, and performance are designed to work with values and dilemmas, from a safe position in a fictive situation (Österlind, 2012). The oscillation between exploring in role and observing out of role creates nurturing conditions for deep reflection. Role playing is becoming more recognised in the research literature on ESD, while other forms, like performance and forum play (as will be discussed in the next chapter), are less known and researched.

Conventional teaching methods in higher education struggle to meet these demands, and it is within this context that this book focuses on the high impact potential of teaching practices informed by a subset of the arts, applied drama, and performance. This book is based on an international project funded by the Swedish Research Council and Liverpool John Moores University, where a group of practitioners and researchers shared, developed, and tested applied drama for sustainability education. The goal of the project was to explore the following questions:

- How might applied drama and performance develop Green Competences among students in higher education?
- How can applied drama and performance be adopted by university teachers with no previous drama experience?
- Which forms of applied drama (e.g. role play, forum play) are more accessible, more likely to be tried out by teachers in fields like science, technology, business, and other disciplines?
- How is such interactive teaching received by the students?
- What do the students learn, and how can the possible impact of applied drama in teaching for sustainability be evaluated in a reasonable and credible?

This book shares the innovative, high impact designs that were tested in practice, as part of our own development.

## How to use this book

The book is designed as a compilation of practices that you can pick up and use as a practitioner or researcher, with some framing and concluding chapters. Although each chapter can be seen as a standalone chapter, we recommend the following sequence:

◼ **Frame the content of this book through Chapters 1–3.** The first chapter (this one, *teaching which makes an impact*) outlines the overall emergency context of sustainability learning and the structure of competence that we have used to label the practices described in each chapter. The second chapter (*introduction to applied drama*) provides more detailed information about the fields of applied drama in education which underpin the majority of the chapters in the book. This chapter is optional but useful for those wanting to learn more about the history and theory of the practices in the book. The third chapter (*before you start*) is a sound foundational chapter for those new to using highly interactive approaches of applied drama, theatre, and performance, particularly in relation to creating a learning environment for safety, exploration, and ethics.

◼ **Explore and dip-in/dip-out of chapters 4-29.** The 26 chapters describe different practices for you to try yourself and have been organised into different **functions**: energising and connecting through icebreakers, exploring perspectives through role play, exploring alternatives through forum play, provoking insight through performance, and deepening insight through drama processes. Within these sections, chapters are organised generally from easiest to most complex. In addition, each chapter indicates which **GreenComp/UNESCO sustainability competence** (as outlined above) the chapter relates to – this means you may want to scan through the chapters to find practices which target particular competences, e.g. promoting nature, systems thinking, and so on. See the table below to help target chapters to consider.

◼ **Consider how you move your own practice forward in Chapters 30–32.** These chapters give you more ideas about how to sustain and innovate your own sustainability teaching for impact. These are optional but give insights from our own research into the ongoing challenges in implementing some of the most interactive and engaging approaches currently embraced in higher ESD.

| Chapter | Valuing … | Supporting fairness | Promoting nature | Systems thinking | Critical thinking | Problem framing … | Futures literacy … | Adaptability | Exploratory thinking | Political agency | Collective action … | Individual initiative |
|---|---|---|---|---|---|---|---|---|---|---|---|---|
| 4 Drama icebreaker: improvisation for beginners | ● | | ● | | | | ● | ● | | ● | | |
| 5 Drama icebreaker: House of Commons | | ● | | ● | ● | | ● | | ● | | | ● |

| | 1 | 2 | 3 | 4 | 5 | 6 | 7 | 8 | 9 | 10 | 11 | 12 |
|---|---|---|---|---|---|---|---|---|---|---|---|---|
| 6 Drama icebreaker: long lists and thinking aloud | ● | ● | ● | ● | ● | ● | ● | ● | ● | ● | ● | ● |
| 7 Drama icebreaker: debate! | ● | | | | ● | | | | | | ● | ● |
| 8 Role play: nature-based solutions – exploring views and values | ● | | | | ● | | | ● | | | | |
| 9 Role play: a serious game to navigate global wicked problems | | | | ● | ● | ● | ● | ● | ● | ● | ● | |
| 10 Role play: playing with power | ● | ● | | | ● | | | | ● | ● | ● | ● |
| 11 Role play: power dynamics in a village logging dilemma | ● | ● | | ● | ● | ● | | | ● | ● | ● | |
| 12 Role play: The Bleeding Water | ● | ● | ● | ● | ● | | | ● | | | ● | |
| 13 Forum play: exploring future energy practices | ● | ● | | | ● | ● | ● | ● | ● | | | ● |
| 14 Forum play: exploring sustainability scenarios and privileged perspectives | ● | ● | | ● | ● | ● | ● | ● | ● | ● | ● | ● |
| 15 Forum play: working with climate anxiety | ● | | | | ● | | | ● | | | ● | |
| 16 Forum play: exploring more-than-human perspectives | ● | ● | ● | ● | ● | ● | ● | ● | ● | ● | | ● |
| 17 Provocation: co-creating a poem about the future | ● | ● | | | | | ● | | ● | | ● | |
| 18 Provocation: Farewell Falsterbo – an audio book walk | ● | ● | ● | ● | ● | ● | ● | | ● | | | ● |
| 19 Provocation: what a load of rubbish! | ● | | | | ● | | | | ● | | | ● |
| 20 Provocation: reflecting on biodiversity loss | ● | | ● | ● | ● | | | ● | ● | | | ● |

| Chapter | Valuing … | Supporting fairness | Promoting nature | Systems thinking | Critical thinking | Problem framing … | Futures literacy … | Adaptability | Exploratory thinking | Political agency | Collective action … | Individual initiative |
|---|---|---|---|---|---|---|---|---|---|---|---|---|
| 21 Provocation: futuring at scale | • | | | | • | | • | | | | • | |
| 22 Provocation: rights of the river | | • | • | | | • | | • | • | • | • | |
| 23 Provocation: the manifold orchard | | | • | • | | | | | • | | • | |
| 24 Drama workshop: Papperssnö | • | • | | | • | | • | • | • | • | • | • |
| 25 Drama workshop: The River | • | • | • | • | • | | • | | • | • | • | • |
| 26 Drama workshop: flood! | | | | • | • | • | | | • | | | |
| 27 Drama workshop: the journey to Dystoplastica | • | • | | | | • | • | | • | | • | |
| 28 Drama workshop: climate activists | • | • | • | • | • | • | • | • | | • | • | • |
| 29 Drama workshop: the climate conference | • | • | • | | • | • | | | • | • | | • |

# References

Annelin, A., & Boström, G.-O. (2022). An assessment of key sustainability competencies: A review of scales and propositions for validation. *International Journal of Sustainability in Higher Education*. https://doi.org/10.1108/ijshe-05-2022-0166.

Chen, J. C., & Martin, A. R. (2015). Role-play simulations as a transformative methodology in environmental education. *Journal of Transformative Education, 13*(1), pp. 85–102. https://doi.org/10.1177/1541344614560196.

Clark, B., & Button, C. (2011). Sustainability transdisciplinary education model: Interface of arts, science, and community (STEM). *International Journal of Sustainability in Higher Education, 12*(1), pp. 41–54. https://doi.org/10.1108/14676371111098294.

Cruickshank, H., & Fenner, R. (2012). Exploring key sustainable development themes through learning activities. *International Journal of Sustainability in Higher Education, 13*(3), pp. 249–262.

European Commission. (2022). GreenComp, the European sustainability competence framework. Publications Office of the European Union. https://op.europa.eu/en/publication-detail/-/publication/bc83061d-74ec-11ec-9136-01aa75ed71a1/language-en.

Fanning, A. L., O'Neill, D. W., Hickel, J., & Roux, N. (2021). The social shortfall and ecological overshoot of nations. *Nature Sustainability, 5.* https://doi.org/10.1038/s41893-021-00799-z

Filho, W. L., Wall, T., Salvia, A. L., Dinis, M. A. P., & Mifsud, M. (2023). The central role of climate action in achieving the United Nations' Sustainable Development Goals. *Scientific Reports, 13*(1), 20582. https://doi.org/10.1038/s41598-023-47746-w.

IPBES. (2019). *Intergovernmental science-policy platform on biodiversity and ecosystem services global assessment report on biodiversity and ecosystem services.*

IPCC. (2023). Summary for policymakers. In: Core Writing Team, H. Lee, & J. Romero (Eds.), *Climate change 2023: Synthesis report* (pp. 1–34). Contribution of Working Groups I, II and III to the Sixth Assessment Report of the Intergovernmental Panel on Climate Change. IPCC, Geneva, Switzerland. https://doi.org/10.59327/IPCC/AR6-9789291691647.001.

Læssøe, J. (2010). Education for sustainable development, participation and socio-cultural change. *Environmental Education Research, 16*(1), pp. 39–57.

Leal Filho, W., Manolas, E., & Pace, P. (2015). The future we want. *International Journal of Sustainability in Higher Education, 16*(1), 112–129. https://doi.org/10.1108/ijshe-03-2014-0036.

Leal Filho, W., & Pace, P. (2016). Teaching education for sustainable development: Implications on 350 learning programmes at higher education. In W. Leal Filho & P. Pace (Eds.), *Teaching education for sustainable development at university level* (pp. 1–6). Springer International.

Leal Filho, W., Shiel, C., Paqo, A., Mifsud, M., Veiga Åvila, L., Londero Brandli, L., MolthanHill, P., Pace, P., Azeiteiro, U. M., Ruiz Vargas, V., & Caeiro, S. (2019). Sustainable Development Goals and sustainability teaching at universities: Falling behind or getting ahead of the pack? *Journal of Cleaner Production, 232,* 285–294.

Lozano, R., María Barreiro-Gen, D'amato, D., Gago-Cortés, C., Favi, C., Martins, R., Ferenc Mónus, Caeiro, S., Benayas, J., Caldera, S., Sevket Can Bostanci, Ilija Djekic, Moneva, M., Sáenz, O., Bankole Awuzie, & Gladysz, B. (2022). Improving sustainability teaching by grouping and interrelating pedagogical approaches and sustainability competences: Evidence from 15 Worldwide Higher Education Institutions. *Sustainable Development, 31*(1), 349–359. https://doi.org/10.1002/sd.2396.

Lundegård, I., & Wickman, P.-O. (2007). Conflicts of interest: An indispensable element of education for sustainable development. *Environmental Education Research, 13*(1), pp. 1–15.

Mezirow, J. (2000). Learning to think like an adult: Core concepts of transformation theory. In J. Mezirow (Ed.), *Learning as transformation—critical perspectives on a theory in progress* (pp. 3–33). Jossey-Bass.

Mueller, M. P., & Tippins, D. J. (Eds.). (2015). *EcoJustice, citizen science and youth activism: Situated tensions for science education.* Springer International.

Ojala, M. (2012). Hope and climate change: The importance of hope for environmental engagement among young people. *Environmental Education Research, 18*(5), pp. 625–642.

Österlind, E. (2012). Emotions – aesthetics – education: Dilemmas related to students' commitment in education for sustainable development. *Journal of Artistic and Creative Education, 6*(1), pp. 32–50.

Richardson, K., Steffen, W., Lucht, W., Bendtsen, J., Cornell, S., Donges, J. F., Drüke, M., Fetzer, I., Bala, G., Werner von Bloh, Feulner, G., Fiedler, S., Gerten, D., Gleeson, T., Hofmann, M., Willem Huiskamp, Matti Kummu, Mohan, C., Bravo, D., & Petri, S. (2023). Earth beyond six of nine planetary boundaries. *Science Advances, 9*(37). https://doi.org/10.1126/sciadv.adh2458.

Rieckmann, M. (2018) Learning to transform the world: Key competencies in education for sustainable development. In *Issues and trends in education for sustainable development* (pp. 39–59). UNESCO. https://unesdoc.unesco.org/ark:/48223/pf0000261802.

Steffen, W., Broadgate, W., Deutsch, L., Gaffney, O., & Ludwig, C. (2015). The trajectory of the Anthropocene: The Great Acceleration. *The Anthropocene Review*, *2*(1), 81–98. https://doi.org/10.1177/2053019614564785.

Stoddard, I., K. Anderson, S. Capstick, W. Carton, J. Depledge, K. Facer, C. Gough, F. Hache, C. Hoolohan, M. Hultman, N. Hällström, S. Kartha, S. Klinsky, M. Kuchler, E. Lövbrand, N. Nasiritousi, P. Newell, G. P. Peters, Y. Sokona, A. Stirling, M. Stilwell, C. L. Spash, & M. Williams. (2021). Three decades of climate mitigation: Why haven't we bent the global emissions curve? *Annual Review of Environment and Resources*, *46*(1):653–689.

Stoknes, P. E. (2014). Rethinking climate communications and the "psychological climate paradox." *Energy Research & Social Science*, *1*, 161–170. https://doi.org/10.1016/j.erss.2014.03.007

UNDP (United Nations Development Programme). (2022a). Human development report 2021-22: Uncertain times, unsettled lives: Shaping our future in a transforming world. UNDP, New York.

UNDP. (2022b). Human development report: Uncertain times, unsettled lives. UNDP, New York.

Van Boeckel, J. (2013). *At the heart of art and earth: An exploration of practices in arts-based environmental education*. Aalto University.

Wall, T., Österlind, E., & Fries, J. (2018). Arts based approaches for sustainability. In W. Leal Filho, et al. (Eds.), *Encyclopedia of sustainability in higher education* (pp. 50–56). Springer.

Wall, T., Thi, N., Foster, S., Phuong Minh Luong, Thi, T., Hindley, A., & Stokes, P. (2024). The spatialization of decent work and the role of employability empowerment for minority ethnic young people in emerging economies. *PLoS One*, *19*(2), e0297487–e0297487. https://doi.org/10.1371/journal.pone.0297487.

# Chapter 2

# Introducing applied drama for learning in higher education

Eva Österlind and Eva Hallgren

## Applied drama for sustainability

Applied drama is a broad term, referring to interdisciplinary drama practices undertaken in a range of settings such as schools, universities, healthcare, community, business, and organisations. It is an educational approach based on interaction and reflection. Here, participants and the facilitator(s) work together to explore a topic by using drama conventions like storytelling and role taking in fictive situations to generate learning. Through such processes, applied drama is a resource which can strengthen sustainability awareness, knowledge, mindsets, and action-taking among individuals and groups within higher education.

Applied drama work may contribute to communicative, emotional, empathetic, and improvisational skills, perspective-making, and civic, critical, and divergent thinking. This clearly relates to the EU's definition of Green Competences – as valuing sustainability, embracing complexity in sustainability, envisioning sustainable futures, and acting for sustainability (European Commission, 2022). Despite this, there are few case and research studies on the generative outcomes of applied drama for sustainability, especially in higher education. The limited number of studies is probably linked to the limited use of drama for learning in higher education, which is why this book is so significant.

DOI: 10.4324/9781003496359-3

## Characteristics of applied drama

The emergence of applied drama can be attributed to 'radical theatre-making' in the latter part of the 20th century, when educationalists aimed to democratise processes of learning (Nicholson, 2005). Applied drama is not the same as but is closely connected to 'drama in education' (i.e. in schools) and 'applied theatre' (or 'community theatre'). Examples of applied drama practices include role play, process drama, forum play, Forum Theatre, and Legislative Theatre. Regardless of genre, applied drama always includes elements of storytelling, theatre, creativity, and playfulness.

The characteristics of applied drama vary depending on national and local conditions. In Sweden, drama has been closely connected to education and includes three main areas.

One area concerns *drama for communicative competences*, such as relational leadership, conflict handling, and group dynamics (e.g. knowledge and conventions about interactive learning: how to listen, to ask questions, to put forward an opinion). This can be described as creating an open atmosphere to promote learning and foster general competences for being a citizen in a democratic society. The area of communicative competence will not be at the centre in this context, although establishing a positive classroom climate is a prerequisite for applied drama. Participants' social skills and the atmosphere in a group often improve as positive side-effects of drama work, which can be related to social sustainability (see Chapter 3 for more details).

Another area concerns *drama as an art form*, where applied drama work might lead to a theatre performance. This area will not be addressed here, as rehearsed theatre performances are difficult to achieve, given that singular drama workshops are more common in higher education. To work more explicitly with dramatic/artistic dimensions and eventually do a performance is of course also always possible, depending on the purpose and circumstances.

A third area concerns *drama for learning in other disciplines*, such as language learning or science education. Here, the facilitator needs to find out what the possibilities are with certain techniques, drama conventions and genres, and how to strengthen learning in a specific subject using drama as an 'extra-ordinary' teaching resource. Applying drama work as an integrated part of learning for sustainability in various disciplines will be at the core of this book, with the intention to inspire the readers to use it in their own academic context.

## Features of applied drama

Learning through drama is not about answering correctly but is more about communicating, asking questions, listening, exploring, and thinking critically and creatively in collaboration with others. In applied drama, the body is a central medium for learning. Through the body, the participants (sometimes in role) express, shape, and use various communicative resources to create meaning. These resources can include verbal language, gestures, spatial placement, movement, costume, and objects.

But it is important to keep in mind that drama activities should be kept simple, with no advanced costume and set design. Learning becomes holistic when the whole person – thought, feeling, action – is involved in the learning process.

Applied drama work can be described as:

- Process-oriented: pre-planned by the university teacher or facilitator but often adapted and/or driven by the participants.
- Interactive: embodied communication in fictive situations.
- Holistic: draws attention to the body, mind, senses, emotions, creativity and imagination.
- Reflective: supports the analysis of actions, reactions, driving forces, and effects at many levels.
- Transformative: integrating personal experiences and theory/literature might lead to questioning what has been taken for granted and generate new ways of understanding.

Applied drama work is often playful, which does not mean that it is lightweight or superficial. On the contrary, addressing challenging topics might need some elements of playfulness in order to stay open, without over-simplifying or denying (e.g. see Chapter 29). Similarly, provocative performances can directly tackle destructive patterns of behaviour in society but still retain a sense of playfulness (e.g. Chapter 19 and 21).

To balance the non-traditional, playful teaching format of drama work, reflection is essential. Through reflection, the fictive situation of the drama is related to the outside world. The possibility to literally change perspective is a key aspect which may increase empathy and provide insights. For instance, a sequence starting with self-reflection (to look inwards), before expressing oneself and taking a stance, followed by joint reflection, allows a critical review of personal and sociocultural values and mindsets (e.g. Lehtonen et al., 2020).

Applied drama appears in many different shapes and sizes, as you will see in this book. It can be just a single game to allow the participants to relax and enter into a more playful mode, to establish a group or to get the body started (see Chapters 4–7). It can also be a whole drama workshop, a role play, a forum play, or a process drama, to develop abilities from role taking to deepening subject content, or even to initiate a legislative or decision-making process. We now introduce a few drama formats or genres which are suitable for higher education, some of which then feature as key sections and chapters of this book.

# Role play

The concept of role play is far more common in higher education than applied drama. However, it is a vague term, and the characteristics of role play may vary significantly. For instance, the kind of preparation required, the degree of predetermined structure, and the emphasis on emotional or cognitive/factual aspects may vary and can be related to factors such as purpose, timeframe, and educational context. Role playing is an integral element of applied drama, although it is not always defined as drama work. In some university disciplines (e.g. biology, economy, engineering, or geography), a role play is often designed as a structured controversy presenting an encounter between stakeholders with different interests and conflicting perspectives.

The definition of role play is often taken for granted, and how it is carried out is seldom described in detail (Österlind, 2018). Role play can be defined as 'an improvisational act of representing characters and behaviours of someone or something as an explorative and creative activity in a dramatic context' (see Chapter 12). Role play can vary from learning a special procedure in a given situation, like flying an aeroplane (through a simulation) to role play focusing on relations and enabling exploration of interactions between participants in certain situations (van Ments, 1994). Sometimes research on role play for sustainability is explicitly based on drama work, and the terminology is more precise (e.g. 'drama-based role play').

A role play is often a single event focused on a particular situation with a fairly straightforward form of role taking. Before conducting a role play, the facilitator needs to plan the activity (e.g. aims, timeframe, and so on) and whether or not there will be a related written assignment. A role play usually includes three phases:

a. Students' **preparation**, which may vary from a few minutes or a couple of days to weeks or even months.
b. **Role-playing** session, from five minutes up to two days.
c. **Reflection** or debriefing session.

The design, profile, and impact of a role play depend on factors such as the context, the academic discipline, the teacher's knowledge, and the allocated time. The four dimensions below may be useful to define what kind of role play you want to design and try out:

■ Long-term commitment versus single occasion.
■ Careful preparation versus ad hoc improvisation.
■ Relatively strict versus more flexible structure.
■ Academic content versus personal, self-reflective knowledge.

The level of structure within the role play may vary considerably, from scripted role plays or role cards which instruct each participant what to say and do from a given perspective (see Chapters 11, 12, and 27) to role plays with minimal preparation based on improvisation 'in the moment' (see Chapter 29). Sometimes the group is divided into smaller groups, working in parallel with the same role play. In this case, comparison can allow fruitful reflection, since all participants will have experienced the same or similar situations. The whole setting can be either predetermined (e.g. a formal symposium attended by different stakeholders, leading to a conflict based on opposing interests) or a more open and personal scenario with less clear-cut roles, representing, for instance, varying lived experiences of a particular issue. Role play can be demanding and time-consuming, but as a student put it 'the learning sticks' (Gordon & Thomas, 2016, p. 14).

Role play in a drama context often has quite a flexible structure and focuses on reflective insights rather than specific academic content. Thus, in cross-disciplinary work it becomes important to relate this kind of role play to the academic course content. In an early study about how to foster connections between humans and the environment, Davis and Tarrant (2014) explicitly address how different knowledge traditions, like drama and natural science, can be integrated. According to their study, a combination of scientific knowledge, experience in the natural environment (e.g. meeting dramatised characters in the forest), and applied drama work was most effective in terms of the students' learning.

## Process drama

In the area of applied drama, a few names need to be mentioned due to their impact on *drama for learning*. Dorothy Heathcote and Gavin Bolton, with backgrounds in drama in education, were pioneers in what is called process drama. Process drama is a whole-group drama where both participants and facilitator(s) step into fictive situations and take on different roles during the drama. The teacher has a 'pre-text', which is a plan for where to start the drama, ideas about how to proceed, and what drama strategies, or conventions, can be useful to enable the participants to explore the theme of the drama. The pre-text is not a strict plan, and the participants are invited to be co-creators (see O'Neill, 1995).

The process drama evolves in relation to the participants' input when inside the fiction and when taking part in the drama strategies initiated by the facilitator. Process drama implies going in and out of different roles in different situations with varying perspectives, defined within a fictive frame, i.e. a story allowing the content to be explored from many angles. This process can be implemented over time, which allows a more complex learning experience. In addition, drama strategies enable different ways of approaching, exploring, and deepening understanding of the content. These can include still images, improvisation, slow motion, thought-tracking, inner thoughts, eavesdropping, conscious alley, and hot seating (some of these are outlined in this book, while others are described and freely available online).

A special drama strategy, *teacher-in-role*, developed by Heathcote (Wagner, 1976), distinguishes this kind of drama from other forms. The strategy does not require the facilitator to be an actor. The role taking is more of a symbolic act and a conscious choice with the aim of building context, influencing, supporting, or challenging the participants in relation to the purpose of the process drama. When planning for teacher-in-role, it is good to think about what status and attitude the

role should have. It might be a high-status role as a leader of the group or as an oppo-
nent to the group or maybe of lower status and in need of guidance or help from the
group, depending on the purpose of the planned activity (Piazzoli, 2018; Wagner,
1976). You will need a simple garment or an object associated with the character to
signal when the facilitator is in role.

When a teacher-in-role initially meets the particpants, s/he often adresses the
group in a *collective role* as if they are all, for instance, villagers living along the River
(see Chapter 25) or journalists travelling back in time (see Chapter 27). The collective role promotes a sense of unity (a *we*), strengthens the sense of belonging, and
ensures that no one feels left out. The collective role contributes to cooperation and
mutual trust. As Piazzoli described, 'when affective space is established, a supportive atmosphere enables participants to take risks within the drama that can trigger
experimental learning' (2011, p. 562).

*Dramatic tension* is a key aspect in this affective space – it becomes the driving
force of the roles and evokes engagement and commitment among the participants.
Dramatic tension gives the character a motive to act in a certain situation. It is the
facilitator who is responsible to frame the situation from a certain perspective, infus-
ing dramatic tension. Dramatic tension can be generated, for example, through an
urgent task, something that must be dealt with, or a conflict between different roles
in the drama, or through withholding information that can be used as a surprise, a
mystery, or a secret (O'Toole, 1992; Piazzoli, 2018).

In a process drama everyone goes in and out of role and also takes on different
roles. It is in these spaces or gaps between fiction and reality that learning can take
place. Thus, it is not only the imaginary experience that creates meaning but the
reflection in and out of role, and shifting between different roles and perspectives,
that contribute to meaning making. This is a well-established principle of learning
through drama, which enables deeper learning. This learning potential is explained
in more detail by Bolton (1979). In contrast, in provocative performances which are
closer to the genre of performance art, this very gap may become blurred, creating a
different kind of tension which is nonetheless generative.

Learning through drama is not about finding the right answer. It is important to
realise that when you invite students into any kind of drama you are inviting them
into what Heathcote called a 'penalty-free zone'. Process drama builds on imagination and ways to express oneself and pure facts are not asked for. A teacher-in-role
asking for correct answers would immediately take the participants out of the playful, penalty-free zone and should rather be called a 'teacher-in-disguise' (Hallgren,
2018, p. 260, referring to Berggraf Sæbø). Then it is no longer *drama for learning*.

## Forum Theatre and Legislative Theatre

Forum Theatre and Legislative Theatre are part of Theatre of the Oppressed, created
by Augusto Boal (2019). Boal also developed several other formats (e.g. Invisible

Theatre and Rainbow of Desire), although in this section, we briefly describe Forum Theatre and how it can be expanded to Legislative Theatre. We also present a Swedish adaptation of Forum Theatre called forum play, suitable for educational settings.

Forum Theatre is the most well-known form of Theatre of the Oppressed (Boal, 1979/2019). It evolved when Boal's theatre company performed for peasants and workers in Brazil during the 1960s. Their performances first presented a conflict ending in a crisis, then the audience was invited to suggest solutions on how to deal with the conflict, and these suggestions were performed by the actors. On one occasion, a spectator who was dissatisfied with how the actor performed the proposed solution was invited on stage. At that moment a significant change took place, as from then on nobody knew what would happen next. This kind of exchange became a core practice in Forum Theatre. The characteristic of audience participation gives a significant presence and authentic flavour to Forum Theatre. It has proven to be a powerful tool, applied around the world (e.g. Ganguly, 2010; Österlind, 2008).

Forum Theatre is a rehearsed play about some kind of oppression, ending in a clash. The purpose is to practice how to counteract oppression, shift the power balance, and find better solutions. The play always includes a protagonist, a 'victim' exposed to injustice or oppression (e.g. an employee who has not received payment or promotion), and an antagonist, an 'oppressor' who maintains the injustice (e.g. rejects the claim). The play may also include characters who support (e.g. work for) the oppressor, and 'by-standers' or witnesses who may or may not support the victim's efforts to change the situation. After the play is performed, the audience is invited to get on stage by a 'Joker', who facilitates communication between the actors on stage and the audience. The Joker encourages the audience to stand up and take on the role of the oppressed (the original actor steps down) to confront the oppression, try to overcome obstacles, and explore different ways of solving the problem. Taking this step transforms a person from being a spectator in the audience to become a *spect-actor* (Boal, 1979/2019), ready to take action. It is not allowed to exchange the oppressor in Forum Theatre, as that would be a 'magic' solution and thus not useful as rehearsal for future actions in real-life situations.

Legislative Theatre (Boal, 2005) is an extended version of Forum Theatre which needs more thorough preparation than Forum Theatre. The theme or issue must be even more carefully chosen, often through a community project, and with a locally engaging problem at its core. The next task is to figure out how to make the problem visible and engaging by creating a rehearsed theatre performance which ends when the situation is at its worst, as mentioned above (see Chapter 22). In Legislative Theatre, the performance is then played for the local community but also for invited lawyers, politicians, and others (e.g. social workers) who have the power to make a change, for instance, to propose new legislation, rules, or routines, in a matter that clearly affects the citizens (see Theatre of the Oppressed NYC, 2019).

Boal also created many warm-up exercises (see Boal, 2022). One example is to ask everyone to write their name with their hand in the air in front of them, continuing with the other hand, then the right leg, the left leg, and finally with their heads. This very simple activity is useful to create a relaxed, playful atmosphere, clearly announcing that this is not going to be an ordinary academic lecture.

## Forum play

Forum play is a concept that does not include a rehearsed theatre performance (Byréus, 2010, 2006; Österlind, 2011) but still incorporates essential elements of Forum Theatre. For instance, just like in Forum Theatre, a fictive, challenging situation is explored. Icebreakers are used to create a playful, encouraging atmosphere (Boal, 2022) where people are ready to step up and intervene, to take action. In forum play, this is followed by values-clarification activities (see Österlind, 2011) to introduce the theme, let participants start to think about their own view and demonstrate that there are many views on a given topic. Then, in smaller groups, the participants prepare a problem scenario, an escalating situation that clearly displays the problem and ends when the injustice/conflict/oppression is at its peak.

The purpose is to show the problem in a way that calls upon the other participants, not to come up with any solutions. This sequence may be rehearsed once or twice before it is shown to the other participants. Then, the same situation is played again. Now the teacher acts as a Joker, by looking for persons in the 'audience' who have an idea on how to respond differently to what they have just seen and invite anyone who is ready to step into the drama and try to find a solution. Only the victim (or a bystander) in the situation should be exchanged, not the oppressor. The person who plays the oppressor must pay attention to the impact of varying interventions from audience members and be ready to adapt if this is in line with the role character.

Forum play enables multiple ways to solve a situation, which is an important experience in itself. However, afterwards, the varying attempts or strategies need to be discussed, not least with the person acting as the oppressor, who can provide valuable insights into how the different interventions affected him/her, and perhaps led to slight improvements or even transformed the situation. Questions explored here might include: *Was there any point you considered 'backing down' or being more flexible? What made you accept a particular suggestion?* In forum play, one may also exchange by-standers, as it can be just as important to practice not only how to act as being 'the victim' exposed to injustice, but also to practice how to interfere when someone else is being treated badly or is offended. As in Forum Theatre, the core is to practice, to rehearse, to think out of the box, and to overcome all sorts of obstacles. On a meta-level, participants may learn that there is always more than one solution to solve a problem.

When the forum play process ends it is important to explicitly get out of role, not least for the person playing the main opponent/oppressor, so no doubts remain that this was a role, not the player's personal attitude or opinion. In fact, the person who takes on this role serves the whole group, making it possible to try out acceptable solutions and to explore precious 'inside information' such as when the oppressor hesitated or began to open up and be a bit more flexible. It is also important to give space for everyone, in their groups or all together, to gain new insights by talking about the process and their experiences.

Forum Theatre and forum play are designed to counteract oppression. Thus, the design draws attention to power dynamics, where institutionalised oppression or social injustice are acted out by individuals. For instance, finding out how to approach, inform, or even convince a climate denier that climate change is for real is a big challenge. Practising in a safe and supportive environment may help to face this outside the drama context. The focus should be on how to argue, motivate, listen, be creative, find common ground, and avoid getting caught in a battle of prestige about who has the strongest personal power. In forum play, conflicts at a personal, individual level are at the forefront. If a wider societal or systemic-level approach is intended in a sustainability context, this needs to be addressed during preparation (see Chapters 1 and 3).

## Making a start

Applied drama invites learning about oneself, including one's own personal preferences, patterns of interaction, and responses to conflict. The learning occurs through taking another person's perspective. Looking at the world from another position affects what we see.

Learning about multiple dilemmas through applied drama connects to the complexity of sustainability and, at its best, encourages participants to think outside what is taken for granted and realise that there is always more than one solution. Applied drama, like role play, process drama, and forum play may thus contribute to learning for sustainability in higher education.

Some key suggestions to help prepare you for the next steps in your journey:

- Consider how to create a safe space for explorative, interactive learning (see Chapter 3).
- Introduce the students to any unfamiliar teaching activities, by telling them about your plan and motives in general terms (e.g. to develop a more varied teaching).
- Inform the students that it is allowed to step in and participate fully or to take a more observational stance if they prefer – In both cases, they may learn something and can contribute to joint reflections afterwards.
- Always try to give clear and concise instructions about the activity, but *do not* mention or predict how it will be received, as that would destroy the learning experience or severely restrict the learning potential.
- If the circumstances allow (e.g. if you will meet the students several times), it might be a good idea to involve the students in the planning.
- Invite supportive colleagues to participate and perhaps act as co-teachers in your lesson when you try something new with your students.

■ Evaluate the interactive teaching both in traditional ways (e.g. surveys) and in less traditional ways (e.g. embodied still images, drawings, letters, poems).

The following chapters offer a rich display of drama formats applied in a range of academic disciplines, as inspiration to further explore applied drama for sustainability in higher education. Section 1 contains icebreakers, Sections 2 and 3 provide examples of role play and forum play in various settings, Section 4 describes how to use dramatic, provocative performances to provoke insights, and Section 5 presents more elaborate drama processes. The final section considers how to sustain future practice.

## Further reading

Patrice Baldwin's books are very user-friendly for readers who are not drama specialists. The titles indicate a specific year group or subject area but are easy to adapt to other educational contexts. For example:

Baldwin, P., & Galazka, A. (2021). *Process drama for second language teaching and learning: A toolkit for developing language and life skills.* Bloomsbury Publishing.
Boal, A. (1979/2019). *Theatre of the oppressed.* Pluto Press.
Bowell, P., & S. Heap, B. (2013). *Planning process drama: Enriching teaching and learning* (2nd edition). Taylor & Francis.

## References

Boal, A. (2019). *Theatre of the oppressed.* Pluto Press.
Boal, A. (2022). *Games for actors and non-actors.* Routledge.
Boal, A. (2005). *Legislative Theatre: Using performance to make politics.* Routledge.
Bolton, G (1979). *Towards a theory of drama in education.* Longman.
Byréus, K. (2010). *Du har huvudrollen i ditt liv. Om forumspel som pedagogisk metod för frigörelse och förändring* [*You play the lead role in your life. Forum play as an educational method for emancipation and change*]. Liber.
Byréus, K. (2006). *Bella – rubble and roses 2: For girl groups.* KSAN.
Davis, S., & Tarrant, M. (2014). Environmentalism, stories and science: Exploring applied theatre processes for sustainability education. *Research in Drama Education: The Journal of Applied Theatre and Performance, 19*(2), 190–194. https://doi.org/10.1080/1356977 83.2014.895613
European Commission (2022). *GreenComp, the European sustainability competence framework.* Publications Office of the European Union. https://data.europa.eu/doi/10.2760/13286
Ganguly, S. (2010). *Jana Sanskriti: Forum Theatre and democracy in India.* Routledge.
Gordon, S., & Thomas, I. (2016). "The learning sticks": Reflections on a case study of role-playing for sustainability. *Environmental Education Research, 24*(2), 172–190. https://doi.org/10.1080/13504622.2016.1190959

Hallgren, E. (2018). *Ledtrådar till estetiskt engagemang i processdrama. Samspel i roll i en fiktiv verksamhet (Clues to aesthetic engagement in process drama. Joint action in a fictional activity)*. PhD dissertation (Summary in English). Stockholm University.

Lehtonen, A., Österlind, E., & Viirret, T. J. (2020). Drama in education for sustainability: Becoming connected through embodiment. *International Journal of Education & the Arts 21*(19). https://doi.org/10.26209/ijea21n19

Nicholson, H. (2005). *Applied drama: The gift of theatre*. Palgrave Macmillan.

O'Neill, C. (1995). *Dramaworlds: A framework for process drama*. Heinemann.

O'Toole, J. (1992). *The process of drama: Negotiating art and meaning*. Routledge.

Österlind, E. (2008). Acting out of habits – can Theatre of the Oppressed promote change? Boal's theatre methods in relation to Bourdieu's concept of habitus. *Research in Drama Education: The Journal of Applied Theatre and Performance, 13*(1), 71–82. https://doi.org/10.1080/13569780701825328

Österlind, E. (2011). Forum play – a Swedish mixture for consciousness and change. In S. Schonmann (Ed.), *Key concepts in theatre/drama education* (pp. 247–251). SENSE Publishers.

Österlind, E. (2018). Drama in higher education for sustainability: Work-based learning through fiction? *Higher Education, Skills and Work-Based Learning, 8*(3), 337–352.

Piazzoli, E. (2011). Process drama: The use of affective space to reduce language anxiety in the additional language learning classroom. *Research in Drama Education: The Journal of Applied Theatre and Performance, 16*(4), 557–573. https://doi.org/10.1080/13569783.2011.617104

Piazzoli, E. (2018). *Embodying language in action. The artistry of process drama in second language education*. Palgrave Macmillan.

Theatre of the Oppressed NYC. (2019). *How does Legislative Theatre work?* https://www.tonyc.nyc/legislativetheatre

van Ments, M. (1994). *The effective use of role play: A handbook for teachers & trainers*. Kogan Page.

Wagner, B. J. (1976). *Dorothy Heathcote: Drama as a learning medium*. National Education Association.

# Chapter 3

# Before you start with drama and performance

Shelley Piasecka

## Learning outcomes and related terms

The drama processes in this chapter aim to develop:

- Awareness of the core principles of drama as a practice-led pedagogy.
- Understanding of the preparation and processes required to run an effective drama session.
- Appreciation of the ethical dimensions of drama as a learning and teaching methodology for sustainability education.

Key terms and definitions:

- Drama: this book refers to the characteristics and processes associated with applied drama in educational contexts. It is not meant to be interpreted as acting techniques or theatre training for actors (see Chapter 2).
- Icebreakers: these are forms of games designed to get to know the group, to learn names, and for introducing drama to non-specialist students. This book offers suggestions for icebreaker games you can play with groups of different sizes.
- Warm-up games: These are games designed for when a group is familiar with each other and are typically played before the main activity as a way of breaking down inhibitions and building teamwork and communication between learners. Warm-up games can be an effective way to end a session.

DOI: 10.4324/9781003496359-4

# Preparing yourself

Drama and performance are a universal pedagogic tool that can be applied in different kinds of educational settings and purposes (see Chapters 1 and 2). It should be stressed that there are no hard and fast rules for using drama and performance; the guidance offered is to support the creation of safe and inclusive learning environments with an emphasis on the activities being fun and enjoyable.

Before introducing drama to teaching, it might be expedient to first discuss this with your line manager or Head of Department. Sometimes, the greatest resistance comes not from the students but from managers. This is not to denigrate those in power but to recognise that managers (and their managers) have wider remits and institutional concerns that lead decision-making and, specifically course design, in particular ways.

Drama and performance can, and do, enrich the learning and teaching environment and, if done carefully, can be integrated into the assessment. Rather than implementing drama behind closed doors, try sharing your observations gained from reading this book with your colleagues and managers. You may be surprised at the response you get.

Drama and performance, as a learning and teaching approach, also have the potential to engage learners in the process of making real and transformative change. Helen Nicholson notes that applied drama has been "troubled by new insights into cultural production and representation of knowledge" (2005, p. 16). Notwithstanding the concerns Nicholson quite rightly points to, the chapters in this volume illustrate a desire to improve the lives and outcomes of participants.

The Brazilian theatre practitioner, writer, and activist Augusto Boal writes, "knowledge is acquired... via the senses and not only the mind. Before all else, we see and we listen, and its thanks to this we understand" (1995, p. 28). The British author and speaker Sir Ken Robinson similarly described the arts as an "aesthetic experience [in which] your senses are operating at their peak. When you're present in the current moment. When you're resonating with excitement of this thing that you are experiencing. When you're fully alive" (2010, n.p.).

There are many examples contained within this book that exemplify these core ideas, drawing upon real case studies to show first-hand the experience of learners and teachers. This chapter marks a starting point of the journey.

# Core principles underpinning a typical session

## *Drama and performance are for everyone*

Anyone, regardless of educational background, subject discipline, or expertise, can lead a drama session. Start by introducing some drama elements in your ordinary teaching and keep adding when you feel comfortable.

Drama, at its heart, is a willingness to enter imaginative and make-believe worlds. It is a facility unique to humans and something we learn as young children. Every time we watch a film, read a book, or listen to music, we exercise our imaginations. Drama builds upon the skills we already possess to foster playful and fun learning environments for our learners.

Drama and performance sessions do not necessarily require participants to be loud, overly confident, or to have prior experience. While prior experience may be helpful, all that is required from those taking part is a willingness to try something new.

## There are no right or wrong answers

Drama and performance encourage us to consider the world, and our place within it, from differing and, often, conflicting perspectives. In drama or performance work, there are no wrong or easy answers.

## Plan, plan, plan

Even experienced drama specialists will tell you that the best-prepared sessions can go awry. Always have a plan B (and C and D), and if something goes wrong simply move on to the next exercise. Some general practices include:

- Icebreakers can be used at any point.
- Reschedule drama activities to another time if learners are preoccupied with forthcoming exams or assessments.
- Avoid replacing a planned conventional lesson with an impromptu drama or performance session.
- It is a good idea to plan lead-in and lead-out sessions, such as developing core themes, with students.
- Plan time for follow-on tasks and projects.

## Enjoy the process!

It is worth remembering that groups respond to material differently, and that what works well for one group may not for another. The playwright Samuel Beckett famously said, "Ever tried. Ever failed. No matter. Try again. Fail again. Fail better" (1983, n.p). The joy is in trying new ideas and above all to enjoy the process.

# Setting up a teaching room for drama and performance

- Before the session, familiarise yourself with the room layout.
- Be prepared to change or revise the session if the space available does not suit the planned activity.

- Consider whether potential noise spill from your session will affect other learners.
- If space is an issue, consider moving the session outside (weather permitting).
- If the room layout permits, move the tables to the edges of the room and arrange chairs in a circle. Give yourself as much space in the middle of the room as possible.
- If it is not possible to move tables and chairs, clear as much space as you can at the front of the room.
- Ask participants to store their coats and bags safely in the corner of the room and to turn off phones.
- Allocate time to return the room to its original layout.

## Icebreakers and warm-up games

- In a notebook, make a list of icebreakers and warm-up games.
- Break the list down into sub-categories, for example, games for small groups, games for big groups, warm-up and warm-down activities (and so on).
- In a 60-minute session, try allocating 5 minutes for icebreakers and 10 minutes for warm-up games before moving on to the main activity.
- Leave enough time at the end of the session for discussion and reflection.
- End with a short warm-down activity.

## Ethical issues to consider

### Emotional well-being

Drama and performance can evoke strong emotions in the participants, particularly if the topic or theme is particularly sensitive or charged. Participants may also become overwhelmed if the lines between fiction and reality are blurred. So:

- Explain the purpose of the session before beginning the activity.
- Remind participants that drama is fictional.
- Intervene and stop the activity if you feel it necessary.
- Have a backup plan.
- Consider taking on the more contentious or challenging roles yourself, at least until the group is familiar with the process.
- Build in enough time for reflection and discussion.
- A warm-down game can help to bring participants out of the drama and into their real lives.

### Group dynamics

A drama session is purposefully egalitarian. However, non-traditional approaches may lead to noisy, talkative, and disruptive sessions if not managed effectively. So:

- Set expectations at the beginning of the session. For example: this activity will require you to work as part of a group, or this activity will require you to work without sound.
- Whenever possible, work in a circle. Not only does this support greater equality between students but also allows the teacher to see all participants (there is no hiding in a circle).
- Use random selection methods to put participants into groups. For example, go around the circle, pointing to each participant in turn, saying 1, 2, 3, 4, where each number represents a group.
- Challenge disruptive behaviour, such as talking, calmly.
- If a session becomes too loud or rowdy, switch to a quiet or reflective activity.

## Power and status

Drama and performance often flatten traditional power hierarchies between teachers and students. To deal with any potential issues arising from conflicts of status, take an active role, i.e. lead from within. Dorothy Heathcote calls this teacher-in-role (Heathcote & Bolton, 1995).

## Participation and consent

An effective drama session relies on participants making informed choices:

- Explain the purpose of the activity and the reasons for using a drama approach.
- Allow participants to contribute on their own terms and without any expectation of dramatic skill or ability.

## Managing differing learning needs and dis/abilities

- Arrange the room layout to facilitate easy access and movability for disabled or wheelchair-using participants.
- Provide clear and unambiguous instructions. This will be particularly helpful for participants with neurodiversity.
- Provide examples of how participants might approach a task or role.
- Be mindful that some participants may feel uncomfortable with touch and proximity.
- Allow participants to contribute non-verbally, such as using sticky notes.
- For participants with ADHD, try running shorter sessions with varied activities.
- For longer sessions, build in time for breaks.
- Provide images, pictures, and diagrams to support participants who find it difficult to visualise.
- Ensure that everyone has an opportunity to reflect on the session.

## Integrating with assessment

As you go through this book, there will be many examples of how to integrate drama into assessment. Before we touch on these, it is worth reminding that the purpose of undertaking applied drama is to facilitate greater communication and collaboration between learners, to encourage deep and exploratory thinking, and to enrich the learning and teaching environment. It is not often a demonstration of acting and dramatic skills. Therefore, by way of example, rather than assessing learners on their portrayal of a role, or characterisation in a role-playing scene, focus on their abilities to create opportunities to promote discussion, debate, deep thinking, and critical awareness and insight.

It is also worth remembering that drama can be emotionally charged. While developing emotional literacy is integral to the drama process, to echo Pamela Bowell and Brian Heap, "the last thing that a teacher wants is a room full of students histrionically role-playing 'fury', and who are then rendered incapable of completing any further talk in a generally constructive way" (2017, p. 91). Assessment, then, should be careful not to prioritise the emoting of expression over deep discussion. Each chapter in this book gives suggestions as to how you might integrate the drama or performance process into assessment.

## Making a start!

For higher education teachers wishing to expand their practical use of drama, the best advice is to simply try out as many games and activities as you can. Many owe their genesis to the techniques and methods of the Brazilian theatre practitioner, writer, and activist, Augusto Boal. And while not all practices can be attributed in this way, the sentiment expressed by Adrian Jackson, translator of Boal's seminal book, *The Rainbow of Desire*, that "the only skills necessary are observation and openness" (Jackson; cited in Boal, 1995, p. xxiii) – is a useful reminder of the purpose of this book.

The games included here are intended to be played, adapted, and re-purposed to meet the specific contexts, disciplines, and individual needs of teachers and students. What follows is not an instruction manual, a list of hard and fast rules, a positioning of values, political leanings, or belief systems. Certainly, follow the guidance suggested by the authors, they are intended to help, but the greatest joy and liberation comes from making the drama your own.

## Further reading

Boal, A. (2015). *Rainbow of desire*. Routledge.

Nicholson, H. (2005). *Applied drama: The gift of theatre*. Palgrave Macmillan.

Whitfield, P. (2022). *Inclusivity and equality in performance training: Teaching and learning for neuro and physical diversity*. Routledge.

# References

Boal, A. (2015). *Rainbow of desire.* Routledge.

Beckett, S. (1983). *Worstward ho.* Grove Press.

Bowell, P., & Heap, B. S. (2017). *Putting process drama into action: The dynamics of practice.* Routledge.

Heathcote, D., & Bolton, G. M. (1995). *Drama for learning.* Heinemann Drama.

Nicholson, H. (2005). *Applied drama: The gift of theatre.* Palgrave Macmillan.

Robinson, Sir K. (2010, October). *Changing education paradigms.* TED Talks. www.ted.com/talks/sir_ken_robinson_changing_education_paradigms

Whitfield, P. (2022). *Inclusivity and equality in performance training: Teaching and learning for neuro and physical diversity.* Routledge.

# ENERGISING AND CONNECTING THROUGH ICEBREAKERS

**2**

## Chapter 4

# Drama icebreaker

## Improvisation for beginners

Shelley Piasecka

### Learning outcomes and related terms

The drama processes in this chapter aim to:

- Apply creative and reciprocal modes of verbal and non-verbal communication with others.
- Develop an understanding of status in relational learning contexts and its impact on sustainability education.
- Apply embodied ways of knowing needed for problem-solving, systems thinking, and adapting to change.

Key terms and definitions:

- Drama impro: impro is a form of improvised theatre or live performance. In this chapter, the term is applied within educational contexts to develop unplanned and spontaneous communication and interaction between participants.
- Offer and acceptance: this term underpins the foundational principles of drama impro. Essentially, it means accepting the other's initiative and offering a reply or action in exchange. This allows interaction and variation of the impro to occur.
- Blocking: preventing an impro from continuing is called blocking. When this happens, the impro breaks down, falters, or stops, usually because the offer

DOI: 10.4324/9781003496359-6

**35**

is not accepted or returned in a generative way, for example: "*Do you want to go to the cinema tonight? – No.*" However, if the response is "*No, I'd like to go dancing*" the impro has a better chance of continuing.

■ Status: in impro, social status affects how we communicate and interact with others. The status you play in a drama impro may not be the same as the status you present to the world in everyday life.

■ Spontaneity: Spontaneity games encourage participants to think fast on their feet and to come up with creative and imaginative ideas in the moment.

| Key sustainability-related outcomes |
| --- |
| **Embodying sustainability values** |
| Valuing sustainability/self-awareness and normative competencies |
| **Embracing complexity in sustainability** |
| Systems thinking |
| **Envisioning sustainable futures** |
| Adaptability |
| Exploratory thinking |
| **Acting for sustainability** |
| Collective action/strategic/collaboration competence |

# Context of application

The impro games and approaches described in this chapter are heavily indebted to the writings of Keith Johnstone (1981). They have been adapted, practised, and re-adapted many times over a 30-year period and applied in university settings, schools, and youth and community groups in the UK. Class sizes have varied from groups of eight or so to groups of more than 30 with students from all kinds of backgrounds and subject disciplines.

The games described here are less concerned with technique or the development of skill. While learning the form is worthy of its own study, the value for non-drama specialists lies in the transferrable benefits of developing communication, reciprocity, collaboration, and teamwork with students.

# Step-by-step guidance

1. Preparation.

   ■ Arrive early to organise the room layout.
   ■ If permissible, move tables and chairs to the edges of the room.

The following games underpin the three core principles of drama impro: (2) offer and acceptance, (3) status, and (4) spontaneity.

2. Offer and acceptance "Yes" Game.

The golden principle for impro is to continue the action. A simple technique is to begin each sentence with "Yes".

■ Organise the participants into pairs.
■ Allocate A and B.
■ Ask them to spread out so that they do not disturb each other.
■ Run the impro for two or three minutes.
■ Ask participants to swap roles or change partners.

Here is the instruction you can give in class:

> *In the scene, two friends, A and B, are debating whether to attend a lecture. A would like to go to the lecture because the teacher will be covering course material for a forthcoming exam.*
> *B thinks going will be a waste of time and besides, it's a nice day. B would rather be outside than in a stuffy lecture room.*

Here is an example of a scene starter you can use:

> A. *Are you ready? I don't want to be late for the lecture. I'm so looking forward to it, are you?*
> B. *Yes, but wouldn't you rather go for a walk and enjoy the sunshine?*
> A. *Yes, it is a lovely day, but I really wanted to go to the lecture. Don't you want to go?*
> B. *Yes, of course, I want to go, but it's so nice outside! Can you hear the birds singing?*
> A. *Yes, they sound wonderful, we could open a window to hear them.*
> B. *Yes, a good idea, but the trees are so far away...*

And so on.
Extension task:

■ Alternate the status of the characters.
■ See what happens if you add props to the impro.

3. Status game.

In an impro session, status, much like in our everyday lives, affects how we communicate and present ourselves to others. This game reverses the usual hierarchical status between a student and a teacher.

■ Organise the participants into pairs, A and B.
■ Participant A plays the role of a university teacher.
■ Participant B plays the role of a student.
■ Run the impro for two or three minutes.

■ Ask the group to swap partners and repeat.
■ Consider asking for volunteers to show their impro to the rest of the group.

Here is the instruction you can give in class:

> *In the scene, the university teacher (A) must give a lesson on a sustainability topic. However, the lesson notes were left on a train. To make matters worse, it is the teacher's first teaching job. The teacher is feeling very anxious and nervous.*
>
> *The student (B) is highly knowledgeable about the sustainability topic. Because the teacher is anxious, the student tries to help the teacher with the lesson.*

Here are some examples of scene starters you can use:

B. *(Looking at the clock) Already 5 past the hour, I wonder where the teacher is?*
A. *(Enters in a fluster) Oh thank goodness you're still here… Now where did I put my lesson notes…?*
B. *Don't panic. Are they in your bag?*
A. *I'm sure I put them in there… Oh no!*
B. *What's happened?*
A. *I took them out to read on the train. I must have forgotten to put them back. They'll be halfway to Stockholm by now. What will I do?*

And so on. Or,

A. *Get out your pens and papers and write, erm, erm…?*
B. *The topic of today's lesson?*
A. *Ah, yes! The topic today is, err, err….?*
A. *Biodiversity and the importance of wetlands?*
B. *Ah yes, Wetlands. Well, the thing about wetlands is that they are very, very…. erm.*
A. *Wet?*

And so on.
Extension task:

■ Try switching the status of characters during the impro.
■ Develop into a longer scene, adding new characters and prompts.

4. Spontaneity games

Spontaneity games encourage participants to think fast and come up with creative ideas in the moment. This game requires participants to come up with quick ideas for a plastic bottle. The game works best when done at speed.

Game 1 "This is not a bottle"

1. Organise the participants in a circle.
2. A participant steps into the middle of the circle, holds up the bottle and says, "*This is not a bottle. It's a hairbrush*".

3. The participant acts out brushing their hair with the bottle.
4. A second participant steps into the circle and says, "*That's not a hairbrush, it's a baby*".
5. The first participant steps out.
6. The second participant pretends the bottle is a baby.
7. A third participant steps into the circle and the process repeats.
8. Each time, participants must improvise different ideas for the bottle.
9. Continue until everyone has had a turn.
10. Possible ideas are a hairbrush, a baby, an aeroplane, a kite, a kitten, a bomb, a sandwich, a television remote (the list is endless).

Game 2 "I am a discarded bottle on a beach"
The game requires participants to create still images in response to a stimulus, in this case a discarded bottle on a beach.
Participants need to create images they can hold until the end of the game.
As with the previous game, it works best when done at speed.
There are no right or wrong answers, participants should jump in with the first idea that comes to mind.

1. Organise the participants in a big circle.
2. A participant walks into the middle of the circle and says, "*I am a discarded bottle on a beach*".
3. The participant then makes a still image, representative of a bottle.
4. A second participant joins them and says, for example, "*I am empty crisp packet, lying next to the bottle*".
5. They then make an image representative of a crisp packet.
6. A third participant enters and says, for example, "*I am a sunbather, who left my rubbish on the beach*".
7. The participant lies on the floor pretending to be the sunbather.
8. A fourth participant enters and says, for example, "*I am a hungry dog looking for food*".
9. And so on. The activity continues until everyone has entered the circle.
10. Hold the picture for a few moments, then relax.

Extension task:

■ Try adding sounds to the still images.
■ Come up with new ideas for a stimulus. Possible suggestions could be a plastic bag floating in the sea, a single tree on a busy traffic island, a lonely recycling bin in the office.

5. Reflection and discussion
Discuss the stimulus and reflect on how you might use drama impro to link to GreenComp and sustainability themes.

# Framing or pre-work

Please see Chapters 2 and 3 in this book.

# When to use and when not to use

Impro works best when groups are comfortable with each other. This is the case for all students, even for those whose specialism is drama and theatre. This is because impro as a form of learning relies on participants working together. Indeed, impro cannot happen, at least the kinds suggested here, without a commitment to reciprocity and teamwork. You can build up teamwork skills using the drama games and icebreakers listed in this book.

Impro games can be noisy, especially when participants are enjoying the session. Check the academic calendar for exams and assessments in nearby rooms – reschedule if necessary or relocate to a more suitable space.

# Reflections from the field

Impro games are often a favourite of students, probably because they are fun and enjoyable. If you take it seriously and spend time developing your understanding of the form, you can expect a lot of laughter in your class or lecture room. The value of which cannot be underestimated when considering the emotional well-being of students.

This said, most participants approach impro for the first time with a great deal of nervousness. There is a feeling that to be good at impro, one needs to be original, funny, and clever. Nothing could be further from the truth; anyone can take part in and indeed enjoy impro.

Johnstone suggests several reasons why impro fails, and it is useful to touch upon concerns of spontaneity and originality. He writes, "At school any spontaneous act was likely to get me into trouble. I learned never to act on impulse, and that whatever came into my mind should be rejected in favour of a better idea" (1981, p. 82). Modern schooling affirms this idea which is not always helpful for students. Of the desire to be original, Johnstone has this to say: "Suppose Mozart *had* tried to be original? It would have been like the man at the North Pole trying to walk north, and this is true of all of the rest of us. Striving after originality takes you far away from your true self and makes your work mediocre" (1981, p. 88; original emphasis).

With this advice in mind, stress to your participants that impro does not require participants to be anything other than themselves. The best impro is when participants enter the spirit of the activity, say or do whatever comes to mind, and remember not to take themselves too seriously.

# Things to consider

There is a tendency for participants to sit and talk rather than getting up and trying out tasks practically. Encourage participants to use their bodies while doing the activity and when preparing the task.

Reassure participants that impro does not need to be good. Sometimes the game will work and other times not. Embracing failure is part of the process.

It is also worth reminding students that we all improvise every day of our lives. Every time we go into a shop, speak to someone we know, grab a morning coffee, and so on, we are improvising. We do this naturally and effortlessly, responding to prompts and stimulus in the moment. Impro games are no different.

If blocking occurs, simply reset and restart the impro.

# Learning extensions

Ultimately, impro is about experimentation and practice; there are no right or wrong ways of doing drama impro. Encourage your students to get into the habit of saying "yes" and to practice moving the activity along. And if it goes wrong – stop the action, laugh, and try again! To extend your understanding of impro, see Johnstone (1981, 2012).

# Integrating with assessment

While students of drama and acting may well be assessed on their skills and abilities of drama impro, it is probably not a good idea to assess non-specialist students in the same way. In this case, the value of drama impro lies in its transferable skills of communication, reciprocity, collaboration, and teamwork. For example, impro could be used as a method of bringing students together for group projects, presentations, seminars, and so on.

For students training to be teachers, they could develop impro workshops for schools and youth groups. Again, the assessment is not concerned with a demonstration of skill, as such, but rather with the application of impro to facilitate collaboration and teamwork.

Impro also develops our capacity for vital and core skills pertaining to the Green-Comp, including to think in the moment and to approach complex ideas and problems from new and imaginative perspectives.

# Further reading

Boal, A. (2005). *Games for actors and non-actors*. Routledge.
Dudeck, T. (2013). *Keith Johnstone: A critical biography*. Bloomsbury.

For a critical overview of Johnstone's work see:

Spolin, V. (1999). *Improvisation for the theatre.* Northwestern University Press.

## References

Johnstone, K. (1981). *Impro: Improvisation and the theatre.* Routledge, Chapman & Hall.
Johnstone, K. (2012). *The last bird: Stories & plays.* Alexander-Verl.

## Chapter 5

# Drama icebreaker

## House of Commons

Lenneke Vaandrager

### Learning outcomes and related terms

The drama processes in this chapter aim to:

- Initiate thinking about a sustainability related-topic such as future energy practices.
- Explore (without preparation) how to view an issue from different perspectives by taking a true or pretend position towards a certain statement (proposition).
- Practice how to instantly formulate arguments and speak up defending a certain position in a playful manner.
- Use body language and position to 'take a stance' and make a non-verbal statement.

Key terms and definitions:

- Word shower: joint associative generation of words similar to brainstorming
- Debate: using verbal arguments in a debate or taking a position in space to discuss or show your agreement or disagreement with a certain viewpoint
- House of Commons: a process where two sides represent two different groups holding different opinions. In a space, these groups sit opposite each other.

DOI: 10.4324/9781003496359-7

**43**

| Key sustainability-related outcomes |
| --- |
| **Embodying sustainability values** |
| Supporting fairness |
| **Embracing complexity in sustainability** |
| Systems thinking |
| Critical thinking |
| **Envisioning sustainable futures** |
| Futures literacy/anticipatory competence |
| Exploratory thinking |
| **Acting for sustainability** |
| Individual initiative |

# Context of application

In 2023 and 2024, a group of 20 PhD candidates participated in a word shower followed by the role play 'House of Commons'. The topic was future household energy practices. The House of Commons role play is a brief and quickly shifting form of role play that takes about 30 minutes to do and can include a reflecting discussion afterwards of 20 minutes. Together with a word shower, which can be created in 10 minutes, it takes in total 60 minutes.

This role play was part of the PhD course Transformative and Participatory Qualitative Research Approaches & Methods (TPAR) of the Wageningen School of Social Sciences (WASS) Graduate Programme in The Netherlands. TPAR provides PhD candidates and early-career scholars conceptual and hands-on methodological engagement with transformative, participatory and action-research approaches that use creative and arts-based research methods and techniques.

These techniques foster the inclusion and engagement of diverse, often marginalised perspectives and to bring into focus, examine and transform narratives, representations, and practices. The course gives students the opportunity to practice using these methods with individuals and groups, as well as to examine and assess these methods in relation to action-oriented engagement and the opportunities and challenges they pose for data analysis and (re)presentation (Ormond & De Vrieze, 2024). PhD candidates participating in this course come from different scientific backgrounds such as health, sustainability, international development studies, and governance.

# Step-by-step guidance

Word shower:

1. Write the topic (e.g. 'future energy practices') on a board or flipchart.
2. Ask the students to pay attention to what comes up in their mind when they hear the words 'future energy practices'. A possibility, when a group is a bit

shy or if certain students tend to be more outspoken than others, is to ask students to first discuss their ideas with another student. However, then it becomes less improvised and associative and more well-considered – like a normal brainstorm.

3. Ask the students to raise their hands and share their words with the facilitator who writes these words in a circle around the central topic.
4. Let the students build upon each other's words. Actively ask for new input.
5. Check with the group whether the word shower is complete by asking 'Did we miss any words?'
6. The outcome is a joint mind map with many different words. Summarise what is shown on the mind map.

House of Commons:

1. Prepare a number of 'propositions' that are debatable. Here are some examples related to future household energy practices:

   ■ The strongest shoulders should bear the heaviest burden.
   ■ For everyone, an electric car in front of your house.
   ■ The rich are showing much better energy practices than the poor: look who has solar panels and heat pumps.
   ■ The technology push represses space for non-technological solutions.
   ■ Cooking a good and tasteful meal for friends and family is more important than saving energy.
   ■ The speed of the required energy transition is more important than that everyone can keep up with that speed (we have to act now).
   ■ The municipality should enforce the energy saving practices.

2. Put an equal number of chairs at each side of the room and place them opposite to each other. The number of chairs depends on the group size. If there are, for example, 16 students, you can put 8 on each side.
3. Appoint a facilitator to manage the process. It can be either the teacher or one of the students.
4. Explain to the group that one side represents proponents, who agree to the proposal, and the other side are opponents, who disagree. The students can pretend to agree or disagree, it does not need to be their real opinion.
5. The facilitator presents the first proposition, e.g. on a PowerPoint slide or a flipchart. Show one proposition at a time.
6. Ask the students to stand up, choose a side and sit down.
7. Brief the participants to stand up when they want to explain why they agree or disagree with a proposition or if they want to react to someone speaking.
8. Summarise viewpoints and invite more participants to react.
9. The facilitator presents a new proposition, and the procedure is repeated.
10. The students may well change sides if they hear a certain viewpoint, or choose to stand in the middle. That is fine too and often results in some laughter.

## Framing or pre-work

The word shower serves to introduce the topic of the House of Commons role play. It is also possible to ask the students to prepare by reading about the topic, in this case future energy practices, before the session, or to connect to relevant literature afterwards.

## When to use and when not to use

The word shower allows teachers to quickly see what the students know about a certain topic. If making a word shower is used as an icebreaker, the teacher could go back to the mind map after the drama activity and see if certain words need to be added or removed from the word shower.

The House of Commons role play is useful to create a safe place and have some fun together. The students can play and pretend they hold a certain viewpoint and develop arguments to defend a specific position. The tool is inclusive as anyone who is less outspoken can join non-verbally or by literally taking a stance, a physical position in the room (agree or disagree).

The tool is not appropriate for large groups (more than 20 participants) or for very sensitive topics. It is also important that the propositions are debatable, that is, the proposition can be seen as being either true or false. If propositions are unclear participants often start to discuss how the proposition is formulated. If everyone agrees or disagrees with a proposition – or in other words if there is nothing to debate – the tool is (also) not effective. Either there are no disagreements on the topic in a particular group, or the propositions need to be a bit more 'edgy'. Then you can just move on to the next proposition, or the facilitator can invite some persons to defend the opposite of what everyone agrees or disagrees with.

## Reflections from the field

In the applications so far, all students were actively engaged. The word shower was created in 10 minutes. Examples of words mentioned included solar panel, electric car, renewable energy, sustainability, energy poverty, climate change, sustainable transport, saving water, recycle, and consumption of local products. For the House of Commons, after one or two participants started to defend their position, others also got involved and there was a lot of energy, playfulness, and laughing. Some participants were clearly more involved than others and also dared to speak up and defend their position. Reflections after the session included:

> "Warming up with the word shower icebreaker and then the House of Commons worked really well to get everyone ready to play."

> "We are getting to know each other in a different way through these playful methods."

"Easier for extroverts and can be intimidating for those who have never done something like this."

## Things to consider

Manage people who are very outspoken and tend to easily take the floor. Actively invite others to voice their opinion. Repeat during the session that the students can pretend that they have a certain (often unexpected or socially less accepted) viewpoint.

## Learning extensions

Word shower:

■ The students can be asked to write words on sticky notes, and these notes can be collected and organised into sub-themes.
■ There are also many word-cloud generators available as software applications (e.g. Mentimeter). They can provide an overview of those words that appear with the highest frequency.

House of Commons:

■ Discuss some debating techniques before you play the actual House of Commons.
■ Ask the students to prepare the propositions themselves.
■ Ask volunteers to take the facilitator role.
■ Collect arguments on a flipchart and discuss them afterwards.

## Integrating with assessment

As the core idea of these activities is to practice argumentation in a creative and associative manner, assessment is not really suitable and can even be counterproductive. If for some reason assessment is mandatory, possible criteria for assessment could be:

■ Quality of the words in the word shower.
■ Level of participation in the debate.
■ Quality of the argumentation.

## Further reading

Brown, Z. (2015). The use of in-class debates as a teaching strategy in increasing students' critical thinking and collaborative learning skills in higher education. *Educational Futures*, 7. https://wlv.openrepository.com/handle/2436/621883

McMonagle, R. J., & Savitz, R. (2022). Active learning: Beyond structured debates in political science pedagogy. *Journal of Political Science Education*, 1–16. https://doi.org/10.1080/15512169.2022.2132164

# Reference

Ormond, M. E., & De Vrieze, A. G. M. (2024). Transformative and participatory qualitative research approaches and methods. *Course Guide 2024*. Wageningen School of Social Sciences. https://www.wur.nl/en/show/transformative-and-participatory-qualitative-research-approaches-and-methods-4-ects.htm

## Chapter 6

# Drama icebreaker

## Long lists and thinking aloud

Mary Ann Kernan

### Learning outcomes and related terms

The drama processes in this chapter aim to:

- Demonstrate and reflect upon collaborative, independent, performative, and creative practices to address complex and wicked challenges including sustainability, as a formative activity towards a related assessment (e.g. 40% of the module credit).
- Develop open-mindedness and enhanced confidence to solve problems in creative and innovative ways and to generate breakthrough ideas and transform problem-solving situations, leading to creative and/or innovative outcomes.
- Participatively explore specific sustainability challenges through the lens of a range of human and non-human actors to understand the challenges that impede the effective sustainability leadership.

Key terms and definitions:

- Still images are representations of scenes using the body to capture the essence of a message (e.g. of an issue, a feeling, or in this case, a power differential).

DOI: 10.4324/9781003496359-8

| Key sustainability-related outcomes |
| --- |
| **Embodying sustainability values** |
| Valuing sustainability/self-awareness and normative competencies |
| Supporting fairness |
| Promoting nature |
| **Embracing complexity in sustainability** |
| Systems thinking |
| Critical thinking |
| Problem framing/integrated problem-solving competence |
| **Envisioning sustainable futures** |
| Futures literacy/anticipatory competence |
| Adaptability |
| Exploratory thinking |
| **Acting for sustainability** |
| Political agency |
| Collective action/strategic/collaboration competence |
| Individual initiative |

# Context of application

This workshop was delivered in 2023 and 2024 to Bayes Business School students completing City's Masters in Innovation, Creativity and Leadership as part of Creativity and the Creative Industries (a 15-credit module). This capstone module was built on the students' knowledge and experience gained in the other modules, which focused on creative writing, interactive design, management and innovation in organisations, organisational psychology, and intellectual property.

The 19 students in 2023 and 22 in 2024 (all at least 25 in age, most 25–35, up to late 50s) were highly international groups, with students from China, India, Indonesia, Korea, Singapore, the Middle East, the Caribbean, the UEA, several Latin American countries, the USA, Canada, Australia, South Africa, and Sweden as well as the UK. Very few of them had previously taken part in drama as adults. This workshop functioned as a formative activity towards an assessed creative group performance, aiming to both support the students' confidence in exploring dramatic processes and deepen their exploration of sustainability themes in the planning and preparation of their assessed group performances.

# Step-by-step guidance

1. Organise groups: if the students are not already in project groups, first create random groups. Groups of four or five are ideal, maximum of six. First

calculate the number of people your total group divides most neatly into (for example, five groups of five and two of four). Ensuring that you have eye contact as you do so, repeatedly count up to your target number of people in each group (e.g. 1, 2, 3, 4, 5), telling them that you are doing so to create groups for an activity. Reassign any who are left over to create groups of no more than six. Direct each group to a space within the room where there are some chairs and safe access to the floor.

2. Agree sustainability scenario: invite them in their groups to discuss and agree a sustainability scenario. In case they need prompts or suggestions, prepare current examples which involve a range of governmental, industry, and community stakeholders, for example, a community issue related to river pollution, air or soil degradation, or recycling in a context that will be meaningful to the participants, and which have human and non-human impacts. If you have the opportunity to provide pre-work, you can set up your project groups before the session and assign pre-research with readings and links, especially with older and more expert groups who could also be directed to readings which highlight complex issues (e.g. examples posted by the UN and local governments and Filho et al., 2023 show how sustainable developments are connected through climate change).

3. Invite the groups to list relevant stakeholders: ask the groups to list the characters or stakeholders involved in that scenario (8–10 minutes). Ask them to identify at least one non-human but primarily human participants. Ensure that all of the groups are on track (and if not, give them a few more minutes).

4. Distribute sticky notes or similar, and brief the students to use these to write a description of each of their characters (5 minutes). If needed, prompt them with suggestions of appropriate 'status' descriptions such as ship's captain, planner, CEO, local mayor, farmer, scientist, purchaser, investor, school, trees, birds, cyclist – emphasising that these are only ideas.

5. While they do this, set up or reveal a flipchart or whiteboard with a heading 'STATUS' and arrows High to Low. To the whole group, then introduce the idea of the status of characters within both real-life and dramatic scenarios. You can add the examples you prepared.

6. Invite someone from each group to place their sticky notes for each of the characters in their scenario on the continuum from High to Low status on the prepared flipchart or whiteboard (3–5 minutes). If you have a large cohort, ask three small groups' representatives at a time to post their sticky notes and allow a few more minutes.

7. As they are doing this, review the outcomes yourself and reposition similar or overlapping descriptions together as well as confirming or adjusting the relative status rankings.

8. Invite the whole group to review the results for a time. Brief them to discuss what they learned through the activity about the status of different stakeholders in their scenario, and ask a volunteer to speak briefly for their group (5–8 minutes, depending on the size of the cohort).

9. Brief the whole group on the next stage of the activity, which is to plan and then show their scenario as a silent still image, using their bodies. Tell them the aim: to allow the rest of the attendees and you as their audience to understand the scenario as well as the role and status of each of the characters within that scenario. Allow 10–15 minutes.

10. As they prepare the presentation, circulate the room to answer any questions and to encourage them to explore how they might use simple props (e.g. chairs or tables) and body positioning to communicate clearly both the scene itself and the status of the characters within that scene. Tell each group that you will also call upon each individual to speak briefly and personally for their character: '*I am the ... [e.g. CEO, villager, heron] and I am [e.g. excited, starving, poisoned]...*'.

11. Invite each group in turn to show their scene, either by inviting volunteers or nominating the groups in term (e.g. working clockwise around the room).

12. Debrief each of the small group's silent images by focusing on each in turn. Allow yourself and the others in the whole group a minute or two in silence to review each still image, then invite each participant in the scene to say who they are and what they are experiencing, starting with the lowest status figure in the scenario. If necessary, ask each participant to repeat their statement briefly and emotively, so the group can hear and understand that character's experience.

13. To briefly wrap up this activity, you could invite the groups to briefly discuss (3–5 minutes) what they have learned about to status of different stakeholders in sustainability scenarios, including non-humans, and invite each group to share an insight with reference to their own or other groups' silent figures. You might also allow time for project groups to note insights that they can build on in later activities – or if part of a portfolio project, you could allow time for individuals to note their own reflections. In your own comments and feedback, aim to be positive, emphasise the power of the process to break down a complex situation into key stakeholders and impacts, and invite applause and celebration (10–15 minutes, depending on the size of the group).

## Framing or pre-work

With the first of these groups, use resources which left no room for doubt about the reality and impact of climate change. At the same time, share the creative potential of the medieval masons' unconditional approach to 'building a cathedral' they would never see completed (Nicholas, 2021), which is arguably what we need now to redress the effects of climate change. The master's and business school context of the cohort described here also gave access to concepts such as the need for leaders to find solutions to wicked or VUCA (volatile, uncertain, complex, and ambiguous) problems, which could be linked directly to the current urgency and complexity of sustainability.

## When to use and when not to use

The processes described here were set within a context of mature students familiar with the challenges of sustainability as well as the requirements of engaged, active learning. The activity was also positioned as a formative activity towards preparing a drama-based group performance assessment related to sustainability. With younger or less confident students, consider using this activity after other of the icebreaker activities described in this book to encourage the participants to feel confident with one another, with participative, embodied learning, and with the willingness to explore hopeful (in contrast to apocalyptic) sustainability outcomes.

## Reflections from the field

In both of my pilot workshops, all of the students participated, and each of the groups developed and showed a sustainability scenario. Their chosen settings included agricultural, organisational, domestic, and natural settings. In one of four groups in 2023 and all of the four groups in 2024, the students opted to explore scenarios which offered no clear indication of who was causing or could address the sustainability challenge and with almost entirely non-human characters (tomatoes, animals, the rain, a river). The level of humour in response to the activity was high on both occasions.

As part of my aim was to encourage them to collaborate, participate, and explore an accessible dramatic format, their enjoyment and engagement were welcome. However, I found that they did not fully engage with and perhaps even resisted the scale of the human challenges and responsibilities implicit in sustainability. I reflected that the initial briefing needed to more clearly require that the scenarios should involve no more than a single non-human character and focus on the roles and potential enactive capacity as well as the status of the human actors in the scenario, e.g. by more explicitly introducing Boal's (2008) language of 'oppressors' and 'oppressed'.

## Things to consider

The activity needs pens, sticky notes, and a whiteboard or flipchart for the debrief. It also needs an open space with a clean floor and, potentially, things to stand on safely. Running it in teaching rooms, I found that the students stood on chairs and even tables as well as lying on the floor to represent status – activities which could lead to health and safety or diversity concerns, especially with larger, less mature groups. Review your organisation's policies. If there are safety limits on space or resources to safely embody the hierarchies in their scenarios, you could encourage the use of masks or simple character representations which the students could create using cards, scissors, and pens. This in itself would be a suitable icebreaker activity before performing.

The activity also assumes participation and touch between the participants and brief public speaking. These aspects might well be problematic for some, so it is useful to have your own strategy for dealing with this. In my case, previous workshops had invited the students to notify me privately if they had any personal or mobility issues with the content of the module workshops. In an environment without that context, consider including this in your pre-arrival material and, again, review your organisation's policies. If individuals do not participate, invite them to take alternative roles in the activity, e.g. reviewing and grouping the sticky notes of the long lists. They could also act as observers of the groups' living statues and share their insights with you or with one another. You could then acknowledge and include their input in your debrief.

The debrief described here also assumes a culture of calm and respectful listening. In a group of strangers larger than around 12 people, these requirements can be included in the initial set-up, and you might need to stop the activity and remind the group as a whole of this requirement before restarting the debrief of the living statues.

## Learning extensions

You can extend the learning from the activity by allowing more time to introduce hopeful case studies or concepts such as 'cathedral thinking' (Kimberley, 2021), or to use examples from popular media, perhaps as pre-reading (also see the further reading section for more examples). Local initiatives and those led by people of similar age, gender, and ethnicity may speak most directly to your students by showing that many successful sustainability initiatives grow from a big idea, start small, and rely on the commitment of local communities.

## Integrating with assessment

Where you need to integrate this activity into an assessment, you can build in a reflective element for this as one of a series of workshop experiences, to be drawn upon as part of a summative project or essay submission.

## Further reading

Filho, W. L., Wall, T., Salvia, A. L., Dinis, M. A. P., & Mifsud, M. (2023). The central role of climate action in achieving the United Nations' Sustainable Development Goals. *Scientific Reports, 13*(1), 20582. https://doi.org/10.1038/s41598-023-47746-w.

Nicholas, K. (2021). *Under the sky we make: How to be human in a warming world.* Putnam.

# References

Boal, A. (2008). *Theatre of the oppressed* (3rd edition). Pluto Press.

Heogh, K. (Ed.). (2010). *Hope beneath our feet*. North Atlantic Books.

Natural History Museum. (2024). *Generation hope: Act for the planet.* https://www.nhm.ac.uk/events/generation-hope.html

Solnit, R. (2016). *Hope in the dark: Untold histories, wild possibilities*. Canongate.

UNFCCC (United Nations Framework Convention on Climate Change). (2024). *Winning projects, UN global climate action awards*. UN Climate Change. https://unfccc.int/climate-action/un-global-climate-action-awards/winning-projects (12 June 2024).

## Chapter 7

# Drama icebreaker

## Debate!

Anna Lehtonen

### Learning outcomes and related terms

The drama processes in this chapter aim to develop:

- Argumentation skills in the context of sustainability.
- Empathy through familiarising with different opinions and orientations to sustainability.
- Self-reflection in relation to various sustainability values and motivations.

Key terms and definitions:

- Debate: to argue a point of view (in contrast to "discuss" which means to consider alternative points, and "dialogue" which means to explore alternative perspectives).

| Key sustainability-related outcomes |
| --- |
| **Embodying sustainability values** |
| Valuing sustainability/self-awareness and normative competencies |
| **Embracing complexity in sustainability** |
| Critical thinking |
| **Acting for sustainability** |
| Collective action/strategic/collaboration competence |
| Individual initiative |

DOI: 10.4324/9781003496359-9

## Context of application

This icebreaker has been applied in various workshop contexts, such as in conferences for both pre-service and in-service teachers, in both national and international settings. This exercise has been used as a warm-up for both getting to know each other and to foster awareness of various opinions and to practice argumentation. The aim of the practice has been to provide participants with skills to engage people with different attitudes about sustainability by generating reflection around why people think as they do, what they value, and how attitudes may be formed and changed.

This icebreaker has worked well with various sized groups from 8 to 30 participants. The ideal size of the group is 10–20 participants, which means there are enough people with different perspectives, and it is easier to get an overview of arguments that may serve to inform idea generation for further collective processes. However, it is also possible to use this practice as an engaging, interactive, and reflective break between lecture times and spaces.

## Step-by-step guidance

1. Learning context.

   You may facilitate this practice in an ordinary classroom or even in an auditorium. However, it is better to have space for the participants to walk around and chat freely with each other. You may also guide them to spread out for their discussions, e.g. in a corridor which allow for more peaceful debate spaces. The issue of debate can be framed either generally to focus on climate change or to a specific issue such as different mitigation strategies.

2. Orientation (10–15 minutes).

   Orientate your participants to the debate by reflecting: "You all might have experienced how discussing sustainability can feel difficult for several reasons like conflicting opinions and attitudes, and the challenging emotions that the topic may evoke" (you may also refer to a study of Norgaard, 2011). Here, like during a lecture, people may not find it easy to talk about their personal opinions. Hence, it is essential to consider how to create a safe space and facilitate an inclusive discussion, where everybody can feel welcome to join without being judged of their opinion. You may emphasise the pedagogical value of this practice, e.g. that facilitating a debate in-role is one way to encourage discussion, manage sensitivities, and avoid real conflicts. The debate in-role fosters awareness of different orientations and simultaneously provokes reflection into how we relate to the issue personally.

   Another crucial point to reflect upon with the participants is what kind of principles are needed for productive learning to feel comfortable discussing sustainability in a group. You may ask the participants to share their ideas with the question: "*What helps you to feel comfortable and safe to express yourself in a group?*" This reflection could be conducted either within the whole group or in small groups, with the participants sitting or standing in pairs or trios for 5–10 minutes. To conclude, emphasise the importance of respect, acceptance, and showing interest, as ground rules for the debate activity.

3. Instructions for the debate (15–20 minutes).

   (a) Ask the participants to think, first, what kind of opinions about ecological sustainability or climate change mitigation they have encountered. Ask: *"Why is sustainability a relevant and important topic for different kinds of people and for you personally? Choose one opinion that either might be relevant for you or that is different and hence you might find it difficult to understand"* (see an example below).

   (b) Next, ask the participants to walk around and introduce themselves to others they encounter in the space by telling them the opinion they have chosen, but by using their own name. For example:

   *My name is Anna and I think that promoting ecological sustainability is clever, because it is an advantage for business…*

   *My name is… and I think…*

   (c) Additionally, you may tell the participants that they may modify their opinions if, while listening to others' arguments, they become impressed and convinced by others' ideas.

4. Post-reflection (10–15 minutes).

   After the debate, ask the participants to share their experiences with the people next to them. Provide them with some questions to help them to deepen their reflections (you can make these questions visible to the participants):

   ■ *What was the debate like? How did you like it?*
   ■ *What kind of different opinions, attitudes, or motives do people have for promoting sustainability?*
   ■ *Were you convinced by others' opinions? Did you modify your argument? Why? How did you feel about that?*
   ■ *What did you learn?*
   ■ *Can you see ways to apply this practice, and if so where?*

To get general feedback quickly, you can ask the participants to show (e.g. with thumbs up or down) whether they liked or disliked this practice, and likewise whether or not they changed their opinions. You may also facilitate a "gallery walk" as a post-reflection, where you ask the participants to write down their reflections on pieces of papers on the tables or walls, spread around the room or corridor, or by using some online application.

You may also introduce some inspirational research such as a survey on attitudes for deepening the learning. One possibility is to use the motivation profiles by Kaitosalmi et al. (2021) (see later in this chapter). If you use such materials, you might ask the participants to compare their opinion in the debate and/or their personal opinions to the outcomes of attitude surveys or motivation profiles.

## Framing or pre-work

This icebreaker needs little framing or introduction and can be used as a stand-alone activity or as a warm-up to other tools outlined in this book.

## When to use and when not to use

This practice works well especially for emotionally sensitive and conflicting issues that people might not feel comfortable to talk about otherwise or share their personal opinions about. It works well as an uncomplicated, easy-going, first-step practice that engages and encourages people simply to talk and debate through empathising with another's perspective. This is a useful practice for engaging people who do not know each other beforehand, and accessible for those who are not familiar or experienced with drama. You can use this exercise just as a creative thought-provocation or hands-on and personal reflection practice, even when you do not use other drama methods.

This activity may be sensitive if debating themes that would evoke personally traumatic experiences, so it is important to be aware of particularly sensitive issues which may emotionally impact individuals in the learning space (in the same way as would be expected in typical learning experiences).

## Reflections from the field

This practice has always worked well. Participants have commented that they have enjoyed and found this practice inspiring, liberating, and eye-opening. The frame of the practice releases tension and gives freedom to debate because the participants do not need to consider what other people think about their own views or worry about possible reactions to their comments. Different types of participants, especially teachers, have considered this practice to be applicable in many contexts and to several disciplines. It works especially well for debating climate change issues as it avoids a level of peer pressure or socially acceptable biases.

To debate from another perspective than your own decreases the threshold to argument and promotes understanding of others' motives and interests. Generally, many people experience talking about climate change as challenging due to emotional, social, and political tensions (Norgaard, 2011). Nevertheless, they like to hear what other people think about climate change. Participants say that have found it interesting to know how widely opinions, aspects, and attitudes to climate change vary, especially with people from different cultural backgrounds. To avoid conflicts in real life it is useful to practice empathy, and this activity promotes role-taking which enables "trying out" different perspectives and explanations, why they think as they do, and why they may deny the problem or resist taking action related to sustainability.

# Things to consider

If you would like to promote awareness of different motivators and interests to sustainability and teach about motivation profiles, then it is better to ask the participants not to adopt an attitude that totally opposes the relevance or denies the whole problem. Then the guidelines could be: *Think how people with different value perspectives could find promoting sustainability as important and an interest for them. Choose a value perspective that you have encountered but might feel strange to you.*

If you have a big group of participants, then it is useful to make visible the main ideas by writing the post-reflections on the tables or walls or by some online application like a polling tool (e.g. Mentimeter, Poll Everywhere).

# Learning extensions

The participants' arguments could be used to prompt deeper discussions on various motivations to sustainability, including why people think as they do or how people form and change their opinion (Rogers & Loitz, 2009; Hopwood et al., 2022). You may also introduce some research data, such as a currently published survey on attitudes for deepening reflection or research on students' attitudes (e.g. Perrault & Clark, 2018).

Another potential source is the motivation profiles based on a profound study by the Finnish innovation fund, Sitra (Kaitosalmi, Tuomisto, & Saarikoski, 2021). Motivation profiles sum up identified factors that get people to make choices that are both meaningful to them and environmentally sustainable. Motivation profiles describe different personal factors related to what people regard as good life. For example, sustainable choices may offer attractive opportunities that fit personal values such as better health, increased well-being, success, and pleasure, time or money savings, or time with loved ones.

Studying motivation profiles could lead to a broadened focus on how to engage and convince different people and this could also be practiced in simulated debates in-role. This could be continued by designing awareness raising campaigns about how to persuade or inspire people with specific motivation or value profiles to become interested and engaged in collective actions for sustainability.

# Integrating with assessment

You might consider asking students to keep a learning journal to capture their insights. This could work well as a tool for assessment of this practice and generally for applied drama. When you use learning diaries, it is useful to schedule some time at the end of the workshop for writing some post-activity notes straight after the practice that can be modified and deepened afterwards. The focus of reflection could be on learning experiences and sustainability competences (see GreenComp, European Commission Joint Research Centre, 2022).

## Further reading

Kaitosalmi, K., Tuomisto, T., & Saarikoski, E. (2021). *Motivation profiles of a sustainable lifestyle*. Sitra. https://www.sitra.fi/en/publications/motivation-profiles-of-a-sustainable-lifestyle/#sources

## References

European Commission Joint Research Centre. (2022). *GreenComp, the European sustainability competence framework*. Publications Office of the European Union. https://doi.org/10.2760/13286

Hopwood, C. J., Schwaba, T., Milfont, T. L., Sibley, C. G., & Bleidorn, W. (2022). Personality change and sustainability attitudes and behaviors. *European Journal of Personality*, *36*(5), 750–770. https://doi.org/10.1177/08902070211016260

Norgaard, K. M. (2011). *Living in denial: Climate change, emotions, and everyday life*. MIT Press.

Perrault, E. K., & Clark, S. K. (2018). Sustainability attitudes and behavioral motivations of college students: Testing the extended parallel process model. *International Journal of Sustainability in Higher Education*, *19*(1), 32–47.

Rogers, W. M., & Loitz, C. C. (2009). The role of motivation in behavior change: How do we encourage our clients to be active? *ACSMs Health & Fitness Journal*, *13*(1) (January). https://doi.org/10.1249/FIT.0b013e3181916d11

Further development of this practice has been a part of the ECF4CLIM project, which has received funding from the European Union's Horizon 2020 research and innovation programme under grant agreement no. 101036505. This article reflects only the authors' views and the Research Executive Agency (REA) and European Commission cannot be held responsible for any use that may be made of the information it contains.

# EXPLORING PERSPECTIVES THROUGH ROLE PLAY

*Chapter 8*

# Role play

## Co-creating nature-based solutions

Viola Hakkarainen

### Learning outcomes and related terms

The drama processes in this chapter aim to develop:

- Understanding of the complexity involved in co-creation processes for nature-based solutions.
- Perspective-taking and deliberation skills.
- Ability to critically reflect on collaborative processes in urban planning and development.

Key terms and definitions:

- Nature-based solutions: are 'actions to protect, conserve, restore, sustainably use and manage natural or modified terrestrial, freshwater, coastal, and marine ecosystems which address social, economic, and environmental challenges effectively and adaptively, while simultaneously providing human well-being, ecosystem services, resilience, and biodiversity benefits' (UNEA, 2022).
- Co-creation: a process that aims to make sustainability change processes more just and inclusive through using collaborative approaches to engage various actors both inside and outside academia. Co-creation of nature-based solutions is used to improve processes from planning to evaluation of the impact of the targeted solutions.

DOI: 10.4324/9781003496359-11

| Key sustainability-related outcomes |
| --- |
| **Embodying sustainability values** |
| Valuing sustainability/self-awareness and normative competencies |
| **Embracing complexity in sustainability** |
| Critical thinking |
| **Envisioning sustainable futures** |
| Exploratory thinking |

# Context of application

The role play was implemented in a nature-based solutions course designed for master's-level students at the University of Helsinki, Finland, during the academic years 2022 and 2023. This course is interdisciplinary and conducted annually, bringing together students from diverse backgrounds such as sustainability science, environmental sciences, and urban planning. It attracts an international student body in addition to Finnish students and is conducted entirely in English. Each year of the course, the role play session on campus comprised approximately 20 students and took place during a 90-minute lecture in a typical university classroom equipped with movable chairs and tables.

The role play was scheduled during a specific week of the course that focused on the co-creation of nature-based solutions, followed by another week concentrating on justice concerns in the planning and implementation of such solutions. The context for the role play was drawn from real-world ongoing development plans for the Malmi Airport area in Helsinki, a subject extensively covered by the media in recent years. This case involves multiple societal actors with diverse values and perspectives regarding the area's development. The negotiation of recreational, cultural-historical, biological, and economic values associated with the area served as a starting point for exploring the complexities of co-creation processes and citizen engagement during the role play exercise.

# Step-by-step guidance

1. Choose a relevant case for your role play, preferably one tied to a real-world context with readily available information. This could, for instance, involve the development of a new neighbourhood in a city or the gentrification of an old neighbourhood using nature-based solutions. Encourage students to familiarise themselves with the case beforehand, perhaps through reports or news articles, and emphasise the importance of considering the diverse views and values expressed by heterogeneous actors in public discussions about the case.

2. Start the class with one or two icebreaker activities to help students feel more comfortable expressing themselves (see Chapters 4–7).

3. At the beginning of the role play, provide a brief introduction to the case to ensure everyone understands the starting points of the activity. Then, divide the students into different roles relevant to the case. For example, in the scenario of the Malmi Airport, roles could include local politicians, residents, aviation enthusiasts, representatives of the Finnish Heritage Agency, environmental activists, and flying squirrels. Involving a non-human role enriches the discussion and enables thinking beyond human needs in co-creation processes. Stress that students will not be judged or held accountable for their role play dialogue.

4. Introduce the 'objective' of the day. For instance, in the Malmi Airport scenario, it was explained that the city of Helsinki had invited various actors to discuss and develop a shared vision for integrating nature-based solutions into the area's development plans. Ask the students to discuss the scenario in small groups with others who share the same group role. Prompt them to articulate their perspectives on the area's development and what they hope to accomplish during the event.

5. Then ask them to 'arrive' at the event in their roles. You now take the role of the formal representative of the city and open and host the event. By this point, everyone should be in character. Encourage participants to mingle and move around, employing an 'eavesdropping' technique to gain insight into ongoing discussions within smaller groups. Eavesdropping refers to only one small group continuing discussion in their roles as if no one else was listening (see Chapter 29 for a longer description of how to do this).

6. After mingling, instruct students to form new discussion groups mixing individuals with different roles. Ask the groups to further explore ideas about the area's future and which nature-based solutions should be implemented.

7. Invite each small group to report back to the city and other groups, sharing both points of agreement and disagreement in their discussions. Encourage cross-group feedback, allowing participants to comment on each other's proposed nature-based solutions.

8. To conclude the role play, ask the students to go back to their original groups (i.e. individuals with the same role). Prompt them to reflect on their experiences during the event, including whether their messages were heard, their impressions of other participants and their agendas, and how the city could better facilitate their involvement in urban development. Use the eavesdropping technique again to gain insights into these discussions.

9. Finally, gather all students in a circle and invite them to reflect on their role play experience. Encourage them to describe how the discussions evolved among participants and identify aspects that were both easy and challenging during the activity.

## Framing or pre-work

Choosing and applying an icebreaker exercise(s) is crucial to establish a friendly and collaborative atmosphere in the classroom (you can explore options for icebreakers in Chapters 4–9).

## When to use and when not to use

This type of role play is effective in courses where you aim to illustrate the complexity of deliberation or citizen engagement. The activity is suitable for medium-sized groups and it is particularly useful in courses where there is limited time to explore multiple applied drama methods but where the teacher wishes to diversify learning approaches.

Role play provides an accessible way of introducing embodied pedagogies to teaching and can help foster a sense of community within the course, especially if implemented early on. It also helps students to become acquainted with each other.

## Reflections from the field

From the teacher's perspective, the role play facilitated the engagement of various learning styles and encouraged discussions surrounding nature-based solutions and co-creation in a comprehensive and practical manner. It ignited creativity and laughter among students. Notably, students who typically remained passive during standard lectures displayed a great ability to express themselves and participate in discussions through their assigned roles.

According to student feedback, the role play was instrumental in enhancing the students' understanding of the complexities inherent in decision-making processes and the trade-offs involved. The students articulated in their written feedback that the activity aided them in formulating arguments, listening to others' viewpoints, and appreciating the diversity of perspectives, even among individuals occupying similar roles. The activity made the intricacies of co-creation and deliberation more tangible from an interpersonal standpoint. Additionally, the students described the role play as an enjoyable and memorable participatory activity that offered a refreshing variation to the more conventional lectures in the course.

## Things to consider and manage

The role play requires sufficient time and space where chairs and tables can be removed or organised in small groups. The students need space to move around. Facilitating a role play necessitates sensitivity to the varying comfort levels of students in taking or acting roles. Potential discomfort may stem from personal anxiety, lack of prior experience in drama methods or, for instance, lack of experience in speaking a foreign language. Therefore, creating a safe and supportive environment through warm-up exercises like icebreakers and reassuring participants that they can step out of the role play at any time is crucial for the success of the exercise.

## Learning extensions

The role play can be used to learn more deeply about a real-world case, such as one introduced in lectures prior to or following the role play activity. With more time than the allotted 90 minutes, the role play could be expanded to include further moments of deliberation and even conducted over various sessions. Small groups could be tasked with reaching a shared conclusion or presenting a collaborative proposal for the development of the area, considering nature-based solutions and evaluating the ecological, social, and economic aspects of the proposal.

Participants could also discuss how they weighed up these aspects in relation to each other and whose voices and values had more weight in the proposal and why. This approach allows for the activity to span multiple lectures, facilitating a more comprehensive understanding of co-creation for nature-based solutions.

The activity described could be applied with more students with modifications in how the small-group discussions are reported back to the whole group. Working with a larger group might require more time.

## Integrating with assessment

The role play does not need to be assessed. However, if the exercise is used to investigate a certain context and topic more deeply, these insights could be followed up and assessed through presentations of the case given in the following lecture in the course.

## Reference

UNEA (United Nations Environment Assembly). (2022). *United Nations Environment Assembly agrees nature-based solutions definition* (2 May). https://www.naturebasedsolutionsinitiative.org/news/united-nations-environment-assembly-nature-based-solutions-definition#:~:text=The%20UNEA%2D5%20resolution%20formally,effectively%20and%20adaptively%2C%20while%20simultaneously

## Chapter 9

# Role play

## A serious game to navigate global wicked problems

Oleksandra Khalaim

### Learning outcomes and related terms

The drama processes in this chapter aim to develop:

- Ability to navigate through conflicting interests and to look for a common ground aiming to embrace the complexity of climate change as a wicked problem.
- Ability to enact transformative societal change as a future professional (Dieleman & Huisingh, 2006).
- Ability to connect personal experiences and attitudes to global, wicked, hardly "graspable" concepts making them more grounded and self-understandable.

Key terms and definitions:

- Serious games: "games that do not have entertainment, enjoyment, or fun as their primary purpose" (Michael & Chen, 2006), where players are immersed in simulated contexts for decision-making transferable to learning (Chandross & DeCourcy, 2018).
- Role play – see Chapter 2.
- Wicked problem: a problem whose social complexity means that it has no determinable stopping point (Tonkinwise, 2015).

DOI: 10.4324/9781003496359-12

| Key sustainability-related outcomes |
| --- |
| **Embracing complexity in sustainability** |
| Systems thinking |
| Critical thinking |
| Problem framing/integrated problem-solving competence |
| **Envisioning sustainable futures** |
| Futures literacy/anticipatory competence |
| Adaptability |
| Exploratory thinking |
| **Acting for sustainability** |
| Political agency |
| Collective action/strategic/collaboration competence |

## Context of application

The described role play took place every fall between 2021 and 2023 as part of a cross-disciplinary three-day event, "Searching for Sustainability", for connection, care, and learning among sustainability teachers and students at Uppsala University Campus Gotland (Sweden). Since 2021, educators from different disciplines have been organising introductory days for six sustainability-related programmes at under- and post-graduate levels, aiming to create a space to meet across disciplinary boundaries in tackling wicked sustainability challenges, as well as to establish a basis for collaborative, creative, and critical learning.

The intention was to start a process that allows new relationships and opportunities in the continuation of individuals' studies. The most recent event took place in September 2023, when 80 students participated. The participants represented a highly multidisciplinary group coming from all over the world. The event is unique in its format as it allows students across different programmes and science domains to connect with each other under the "sustainability umbrella".

## Step-by-step guidance

1. The board game "Keep Cool" (see Figure 9.1) focuses on international climate change negotiations. The aim is to link students' personal experiences and emotions related to global sustainability wicked problems with situational decision-making through role play. One game session lasts on average one and a half to two hours, with up to 35 participants. In the game, three to six players

(individual players or combined in small groups) represent country regions such as Europe, USA and partners, OPEC, or the developing countries. They can choose between "black" and "green" economic growth in terms of energy sources (represented by colour of the factories they buy in the game). At the same time, they also have to adapt to inevitable climate impacts like droughts or floods. The strength of these increases when the world temperature rises. Additionally, lobby groups like the oil industry or environmental groups are integrated into the game and have to be considered. The winner is the player who most efficiently reconciles climate protection with lobby interests. If some players are too ruthless, everybody loses.

2. Since it is a board game, participants sit at one table around the game map (see picture below). Detailed instructions for the game facilitation are available at the game website (see further readings).

3. There is some advice for facilitators: at the beginning, the facilitation should be proactively intense, to get the participants on board, to create a trusted and engaging atmosphere for everyone, and to clarify the rules and game sequence. In the middle of the game, the facilitator's role is more to navigate players through the game stages, helping them to avoid being stuck in unproductive or lengthy discussions, as well as to speed up the process in general to be in line with the timeframe. At the end of the game, it is important for the facilitator to appreciate the shared work, and to let participants provide their feedback regarding both the game process and the educational content. Since it is an educational game, this last part is the most valuable part as it contributes to the learning process.

4. There are some suggestions for facilitating the "check-out and appreciation" round.

   a. Firstly, you can ask participants to recall and describe what happened in the last 100 years on our planet (in the game). Key points are written on a flip-chart and will be used later for connecting with game results, for example: "*Our (game) economies suffered from climate change. It was easy to make money at the beginning of the game, but the turnaround from black to green was difficult: we didn't trust each other enough to agree to reduce the amount of black factories*".

   b. As a second stage, initiate a reflective discussion on learning from the game and how it helped to better understand the process of climate negotiations and its difficulties. In addition, you can explore with the participants which processes in the game did not reflect reality (e.g. because they may be too simplistic or modelled in a strange way).

5. Finally, you can connect the game outcomes with the daily lives of participants by asking them to identify "green" and "black" elements in their live (metaphorically), in relation to ecological issues and energy use.

**Figure 9.1 Photograph of the game "Keep Cool".**

*Source:* The author, used with permission.

## Framing or pre-work

It usually takes some time for the participants to warm up and understand the rules for playing their roles at the initial stage. They may ask many clarifying questions and some may remain silent, seemingly not engaged in the process. After the first round of the game (approx. 30 minutes), the majority become more comfortable with the rules and their roles; they act freely, initiate discussions, and become more immersed in their roles.

It is helpful to let them make a small speech on behalf of their country region during the first round; for that they need to pretend to be presidents of their countries and behave accordingly. After every speech, ask the audience to give them a round of applause so it feels like something meaningful but still in a playful manner. To keep the role play atmosphere, it is helpful to visualise the roles by assigning every player (small group) representing a country region a name linked to a political leader coming from this region (for example, Joe Biden for the USA). Placing corresponding name cards near each player will support the role play atmosphere for the duration of the game.

## When to use and when not to use

The game does not fit groups larger than 35 persons. Since it simulates a decision-making process and connects personal experiences with global wickedness of climate change as well as enables active self-reflection, it is worth organising it at the beginning of the study course. In this way, the teacher can raise interest in the complexity of interrelated topics that can be further developed throughout the course, with the possibility to return to the joint experiences of the game during course lectures and seminars, linking theories and social learning outcomes.

## Reflections from the field

Students looked very engaged. During the game, they constantly interacted with each other (the idea of the game is to model a process of international climate negotiations). They actively communicated during the rounds of the game and seemed quite comfortable with the format. Even though the students had a lot of fun when playing the game, they demonstrated very serious discussion during the debriefing session (e.g. about the wickedness of climate change as a global problem) and tried to extrapolate the game results to what is happening in the real world. They reached very good conclusions on negotiation failures as well as on finding a balance between climate ambitions and economic growth for their country's regions.

At the final stage of the workshop, students said the game "*reflected a reality outside the classroom*" and "*it was fun yet challenging to negotiate with others on climate and economy under time pressure and climate catastrophes*". The role play format deepened the sustainability-related discussions after the game, as students were able to connect their own experiences gained during the game with the theory and information that they were studying in their programs. Usually, the reflection process that is initiated after the game continues throughout their studies and students come back with new insights related to the game later in the academic year.

## Things to consider

Use the original game toolkit or to follow the open-access online version of the game (see links to both versions below). Try facilitating the game with a group of friends or colleagues before running it with the students for the first time.

## Learning extensions

To deepen the learning, you can also direct students toward reflecting on the process, not only outcomes. The teacher can ask questions that help to structure students' individual reflective thinking, for example:

■ *How was your learning process evolving during the game? What thematic linkages have you built in between theories/concepts/cases?*
■ *What do you find the most/least useful and relevant in the game? Why?*

■ *How do you think the new information/knowledge/skill you have learned will support your individual learning?*
■ *What would you like to learn more about, related to the game content?*
■ *What has worked well in the game process and group discussions in terms of the learning process? What hasn't?*

## Integrating with assessment

A learning journal that reflects on the learning process (and the questions above) can be a good assessment tool in this case. The purpose of the learning journal is to record the students' reflections and learning experiences throughout the game. It is not just a diary or record of what was done during the game, but a record of what has been learned, tried, and critically reflected upon. It helps to personalise and deepen the quality of learning by means of writing reflectively.

One of the most important things the diary contains is reflections about how what has been learnt is relevant to the student and how s/he will use the new information, knowledge, skills, and techniques in current and future practice.

## Further reading

More details about the *Keep Cool* game and its rules: https://www.climate-game.net/en/the-board-game/, and the online version: https://www.climate-game.net/en/keep-cool-mobil-2/.

## References

Chandross, D., & DeCourcy, E. (2018). Serious games in online learning. *International Journal on Innovations in Online Education, 2*(3). https://doi.org/10.1615/intjinnovonlineedu.2019029871

Dieleman, H., & Huisingh, D. (2006). Games by which to learn and teach about sustainable development: Exploring the relevance of games and experiential learning for sustainability. *Journal of Cleaner Production, 14*(9–11), 837–847. https://doi.org/10.1016/j.jclepro.2005.11.031

Michael, D. R., & Chen, S. (2006). *Serious games: Games that educate, train and inform.* Course Technology/Cengage.

Tonkinwise, C. (2015). Design for transitions – from and to what? *Design Philosophy Papers, 13*(1), 85–92. https://doi.org/10.1080/14487136.2015.1085686

## Chapter 10

# Role play

## Playing with power

Leif Dahlberg

### Learning outcomes and related terms

The drama processes in this chapter aim to develop:

- Intercultural communication competence.
- Cultural self-awareness and respect for cultural differences.
- Power dynamics.

Key terms and definitions:

- Intercultural communication is the study of cultures and cultural differences, as well as the means to communicate across cultural differences.
- Intercultural communication competence is the cultural awareness and communication skillset that enables an individual to communicate across cultural divides.
- Concepts of power: traditionally, power is considered an external force that exerts influence on other bodies, e.g. in the juridical system, the judge is inserted into a hierarchical structure of power relations and is invested with the power to decide legal cases (see Cover, 1986). This form of juridical power can be contrasted with an understanding of power that functions in and through a multiplicity of social relations to form a field of force relations (see

DOI: 10.4324/9781003496359-13

Foucault, 1991, 2003). Here power is seen as socially constructed, internalised as a form of discipline; power is viewed as productive and the modern subject is constituted as a vehicle of power. In traditional conceptions of power, there is also a tendency to separate power and knowledge (e.g. Habermas, 1994). Foucault again offers a contrasting perspective, arguing that there is not "any knowledge that does not constitute at the same time power relations" (Foucault, 1991, p. 27).

■ Power distance is the unequal distribution of power between individuals in organisations and institutions, and the level of social acceptance of that inequality (Hofstede, 2010, 60–61). The concept of power distance is used in intercultural communication to describe the relationship between individuals with varying power, and the effect this has on society. The Power Distance Index (PDI) is used to measure the level of acceptance of power distance in any given culture: it may be low (egalitarian culture), moderate, or high (hierarchical culture).

| Key sustainability-related outcomes |
| --- |
| **Embodying sustainability values** |
| Valuing sustainability/self-awareness and normative competencies |
| Supporting fairness |
| **Embracing complexity in sustainability** |
| Critical thinking |
| **Envisioning sustainable futures** |
| Exploratory thinking |
| **Acting for sustainability** |
| Political agency |
| Collective action/strategic/collaboration competence |
| Individual initiative |

# Context of application

The pedagogical context of this role play is a university course in Intercultural Communication in Sweden. In the course, we use role play as a way for students to apply the concepts and theories they learn in concrete situations. In this way, the learning outcomes are more practice-oriented than in traditional courses with lectures, discussion seminars, and reading assignments. This particular role play borrows some elements from forum play (Österlind, 2010) and forum theatre (Boal, 2019); it is a variation of pedagogic role play used to teach students to constructively and critically engage with a situation. The exercise is conducted in a seminar group with 10–20 students.

# Step-by-step guidance

1. Preparations. It is helpful to provide the students with written instructions, either in digital form before the class or as a handout during the class.
2. After greeting the class, begin by doing a couple of simple warming-up drama exercises.
3. Describe orally the content and purpose of the exercise to the students. For instance: "*Today we will do a role play that thematises power distance in different cultures and how to do power (power as technique). We will also analyse how to approach and deconstruct cultural differences and different power techniques. In contrast to ordinary role play, it will be possible for the audience to suggest changes and also to act out the suggested changes. This is a variation of role play inspired by forum play and forum theatre*". It is recommended also to have written instructions available to handout.
4. Organise the students in groups of 5–6 students.
5. Give the students a written description of a situation in which people from different cultures should interact with each other. In this exercise, the situation involves both power dynamics and power distance within and between cultures. The description of the situation should be quite precise without being detailed. The characters the students should play are also described in the scenario, as is the type of interaction (e.g. decision-making in a company; conflict resolution; discussion of how to do an oral presentation). For instance:

> In the seminar we will do a role play focusing on conflict resolution in the context of intercultural communication. Interpersonal conflict is a typical – and difficult – situation in which power distance and power dynamics are at play. The setting is a meeting room with a table and chairs. There are 5–6 people in the room. Two persons are engaged in a conflict. One person has the role of conflict resolver. The remaining persons can either play observers or support persons. The conflict is related to work. One of the persons engaged in the conflict is a man in his early thirties. He is an engineer and from Germany. The other person involved in the conflict is a woman, middle aged. She is a designer, from Japan. She is married and has two children. The conflict resolver is external to the company and does not know the two persons engaged in the conflict.

The description of the scenario and the characters can be more detailed, including details of personal history and class and psychological traits. The nature of the conflict can be predefined in the written scenario or can be left for the students to invent and define. Similarly, the power techniques used by the parties and the conflict resolver can either be described in the written scenario or be left to the students. (For studies of conflict resolution in the context of intercultural communication, see e.g. Ting-Toomey & Oetzel, 2001.)

6. The students should then study the cultural characteristics of the characters, e.g. the eight-scale model in Erin Meyer's *The Culture Map* (2016), with emphasis on social constructions of power and power distance in different cultures (Meyer, 2016, Chapter 4). Next, the students should write a short script, including key spoken lines. Here the students create characters and possible developments, thereby applying their theoretical understanding to a concrete situation. The script should also include descriptions of gestures and posture. It is recommended that students play someone else than themselves, culturally speaking, otherwise it is not really role play. There is usually no time to rehearse, so this will be improvisation. Depending on the scenario, there could be anything from 3 key lines per character to 10 lines. Since there may be students who feel uncomfortable to act, the script could include non-acting characters who do not say anything.

7. The students then perform the role play for the other students.

8. After the first performance, the students perform the play a second time, but this time the audience is allowed to interrupt the performance with questions and suggestions to change the script and the dialogue. The student in the audience who proposes a change can also take over the character and play the role differently. The other actors on stage must adjust to the new suggestions if their role "feel" that the actions affect them. The teacher functions as a moderator. The teacher can also have a more active role by asking questions both to the audience and to the actors (i.e. as a "joker", see Chapter 2).

9. The role play ends with a debriefing session in which the students discuss what happened and what they learned from the exercise. Key concepts in this exercise are the social construction of power, i.e. that power is constructed together (co-constructed) in a given context, which may well be transformed in the process, as well as power distance in and between cultures. In the discussion, encourage movement between concrete situations to abstract notions and back again. In the debriefing session, it is also important to listen to what the actors felt when playing different roles and also when the roles were altered by the audience.

## Framing or pre-work

This role play takes place in the context of a course on Intercultural communication in which role play has been used several times already. Warming-up exercises are useful in the early stages of the course when the students are new to drama pedagogy. In later stages, they may be skipped or made more connected to the content of the session. You could use, for instance, freeze frames (or still images) where participants in groups of four use their bodies to illustrate the meaning of concepts that will be used during the session; power, power distance, intercultural communication, cultural awareness, cultural self-awareness. This can be a way of tuning in to the topic in a light-hearted way. If one decides to do a role play thematising conflict resolution (the example given above), it may be helpful to provide the students with some reading material covering this topic beforehand (e.g. Ting-Toomey & Oetzel, 2001).

## When to use and when not to use

This role play exercise is designed for the use in a university course on Intercultural Communication in which role play already has been used several times. The participating students have read texts on the social construction of power and power distance, so they are familiar with these notions. These factors probably affected the successful outcome of the exercise.

## Reflections from the field

In my experience of role play, the most engaged discussions happen when the students work on the situation in small groups, imagining the characters and possible developments and writing a script. Here, they apply their theoretical understanding to a concrete – albeit fictional – situation, and also engage creatively and critically with the question of power. Secondly, in this role play, inspired by forum play, the enacted situation is interrupted and the script may be altered by the audience. Here alternative actions change the relationship and the development of the situation. Thirdly, in the final debriefing session, it is clear that the students learn from the activity in many ways. This is apparent not only from the comments made by students, but also from the focused attention and pensive silence following the discussions – no one is checking their mobile phone for updates.

A key feature that distinguishes forum play from ordinary pedagogic role play is interruption. As noted by Walter Benjamin in an essay on Bertolt Brecht's epic theatre, the use of interruptions is an artistic device used to break with the traditional theatre form (Benjamin, 1998, pp. 3–4), that is, whereas in traditional theatre there is focus on the development of dramatic action, epic theatre "does not so much have to develop actions as to represent conditions". (Benjamin, 1998, p. 4, trans. modified ["*Dies epische Theater [...] hat nicht so sehr Handlungen zu entwickeln, als Zustände darzustellen*".]) According to Benjamin, the interrupted action also has a tendency to produce and emphasise gestures, that is, actors make use of repeated gestures to signal connections between scenes. Benjamin's reflection on the dramatic gesture can also be applied to role play and forum play.

## Things to consider

In the beginning, when one introduces pedagogic role play in teaching, there may be hesitation from some students. Some may not be comfortable with acting in front of their peers, others fail to see that playing is a form of learning activity. For this reason, it is important to explain what is going on and why drama pedagogy is useful as a complement to traditional forms of teaching. It is also recommended to talk about and reflect on the interface between theoretical knowledge and practical knowledge, and the difference between learning by reading and discussing, and learning through performing. It is important to listen to the students' reactions and reflections. How can one design the role play in ways that make them feel more comfortable? At the same time, the students should be given space to explore and become familiar with the format.

It is also valuable to indicate how techniques in role play can be used in other contexts. For instance, in this forum play inspired role play, students become familiar with the device to interrupt a dramatic situation, comment on it, and suggest alternative ways of interacting and doing things. How can this be applied in other, non-pedagogical contexts? What are the risks and limitations of interrupting action? Also, the focus on gestures as symbolic action will make the students conscious of body language and proxemics (the physical distance to other people, and the meaning of touch).

## Learning extensions

In my experience, using role play throughout a course, or at least as a recurrent element, increases the chances that the students engage with the learning activities. There are different ways of extending and deepening the learning experience (see transformative learning, Dirkx, 1998). Several times, I have had students go through personal development in courses where role play is a central element. To the extent that this is an intended learning outcome, you may want to reflect on the means and conditions of transformative learning.

## Integrating with assessment

This particular exercise is designed as a learning activity and as part of a course. Role play can be used as assessment in a course, for instance, the students can prepare a role play, perform it, and then critique it. The teacher needs to define transparent grading criteria before grading it, and the performance assessment can take place several times during the course, and/or at the end of the course. You can also ask students to submit written reflections on their work (individually or as a group) and on the work of other students.

## Further reading

Boal, A. (2019). *Theatre of the oppressed*. Trans. A. Charles, M.- O. Leal McBride, & E. Fryer. Pluto Press.

Meyer, E. (2016). *The culture map*. Public Affairs.

Österlind, E. (2010). "Forum Play. A Swedish mixture for consciousness and change". In S. Schomann (Ed.), *Key concepts in theatre/drama education* (pp. 247–251). SENSE Publishers.

# References

Benjamin, W. (1998). *Understanding Brecht. Trans.* A. Bostock. Verso.

Cover, R. (1986). Violence and the word. *Yale Law Journal, 95*, 1601–1629.

Dirkx, J. (1998). Transformative learning theory in the practice of adult education: An overview. *PAACE Journal of Lifelong Learning, 7*, 1–14.

Foucault, M. (1991). *Discipline and punish. The birth of the prison.* Trans. A. Sheridan. Penguin.

Foucault, M. (2003). *"Society Must Be Defended". Lectures at Collège de France, 1975–1976.* Trans. D. Macey. Picador.

Habermas, J. (1994). *Theory of communicative action.* Vol. 1. Trans. T. McCarthy. Beacon Press.

Hofstede, G., Hofstede, G. J., & Minkov, M. (2010). Cultures and organizations. *Software of the mind.* McGraw Hill.

Ting-Toomey, S., & Oetzel, J. (2001). *Managing intercultural conflict effectively.* Sage Publications.

# Chapter 11

# Role play

## Power dynamics in a village logging dilemma

Michelle Dyer and Tim Daw

### Learning outcomes and related terms

The drama processes in this chapter aim to develop:

- Appreciation of cultural embeddedness of power dynamics such as gender norms.
- Role play and applied drama as a method to support learning and reflection.
- Personal experience of the power and/or frustration of social and cultural norms.

Key terms and definitions:

- Gendered power dynamics: the effect of gender on the ability of individuals to exercise autonomy, make decisions, and have influence in relationships and interpersonal interactions mediated by social and cultural context.
- Global commodity chains: the trade networks that extract and transport raw materials from source areas (often in the Global South) to where they are demanded (in rapidly developing economies or in the Global North).
- Making the familiar strange and the strange familiar: the Anthropological idea that learning about a culture different from our own can lead us to reflect on our own culture with a new lens.

DOI: 10.4324/9781003496359-14

| Key sustainability-related outcomes |
|---|
| Embodying sustainability values |
| Valuing sustainability/self-awareness and normative competencies |
| Supporting fairness |
| Embracing complexity in sustainability |
| Systems thinking |
| Critical thinking |
| Problem framing/integrated problem-solving competence |
| Envisioning sustainable futures |
| Exploratory thinking |
| Acting for sustainability |
| Political agency |
| Collective action/strategic/collaboration competence |

## Context of application

The role play concerns residents of a small coastal village on tribal lands in Solomon Islands, where a foreign logging company wishes to log the forest above the village. The role play is a meeting to discuss the logging proposal.

This role play has been used in a range of higher-education settings from an introductory sustainability science course within an undergraduate programme in Business Ethics and Sustainability to a master's course on Social-Ecological Resilience in Sustainable Development. The undergraduate course includes 80 students (divided into four seminar groups each led by a teaching assistant) with no background knowledge of sustainability. Here, the role play aimed to introduce questions of power and gender dynamics in the context of globalisation. The master's class was a small group of highly motivated students who have previously had two months of intensive sustainability science teaching. Here, the role play was used within a module about how people benefit from ecosystems and support lectures on governance, equity, and environmental justice, by illustrating how power dynamics lead to unequal voice and unequal benefits from ecosystems. The role play can be run with 12–25 students.

## Step-by-step guidance

### Setting up the role play

Before meeting the students, prepare some written materials, like printed briefing sheets for all students. You also need to print role descriptions and distribute one (single) role card for each student. These materials are presented below.

You also need large visible name badges for each role - one per student. These include the title of the role as well as a letter A, B, or C (see list below) or colours to indicate the speaking hierarchy – which the chair of the meeting is instructed to follow, but without explaining this to the rest of the villagers.

Finally, you need a room with tables aside and chairs in a circle – ask early students to help.

## *Running the seminar*

Welcome the students and inform them that you will do a role play which will be fun, and that applied drama like this can be an effective way to explore, experience, and learn about different perspectives in sustainability dilemmas. Applied drama is used not only in education, but also in research and development interventions with stakeholders to help facilitate understanding and learning. So, explain that in this lesson you will learn about a real situation, but also a novel method that can be used in sustainability science (for more detailed guidance about role play, see Chapter 12).

1. Warm-up (5 minutes).

   a. Stand in a circle – draw your name with your hand in the air. Then with your opposite hand, with your foot, with your other foot, and with your head.

   b. Now each person thinks of a short phrase, e.g. a line from a children's song and stands in a circle facing *outwards*.

   c. Everyone says their phrase at the same time, then repeat it again and again, with a voice characterised by different situations, such as

   i. *Like you are telling someone a secret*
   ii. *Like you are talking to a room full of people*
   iii. *Like you are a child learning to read*
   iv. *Like you are very busy and bossy*

2. Distribute the briefing sheet to everybody (this could also be circulated in advance). Hand out the instructions for each role, one per student, and point out they should not share them with anyone else. The sheets state the role as well as speaking rules, such as *"You must never directly disagree with someone with an A"*, *"You should speak at length frequently"*, or even *"You may not speak at this meeting"*. Give the students time to read (5 minutes).

3. Preparing for the meeting (5 minutes).

   a. Stand up and find two others who also agree or disagree about the logging.

   b. In this group of three (or four) talk about why you (dis)agree with the logging.

Use your imagination and improvise. The reasons can be related to personal interests or to what is good or fair for the village, now or in the future.

4. The role play (40 minutes).

   a. Return to the seats and put on badges – ask everyone to say briefly who they are (e.g. *I'm a landowner*).
   b. Instruct the meeting chair to open and initiate the meeting.
   c. Let "the villagers" (students in the groups) discuss for about 30–40 minutes depending on how it is going, and then ask the chair to close the meeting.

5. Debrief (20 minutes).

   a. The players should stay in their roles and have a brief round to express what they are thinking/feeling. You may invite the "anthropologist(s)" (a role) to comment on what they saw.
   b. Then ask the students to stand up, walk around their chair, and sit down again to leave their role – now everyone is *out* of role.
   c. What was happening in the meeting?

      i. At some point, allow the class to notice the difference between A, B, C is not just due to elder or landowner status – let them guess until they realise that speaking order is being driven by gender. Explain that gender was kept hidden to reflect that we are all influenced by rules and norms that we may not be aware of (e.g. an unconscious bias that men are more authoritative).

         1. Point out that the elder, land-owning man with an authority position is at the top, and an in-law, non-land-owning woman is at the bottom. So, gender and land ownership intersect to determine the power of each individual.
         2. Ask "*how does this affect how environmental disputes are resolved?*" What about for "*community engagement*" or projects "*for the local community*"?

      ii. Anthropologists make the "strange familiar and the familiar strange" – having learned about the gendered dynamics in this village meeting in Solomon Islands, ask the students to reflect on their own context. For example, in this class, what are the unwritten rules about whose voices are heard, and how does that affect outcomes? Thinking more broadly, what is said and not said in environmental disputes? How might different voices be heard?

   d. Finally ask for a round of reflections on the seminar.

**Logging role play briefing sheet**

## Story outline

You are a group of village residents of a small coastal village on tribal lands in Solomon Islands. The 200 people in your village are a mix of landowners and non-landowners and some with very specific land rights.

There have been two previous logging operations by foreign companies in your village. The first one was in the 1970s. Decision-making and distribution of benefits from the logging were made through the elder system of authority. The second round of logging took place around 10 years ago. Decision-making was through the larger tribal group, and tribal land chiefs again served as trustees on the logging licence.

Village residents felt they did not get fair benefit from this round of logging, but even though they complained about this second logging project, many people received money, timber, and some other benefits. There were also negative effects from this logging: the village water supply was dirtied and the hydroelectric scheme was rendered non-functional by illegal logging too close to the watershed boundaries.

Currently, another foreign logging company wishes to log the forest above the village. They have approached the Prime Minister, who is a member of the wider tribal group of which your village is a part, and he is pushing for the logging operation to happen. The PM's representative claims that the current licence is simply a renewal of the previous logging licence and therefore there is no need to go through the wider tribal consultation process as required by both legislation and customs about decision-making on customary land. There are other legal irregularities in the way the licence has been obtained.

Three land-owning men from your village have already signed as trustees on the logging licence giving access to money. They have already accepted money from the logging company. Other landowners are opposed to the logging and are angry that the three other tribal members have become trustees without their permission and without wider discussion in the group.

The role play is a meeting to discuss the logging proposal. There have been underlying tensions prior to the meeting because of the appointment of the three trustees. Family groups are divided over the issue and people are feeling angry.

Due to the local culture the meeting is governed by a system of speaking rights. Each role play card gives you certain rules for the meeting and interaction with other groups – *do not share or refer to these instructions* in the meeting but use them to guide how you act.

Regardless of the rules of your role play card, your personality will also affect how you behave in the meeting. You may disobey your rules of engagement but there may be social consequences.

*Source:* Based on the anthropological fieldwork of Michelle Dyer, with modifications by Tim Daw and ideas from Eva Österlind.

## Roles to print and distribute to students

| | |
|---|---|
| Meeting chairman | You must allow all members at the meeting who wish to speak to make contributions.<br>However, you will give priority to speakers labelled A first and C last. For example, if you see an A and a B member wishing to speak at the same time, you will allow the A member to speak first. If you see a B and C member wishing to speak at the same time you will allow the B member to speak first. You may also ask someone to speak from any group.<br>Let the labels A–C guide who you let speak, *but do not refer to these groups in the role play.*<br>After any number of contributions have been made, you may give a summary of issues giving greater value to opinions of A members who are NOT in favour of the logging. You may do this as often as you like.<br>If necessary, you can remind the meeting that members should be given the word by you as chair before contributing. |
| Elder landowner A<br>x 2–3 in favour<br>or against the<br>logging | You ARE/ARE NOT in favour of the logging operation. You may speak at length and as many times as you like during the meeting to persuade others to your view. You may openly disagree with anyone else at the meeting. |
| Landowner A<br>x 2–3 in favour<br>or against the<br>logging | You ARE/ARE NOT in favour of the logging operation. You may speak at length and as many times as you like during the meeting to persuade others to your view. You may openly disagree with anyone else at the meeting except elders labelled A. |
| Elder B<br>x 2–3 in favour<br>or against the<br>logging | You ARE/ARE NOT in favour of the logging operation. You may make up to 3 contributions to the meeting. You may openly disagree with anyone except elders labelled A. |

| | |
|---|---|
| Landowner B<br>x 2–3 in favour<br>or against the<br>logging | You ARE/ARE NOT in favour of the logging operation.<br>You may speak at the meeting but only after members<br>labelled A have had a chance to speak. You may make up to<br>two contributions to the meeting. You may NOT disagree<br>with anyone labelled A. You defer to elders labelled B. You<br>may openly disagree with anyone labelled C. |
| In-law B<br>x 2–3 in favour<br>or against the<br>logging | You ARE/ARE NOT in favour of the logging operation. You are<br>married into this village. You are not a landowner. You may<br>make as many contributions as you like during the meeting<br>but must always defer to the opinions of Elders labelled B.<br>If you have an opinion that disagrees with people labelled<br>A you can only do this in very circumspect and respectful<br>terms. You may openly disagree with anyone labelled C. |
| Observer<br>Can be two if large<br>class | You are an anthropologist. You will listen and observe<br>the interactions between the participants throughout the<br>meeting. You must decide what to do if you are asked to<br>make a contribution. You will make a note of how many<br>contributions are made by the participants. You will be<br>asked at the end of the meeting to give your opinion on<br>the meeting dynamics and give your understanding of the<br>interactions that took place during the meeting.<br>Pay close attention to what is going on. Who is speaking<br>and how they speak can be more important than what they<br>say for understanding social interactions. |
| In-law C<br>x 2–3 in favour<br>or against the<br>logging | You ARE/ARE NOT in favour of the logging operation.<br>You are married into this village. You are not a landowner.<br>You may not speak at the meeting. |
| Village chairman A | You are NOT in favour of the logging operation. You are<br>a landowner. You may make as many contributions to the<br>meeting as you like but you do not dominate the main<br>discussion. You keep your comments to challenge those<br>elders and landowners labelled A who are in favour of the<br>logging and also those labelled C. |
| Church elder A | You are NOT in favour of the logging. You are not a<br>landowner. You are married into the village. You may make<br>as many contributions to the meeting as you like. You may<br>not openly disagree with elders labelled A. You do not<br>openly disagree with anyone from group C. |
| Land rights<br>holder C<br>x 2–3 all in<br>favour of the<br>logging | You ARE in favour of the logging operation. You are not<br>a landowner, but you have land rights to the place the<br>logging company wants to build their log point. You may<br>speak at length and as many times as you like during the<br>meeting to persuade others to your view. You may openly<br>disagree with anyone else at the meeting. |

## Framing or pre-work

Optionally, ask the students to read Dyer (2017, 2018) describing the context. You might want to read more about role play (e.g. Chapters 2 and 12) or about other warm-up activities (e.g. Chapters 4–7).

## When to use and when not to use

This activity is suitable when students have sufficient trust and confidence to embark on a role play. The learning from this exercise depends crucially on the debrief but also tends to be richer and more profound with more advanced and engaged students (i.e. with the master's class).

## Reflections from the field

This exercise generally elicits engagement and interest amongst the students and allows them to feel power dynamics that they may not have reflected on before. Feedback from undergraduate classes show that most students reflect on this issue and state that experiencing unequal power in the discussions supported their learning. Keeping gender hidden helps to add surprise and impact to the learning. For example, one reflected that during the role play she suddenly realised that she subconsciously assumed that her character was a man.

The separate round of reflections first in-role added a great additional opportunity to hear the perspectives of each participant – especially those with limited or no speaking opportunities. It also provided dramatic energy giving the students the chance to imagine and reflect on their characters.

The engagement and experience seem to vary with the level of the students. At the master's level, the students engaged more in the role play, reflected more actively, and drew more learning and insights from the exercise. On a five-point scale of agreeing that taking part in the role play helped to learn about sustainability, the 14 master's students gave an average of 4.2 and a minimum of 3, whereas the 32 undergraduate students gave an average of 3.2 including three students who gave a minimum of 1.

A minority of students from the undergraduate class were unaccustomed to and resisted the role play. Sometimes the undergraduate students invested less in following their roles. Thus, in lower-stage classes more encouragement and support from the teacher may be necessary. The teacher may also want to emphasise that the experience is best if people try to follow their roles.

## Things to consider

The gender roles should be hidden from the students and only become apparent in the debrief – this is because we all have an unconscious bias that men will be in charge. When you do not know you are playing a man or a woman, you feel the personal injustice of being silenced or of silencing others. The point is to feel this personally, as yourself, so that you realise what it feels like.

Students need to understand why role play is a legitimate and effective teaching method.

We usually allocate all roles randomly, but with less engaged students, it may be appropriate to have a volunteer to chair the meeting, as this is such a key role.

Some students found the strong sense of empowerment/disempowerment unsettling. There is a need to have a proper debriefing and stepping out of roles to settle feelings of frustration and anxiety. As such, ensure that there is sufficient time for the debrief, and that students reflect on power dynamics in their own contexts.

## Learning extensions

Providing the context in which the dispute takes place can create a more immersive experience for students. When students know more fully what they are arguing for or against they feel more invested in their allocated role. This results in their wanting to succeed in influencing the outcome of the discussion in favour of their allocated role and thus subsequently experiencing more personally the power or lack of that results from circumstances outside of their control – like their gender, kinship ties, and so on. Greater contextual knowledge also reveals students' personal assumptions about what factors should be most important in interpersonal interactions. Understanding the cultural context of the role play foregrounds these culturally mediated power dynamics with the critical realisation that these cannot be assumed across cultural contexts.

## Integrating with assessment

The undergraduate course includes a weekly reflective log, which is compulsory but ungraded. At the end of the week in which the role play happens, students are instructed to contrast the experience of the role play with another seminar in which they deliberate about a sustainability question anonymously online (i.e. with almost no identity-based power relations). The final assignment of the module includes instructions for the students to draw on their reflective log to describe their learning. Some students have chosen to refer to this seminar.

## References

Dyer, M. (2017). Eating money: Narratives of equality on customary land in the context of natural resource extraction in the Solomon Islands. *The Australian Journal of Anthropology*, *28*(1), 88–103. – a study that gives the background to the case.

Dyer, M. (2018). Transforming communicative spaces: The rhythm of gender in meetings in rural Solomon Islands. *Ecology and Society*, *23*, 1–10. – a study of the meeting on which this role play is based.

## Chapter 12

# Role play

## The Bleeding Water

Marianne Ødegaard

### Learning outcomes and related terms

The drama processes in this chapter aim to:

- Provide participants with an embodied experience of a 'wicked problem' associated with sustainability.
- Discuss the role of science in addressing sustainability dilemmas and socio-scientific issues while also recognising the significance of such topics.
- Explore how these experiences can contribute to scientific literacy.

Key terms and definitions:

- Role play: an improvisational act of representing characters and behaviours of someone or something as an explorative and creative activity in a dramatic context (also see Chapter 2).
- Citizenship: citizens' active participation in society. Environmental citizenship refers to pro-environmental behaviour driven by the belief in the fair distribution of environmental goods. Citizens can act in different ways in terms of balancing between maintaining individual rights and the responsibility for the common good (Dobson, 2007; Ødegaard, 2023).

DOI: 10.4324/9781003496359-15

| Key sustainability-related outcomes |
| --- |
| **Embodying sustainability values** |
| Valuing sustainability/self-awareness and normative competencies |
| Supporting fairness |
| Promoting nature |
| **Embracing complexity in sustainability** |
| Systems thinking |
| Critical thinking |
| **Envisioning sustainable futures** |
| Adaptability |

# Context of application

The Bleeding Water role play has been implemented in various educational settings, involving in-service science teachers, student teachers at the university level, and upper secondary students. This immersive role play draws inspiration from the novel *And the Waters Turned to Blood* by Rodney Barker, which is based on a true scientific story. The narrative revolves around the dinoflagellate (algae) *Pfiesteria piscicida*, commonly known as 'the cell from hell'. This organism, dormant for centuries, was awakened by human pollution in the rivers and coastal waters of the eastern US. Given the captivating nature of this scenario, it was deemed ideal for a role play.

The primary objective of the role play activity was to explore alternative approaches to science education while simultaneously providing participants with an embodied experience of a 'wicked problem' associated with sustainability (Lehtonen et al., 2019; Lönngren & Van Poeck, 2021). Through engaging in this role play, students and teachers were prompted to discuss the role of science in addressing sustainability dilemmas and socio-scientific issues, while also recognising the significance of such topics in their context (i.e. science education). Moreover, the role play activity fostered a deliberate exploration of how these immersive experiences can contribute to scientific literacy (Ødegaard, 2008, 2023; Valladares, 2021).

# Step-by-step guidance

1. The setting.

   In this role play, students take on the roles of a family tasked with making a crucial decision regarding whether to support a petition from local doctors urging the immediate closure of the nearby New River for all human activities. This action is prompted by suspicions of a deadly algae outbreak linked to water pollution. Reports suggest that the algae are responsible for fish mortality, human injuries, and the discolouration of the water. Dr. JoAnn Burkholder's scientific research on the harmful dinoflagellate, *Pfisteria*, lends support to the hypothesis of potential harm to humans.

The setting for the role play is a family dinner at William Smith's residence, and the participants include:

*William Smith*: A fisherman reliant on the New River for his livelihood, who is aware of the need to wear gloves when the water turns red.

*Sarah Smith*: William's daughter, a student of aquatic biology who has recently joined Dr. JoAnn Burkholder's research group for her master's studies.

*Karen Jorgensen*: William's sister and a mother of two, whose family has experienced unusual muscle symptoms following their summer vacation spent by the New River. Her husband, who did not swim in the river, has not exhibited any symptoms.

*Samuel Smith*: Karen and William's brother, a pig farmer with a large farm adjacent to the river. His farm has generated numerous employment opportunities for the community, and he is distressed by the accusations of polluting the river.

*Patricia Griffith*: Samuel's girlfriend and the tourism manager in the municipality, who is concerned that rumours of local business emissions causing algal blooms, leading to fish mortality and health issues, may incite panic among potential tourists and result in significant revenue loss for the municipality.

Each participant is provided with a role card containing supplementary information, *without* predetermined attitudes or opinions, serving as a starting point for discussion (the role cards are below).

The role play typically spans about 20–30 minutes (including preparation and debrief), but due to its facilitation of both academic and ethical discussions, it is recommended to allocate additional time, at least 60 minutes in total, to allow a more in-depth exploration of the issues afterwards.

2. Introduction to the role play.

The students should be briefly introduced to role play in general and the specific role play situation. The text in *italics* serves as examples of what can be said.

*Today, we will be engaging in a role play activity that revolves around an ecological mystery. This scenario is based on a real-life situation that took place in the US some years ago, but the individuals you will be portraying are fictional. Please keep in mind that this is not about acting skills. Instead, think of this as an opportunity to initiate a discussion and gain a deeper understanding of different perspectives. There are five roles available, and you can choose which one you would like to take.*

Choosing a role is voluntary. At this point, the role cards have not yet been introduced, so role selection is superficially based on gender, age, and occupation. If there are more than five participants in a group, the extra participants can take on the roles as observers. This is an important, useful, and fascinating role to have. If there are fewer than five participants in a group, Patricia's role can be omitted. The role of Sarah is essential and requires a bit more reading than the others as she has some scientific documents to look through. This might be considered when choosing roles.

*I will now distribute a role card to each of you. Please do not show it to anyone else; it is for your personal use only. If you have any questions about your role, feel free to ask me. Once you have read your role card, we will begin with the improvisation. I will indicate when to start.*

*Remember, you are not performing for an audience, and there is no predetermined dialogue. This is improvisation, meaning you must come up with everything you say in the first person. Focus on your character's attitudes and try to avoid creating stereotypes. Use your inner knowledge and empathy to put yourself in your character's shoes and explore the situation.*

Now, the role cards can be distributed and about 5–10 minutes are given for reading through them. In addition to the role cards, 'Sarah' is handed the science articles about *Pfiesteria* by JoAnn Burkholder. There is no time to read through everything, but once the play has started Sarah can show them to the others. Tell Sarah that she should attempt to make a personal decision about signing the petition or not. She should also encourage the others to do so. This creates drive and engagement during the play. By setting a timeframe for the game, the roles are encouraged to engage in a meaningful dialogue. The improvisation should last for 10–12 minutes.

3. Conducting the role play.

*Excellent! Now, let's begin. Remember, the role play will last for approximately 10–12 minutes, and I will notify you when it is time to stop. The Observers and I will not participate in the game, so please do not address us. We will observe quietly and take note of any interesting arguments that can be discussed later. Speak in the first person and be open to exploring the situation! Karen, Samuel, and Patricia, please physically arrive together at the dinner party. William, you can start with the opening line: 'Hi Karen! So good to see you. How are you? Are you sick?' Begin when you're ready, William. Please proceed.*

After 10–12 minutes, depending on how the dialogue goes, the game will be stopped.

(Clap your hands) *Please freeze the situation! It's time to stop the role play for now. Well done, everyone! Thank you for your participation and engagement. Let's take a moment to reflect on the subtext of the discussion and what was happening between the lines. Observers, feel free to share any interesting points you observed during the role play. Now, I'll ask some questions to further explore the situation. Karen, how do you feel about the discussion at this point? Have you made a decision about signing the petition? What have you decided, and why? And William, how do you feel about the situation? Please share your thoughts.*

It is desirable for everyone to say something.

## Information for participants

## Role play – THE BLEEDING WATER

*by Marianne Ødegaard*

(Inspired by the novel: *And the Waters Turned to Blood* by Rodney Barker)

In the rivers and coastal waters of the eastern US, an ancient and deadly organism was awakened by human pollution. Could it become the ultimate biological threat...? This is based on a true story of the dinoflagellate *Pfiesteria piscicida*, or "the cell from hell" as it has been called. (Dinoflagellates are algae.)

The role play takes place in the state of North Carolina, US, at a dinner party hosted by William Smith. There are five people present:

*William Smith* (a fisherman), *Sarah Smith* (his daughter and biology student), *Karen Jorgensen* (his sister, has two children), *Samuel Smith* (his brother, pig farmer), *Patricia Griffith* (Samuel's girlfriend, tourism director)

Karen and Sarah have come to visit their hometown. The others live here. Today, they all received a troubling announcement from the local health authorities in their mailboxes. The role play begins as they arrive at William's dinner party.

(Please contact marianne.odegaard@ils.uio.no for extended role card versions)

**NCHA** PETITION FROM LOCAL HEALTH AUTHORITIES (doctors) IN NORTH CAROLINA STATE!

In recent times, there have been rumors circulating regarding a possible connection between fish deaths and health injuries in humans.

We hereby urge the National Health Authorities to immediately close New River for swimming, boating, and fishing, i.e. all human activities, due to Dr JoAnn Burkholder's research on the killer dinoflagellate and her hypothesis that it may be harmful to humans. The fish deaths might be related to water pollution.

It is crucial to be cautious!

Please sign this petition, which will be forwarded to the National Health Authorities.

Signatures:

**Role cards (short versions)**

Your name is **Sarah Smith**, you are 24 years old, and you are a student in aquatic biology at North Carolina State University. Today, you are quite excited because you spoke with Dr. JoAnn Burkholder about joining her research group as a master's student. Dr. Burkholder is a renowned researcher and an expert in her field of toxic dinoflagellates. Her research has indicated that the outbreak of toxic algae, *Pfiesteria piscicida* (which can turn the water red), is related to polluting discharges. She gave you some articles to read. Since your father is a fisherman, life in water has always been a topic you liked. You are excited to share the prospect of working with Dr. Burkholder with your family. It will be nice to see Aunt Karen again! She is visiting from Atlanta, and you look forward to telling her about your studies.

  Scientific articles: https://www.nature.com/articles/358407a0

  https://aslopubs.onlinelibrary.wiley.com/doi/abs/10.4319/lo.1997.42.5_part_2.1052

Your name is **Karen Jorgensen**, you are 40 years old, and the mother of Soren (6 years old) and Carolyn (12 years old). You are a stay-at-home mom. Just over a year ago, you started feeling some strange symptoms. Suddenly, it feels like the blood in the lower part of your body is getting cold, and you have muscle spasms that burn. The symptoms come and go. Both Soren and Carolyn have similar symptoms. Lately, Soren has been absent-minded and forgetful at times, and you are extremely worried. You have been to the hospital and undergone all possible tests, but they found nothing. The symptoms started after the last vacation you had to North Carolina to visit Uncle William, your brother. You all had waded in the water for several hours, except for Tor, your husband, who had stayed on land. He hasn't been sick. Now you are visiting William and Sarah, your niece, to try to find out more information about the situation. Tonight, you need to talk to your brothers to see if they know anything about this.

Your name is **William Smith**, you are 49 years old, and you are a fisherman. Your daughter, Sarah, is studying marine biology, and you are very proud of her. Today, she's coming home for dinner because your sister, Aunt Karen, is visiting. You also invited your brother, Samuel. Apparently, he's bringing his new girlfriend. In your mailbox today, you found a petition and a signature campaign. Some people want to close the New River, where you fish, due to fear of health issues caused by human activity. They can't just shut down the river where you make a living, right? What will you live off then? You've never gotten sick from working there. But it's something all fishermen in the family have known that when the water turns red, you must be extra careful. The fish also die in those conditions.

*Opening line:* Hi Karen! So good to see you. How are you? Are you sick?

Your name is **Samuel Smith**, you are 45 years old, and you're a pig farmer. However, today you are very upset because you found a petition in your mailbox calling for the closure of all human activity in and along the New River, where you live, based on some vague research findings suggesting that the occasional fish deaths are caused by pollution from pig and chicken farming in the local area. How ridiculous! You have created many much-needed jobs in the community and built a successful business that provides the local population with healthy locally produced food. No, this must be stopped! Tonight, you will discuss with William, your brother, about what to do. You're excited to introduce Patricia, your girlfriend to the family.

Your name is **Patricia Griffith**, you are 33 years old, and you are the tourism manager in the municipality. It's a beautiful place with so much potential for tourism! Where the river meets the sea, there's an amazing estuary where people can swim, fish, or go for walks. But now you've heard rumours that some researchers claim that emissions from local businesses, like pig farms, are causing algal blooms, which could lead to health problems and fish deaths. This will only create panic and make people not want to use this beautiful area for recreation. Today, your boyfriend Samuel, who runs one of the most successful pig farming businesses here, asked if you would like to meet his family!

# Things to consider

Following this round, it is essential to provide a brief debriefing session. During this time, the students are encouraged to transition out of their assigned roles. This allows for personal reflections and reactions to be expressed freely. Some may feel the need to reassure others that their role play behaviour was in fact fictitious, while others may be reminded of real-life situations they wish to share with the group. It is crucial not to skip this debriefing, as neglecting it may result in participants feeling vulnerable, exploited, with their emotional responses disregarded. However, it is important to keep this debriefing concise and efficient.

# Learning extensions

After the debriefing, it is time to facilitate a reflection on the events of the role play and encourage participants to share their perspectives on the ethical dilemma presented. If there were any observers within the groups, they should initiate the discussion.

During this phase, the teacher must distinguish between the character and the person portraying them. This differentiation is crucial when discussing questions that emerged during the role play, always maintaining a direct reference to the characters' viewpoints. For example, '*Samuel mentioned this and that... What do you think he meant?*' The teacher should never assume that participants share the same opinions as their respective characters.

Additionally, addressing academic and scientific inquiries is necessary to ensure that ethical decisions are based on sound reasoning. Specific attention should be given to ensuring that all participants comprehend Dr. Burkholder's scientific work. Did the arguments shift during the role play when scientific information was introduced? Scientific comprehension is intrinsically linked with ethical reasoning.

So far, the role play discussion has focused on exploring personal values and actions, such as what decisions should be made and whether the scientific evidence supports closing the river. Other potential resolutions and ethical dilemmas should be explored as well. By carefully guiding the discussion, it can be elevated from a personal to a more interpersonal and societal level. This may involve deliberations on which experts to trust, negotiation of cultural values to pursue, and ultimately, engaging in a decision-making scenario.

Ødegaard (2023) has described different levels of dramas for examining sustainability: *little dramas* for exploring personal levels, *middle dramas* for exploring interpersonal levels, and *big dramas* for exploring symbolic levels. The Bleeding Water role play can effectively serve as both a little and middle drama. By first assessing the situation at a personal level, a discussion regarding societal perspectives will be grounded in an empathic understanding of the stakeholders involved.

# Reflections from the field

Student teachers perceived the role play as a fitting learning activity for cultivating citizenship in science education and sustainability. This perspective was informed by their observed interaction between scientific knowledge, argumentation, ethical reasoning, and critical thinking. However, these future teachers were confronted with a study of upper secondary students implementing the same role play. Despite the evident display of future citizenship in their discussions, the teacher's own students did not personally connect this competency to science education (Kristoffersen, 2021). An implication for the student teachers discussed was the necessity for future teachers to explicitly address citizenship and sustainability as desired outcomes when conducting socio-scientific role plays in science education, particularly during post-role-play discussions (Ødegaard, 2023).

# Further reading

Barker, R. (1998). *And the waters turned to blood.* Simon & Schuster.

# References

Dobson, A. (2007). Environmental citizenship and pro-environmental behaviour: Rapid research and evidence review. *Sustainable Development, 15,* 276–285. https://doi.org/10.1002/sd.344

Kristoffersen, K. D. (2021). *Rollespel i naturfag Eit reiskap for utdanning for medborgarskap?* [Roleplay in science. a tool for citizenship education?] Master's thesis, University of Oslo.

Lehtonen, A., Salonen, A. O., & Cantell, H. (2019). Climate change education: A new approach for a world of wicked problems. In J. Cook (Ed.), *Sustainability, human well-being, and the future of education* (pp. 339–374). Palgrave Macmillan.

Lönngren, J., & Van Poeck, K. (2021). Wicked problems: A mapping review of the literature. *International Journal of Sustainable Development & World Ecology, 28*(6), 481–502. https://doi.org/10.1080/13504509.2020.1859415

Ødegaard, M. (2008). Dramatic science: A critical review of drama in science education. *Studies in Science Education, 39*(1), 75–101. https://doi.org/10.1080/03057260308560196

Ødegaard, M. (2023). Using drama in science education and for sustainability issues. In D. McGregor & D. Anderson (Eds.), *Learning science through drama: exploring international perspectives* (pp. 69–86). Springer.

Valladares, L. (2021). Scientific literacy and social transformation: critical perspectives about science participation and emancipation. *Science & Education, 30*(3), 557–587. https://doi.org/10.1007/s11191-021-00205-2

# EXPLORING ALTERNATIVES THROUGH FORUM PLAY

**4**

## Chapter 13

# Forum play

## Exploring future energy practices

Lenneke Vaandrager

### Learning outcomes and related terms

The drama processes in this chapter aim to develop:

- Understanding of a social and often unfair or unjust problem situation, in this case related to future energy practices.
- Improvisation towards, and experience of, different possible solutions.

Key terms and definitions:

- Icebreaker: please see Chapter 2.
- Forum play: please see Chapter 2.

| Key sustainability-related outcomes |
| --- |
| **Embodying sustainability values** |
| Valuing sustainability/self-awareness and normative competencies |
| Supporting fairness |
| **Embracing complexity in sustainability** |
| Critical thinking |
| Problem framing/integrated problem-solving competence |

DOI: 10.4324/9781003496359-17

| Envisioning sustainable futures |
| --- |
| Futures literacy/anticipatory competence |
| Adaptability |
| Exploratory thinking |
| **Acting for sustainability** |
| Individual initiative |

# Context of application

In 2023 and 2024, a group of 20 PhD candidates participated in a workshop as part of the PhD course Transformative and Participatory Qualitative Research Approaches and Methods of the Wageningen School of Social Sciences Graduate Programme in The Netherlands. The course provides PhD candidates and early-career scholars conceptual and hands-on methodological engagement with transformative, participatory, and action research approaches that use creative- and arts-based research methods and techniques. These techniques foster the inclusion and engagement of diverse, often marginalised perspectives and to bring into focus, examine, and transform narratives, representations, and practices. The course gives students the opportunity to practice using these methods with individuals and groups, as well as to examine and assess these methods relative to ethics of action-oriented engagement and the opportunities and challenges they pose for data analysis and (re)presentation (Ormond & De Vrieze, 2014). PhD candidates participating in this course come from different scientific backgrounds such as health, sustainability, international development studies, and governance.

# Step-by-step guidance

1. Icebreaker: "Person, House, Hurricane".

   - ◼ This game can be played inside or outdoors, but you need enough space to move around.
   - ◼ Ask everyone to stand up and make groups of three players.
   - ◼ Explain that two players are the two walls and roof of a house and one person is the inhabitant of the house. Two persons build a house by standing face to face, lifting their arms up, and putting their hands together. The inhabitant moves into the house.
   - ◼ Explain that a student who is neither inhabitant nor part of a house will call out either "Person", "House", or "Hurricane".
   - ◼ When you call "Person", the inhabitant/s must leave their house and find another house. Practise this a few times.
   - ◼ When you call "House", the two players who formed the house break up and make a new house with somebody else, around another inhabitant

(Note: all inhabitants stay where they are). Practise this a few times and also use the command "Person".

■ When you call "Hurricane" everyone must move around and form new houses with new inhabitants. Here a former "Person" can change to be a "House" and vice versa.

■ The student who is calling tries to move into a house or become a house so that whoever is left becomes the one calling.

■ You can now use all three commands.

2. Forum play:

Forum play (see Chapter 2) encourages audience interaction and explores different options for dealing with a problem or issues (Österlind, 2011). This forum play concerns future energy practices, which are often characterised by an unequal distribution of benefits and burdens, and different groups have different perspectives. The workshop consists of four phases:

1. Present four different conflict-oriented issues (if you want to have four groups), in this case related to future energy practices. Ask the students to choose which issue they prefer to work with, and form four groups. Then let each group decide about personalities and prepare a short improvised role play which will allow the spectators to understand the issues or conflict. The groups do not have to develop solutions but need to focus on showing the escalating problem, conflict, or dilemma. It should include some movement and small talk, and everyone should have a role. Tell the groups they should do a rehearsal of the scene they want to perform.

2. The first group performs their play until the conflict has escalated to a crisis. The teacher stops the performance and asks everyone present, "*Is this resonating?*" and "*Who is the most exposed or oppressed here?*"

3. Play the scene(s) again and explain to the spectators they can shout "*stop!*". One person then enters the scene by exchanging with the most oppressed (or a bystander) and tries to change the situation through new arguments or (unexpected) actions to come to a better ending. This step is repeated a few times, depending on the level of interaction and timeframe.

4. Each time, invite different people to step in to the scene and discuss the unfolding scenario with the whole group using questions like "*What happened?*", "*How do we think about the alternative scenario?*" and "*What made it different?*" Steps 2, 3, and 4 are repeated by the following groups with a different dilemma so that everyone gets a chance to both perform and step in.

# Framing or pre-work

The "Person, House, Hurricane" is an energiser that can be used at any time (see Chapters 4–7). Household (future) energy practices are a suitable issue for forum play to explore how (in)justices are reproduced in household energy practices in the present and future. Related readings can be added and discussed, before or after the workshop.

## When to use and when not to use

"Person, House, Hurricane" can be useful in various contexts as long as there is sufficient place to move and run around. For forum play, students need to feel safe to participate. It is fine if some do not step in and act. Instead, they may give suggestions to the oppressed character on how to act. There also needs to be sufficient time to do some icebreakers, some role play, the preparation of the scene, the actual forum play, and the reflection. It is advisable to have at least two to three hours available (including a break).

## Reflections from the field

The icebreaker and forum play were used in March 2023 and 2024. All of the students were actively engaged in the icebreaker "Person, House, Hurricane", and it created a lot of energy and laughing. It was a good warm-up for the forum play. In 2023, there was more time available for the workshop (three hours) than in 2024 (two hours). The 2024 workshop felt a bit rushed and some students also expressed they felt some pressure and had too little time to prepare their scene.

The four options presented represented the following conflict areas:

- Family dilemma: conflict about cutting expenses and saving energy.
- Researchers: have new technical solutions, eagerly searching for start-ups, business partners ready for production.
- Local politicians: trying to convince other politicians/local board to become a gas-free community.
- Open option: what would be the most problematic scenario?

Each of the conflict issues attracted a group and all of the groups prepared scenes. Some scenes were clearly more "explosive" than others. Sometimes it took some time for a volunteer to call "*stop!*" and jump in. The different scenes clearly facilitated new ways of thinking, enlarged frames of reference, and made the students conscious about the injustices but also about alternative, fairer solutions. Student reflections included:

> "This can be a powerful tool if the audience deeply connects with the situation and is comfortable with others in the group."

> "As the audience, you get to watch it externally at first, and this gives you a way to have a broader perspective, potentially allowing you to see creative solutions (instead of when you're too 'in' the problem itself)."

"Diversity of perspectives that arise increased perceptiveness to other's experiences."

"I think, by building up a conflict situation, you can make it absurd, which makes it fun but potentially unrealistic, at which point it might lose value."

## Things to consider

It is important to explain the icebreaker "Person, House, Hurricane" step by step and practise the different steps. The game should be short and engaging. In the forum play, some participants may need extra encouragement to perform, whereas others can dominate a scene. It is your job to ensure that these issues are managed – you can walk around when scenes are being prepared and give suggestions, e.g. about everyone having the opportunity to perform, and to encourage volunteers to step in.

## Learning extensions

■ Ask the students to do some reading about injustice related to future energy practices.
■ Use a structured evaluation format asking all participants to individually write their (1) thoughts, (2) questions, (3) "aha!"-moments, and (4) pitfalls on a sticky note. Each participant shares their experience in the group.
■ Give participants the opportunity to organise and facilitate a forum play workshop on a topic they choose.

## Integrating with assessment

The script and the acting could be a part of assessment. However, this might also hinder creativeness and feelings of safety. Students can also be asked to write a reflection about their experiences afterwards.

## Further reading

Chlup, D. T., & Collins, T. E. (2010). Breaking the ice: Using ice-breakers and re-energizers with adult learners. *Adult Learning*, *21*(3–4), 34–39. https://doi.org/10.1177/104515951002100305

Conrad, D. (2004). Exploring risky youth experiences: Popular theatre as a participatory, performative research method. *International Journal of Qualitative Methods*, *3*(1), 12–25. https://doi.org/10.1177/160940690400300102

Enria, L. (2016). Co-producing knowledge through participatory theatre: Reflections on ethnography, empathy and power. *Qualitative Research*, *16*(3), 319–329. https://doi.org/10.1177/1468794115615387

Midha, G. (2010) *Theatre of the oppressed: A manual for educators*. [Masters thesis, University of Massachusetts-Amherst].

# References

Ormond, M. E., & De Vrieze, A. G. M. (2024). Transformative and participatory qualitative research approaches and methods. *Course Guide 2024*. https://www.wur.nl/en/show/transformative-and-participatory-qualitative-research-approaches-and-methods-4-ects.htm

Österlind, E. (2011). Forum Play – a Swedish mixture for consciousness and change. In S. Schonmann (Ed.), *Key concepts in theatre and drama education* (247–251). Sense.

## Chapter 14

# Forum play

## Exploring sustainability scenarios and privileged perspectives

Mary Ann Kernan

### Learning outcomes and related terms

The drama processes in this chapter aim to develop:

- Embodied, active engagement with drama as an accessible and potentially powerful medium to explore the resolution of conflict related to sustainability.
- Enhanced student confidence about how they could apply established dramatic practices to develop their own group plays on a sustainability theme.
- Informed student understanding of sustainability scenarios and stakeholders.
- Applicable formative insights about how to use dramatic techniques, including improvisation, to inform the development of related module assessments.

Key terms and definitions:

- Forum play: see Chapter 2.

DOI: 10.4324/9781003496359-18

| Key sustainability-related outcomes |
| --- |
| **Embodying sustainability values** |
| Valuing sustainability/self-awareness and normative competencies |
| Supporting fairness |
| **Embracing complexity in sustainability** |
| Systems thinking |
| Critical thinking |
| Problem framing/integrated problem-solving competence |
| **Envisioning sustainable futures** |
| Futures literacy/anticipatory competence |
| Adaptability |
| Exploratory thinking |
| **Acting for sustainability** |
| Political agency |
| Collective action/strategic/collaboration competence |
| Individual initiative |

## Context of application

The activity described in this chapter drew on the research work of Eva Österlind (2018, 2022) and her collaborators. Österlind presented the rationale for this approach and led the group in an active exploration of its impacts as part of the Explorative Workshops project in 2022. The processes outlined here were applied in a workshop in 2023 with a group of 20 Bayes Business School students completing City's Master's in Innovation, Creativity and Leadership (MICL) as part of a 15-credit capstone module, Creativity and the Creative Industries. This cohort consisted of primarily international students aged between 25 and 50, many of whom first encountered the nature and urgency of the UN's Sustainable Development Goals and sustainability challenges while studying for their master's (see also Chapters 6 and 14).

## Step-by-step guidance

1. Before the session, clear tables to the side of the room, and put chairs in a circle (or a semi-circle if you will be showing slides). As the students enter, invite small groups to sit together if they are already established, or to take any seat.
2. As a first stage of this activity, debrief any pre-work by inviting discussion in pairs or threes (2–3 minutes).
3. To set up the forum play activity, briefly summarise the background to Forum Theatre (around 5 minutes, see Chapter 2). You might, for example, emphasise how Boal (2008) built on this experience to devise Forum Theatre. He and his collaborators took actors onto the streets to enact current political conflicts

and invited members of the audience to join in the drama and contribute to finding solutions. Additionally, you might say that today's activity uses forum play, an applied version of Forum Theatre developed in Sweden for use in educational settings (Österlind, 2011).

4. If not already assigned, create groups of four or five members, maximum six (see Chapter 6 for some ways to do this). Invite the small groups to sit together. Ensure that they can all hear you for the activity briefing.

5. Next, brief their preparation for the forum plays. You might say:

■ *In your small groups, decide on a sustainability scenario and the characters in it, then plan an improvised forum play, about three to five minutes in length, to explore the scenario, its issues and impacts, and who has the highest and lowest status to resolve the conflicts it involves.*

■ *Ensure that we will understand your sustainability scenario. Choose one which involves tension, where at least one participant is being oppressed by others, and where the characters can be passionate about the issues. The ending should escalate to a conflict between the people involved.*

■ *Plan how your characters will talk for your non-human stakeholders, remembering that the focus of a forum play is on realistic human action (no talking trees, evolution as a solution, or escapes to Mars?).*

■ *You will first perform your forum play to the rest of the group before we invite others to join a second performance as spect-actors.*

■ *As props, you can use the tables and chairs in the room, as well as paper, pens, and sticky notes to make signs or props if you wish.*

■ *This is not about being actors – you can have fun with it and do not need to prepare a script. We do need to hear you: practise speaking more slowly and loudly than feels natural, and remember that silent gestures, body posture and sounds will help to tell your story.*

■ *You have up to 15 minutes to prepare.*

6. As they work, circulate around the room to answer any questions, ensure that they are working to the brief, and direct them towards the flipchart paper, pens, and sticky notes if helpful. Give reminders after 5 and 10 minutes (you might allow up to 20 minutes if their discussions continue to be active).

7. When most of the groups appear to have prepared their plays, move into the performance segment. Invite the participants to move their chairs into a semi-circle facing a designated part of the room to act as the stage, and to sit with their small group. Ensure that the whole group will be able to see and hear the performances.

8. It is important to establish ground rules for running the plays. Invite the group to listen with their hearts as well as minds to each other's plays, to be curious about the characters and how they might feel, to follow the events carefully, and to note which of the characters might resolve the conflict and at when in the scene they might do so. Remind them that after the first group has

performed, you will invite them to volunteer to take the place of a character who is oppressed or being treated badly.

9. Invite a volunteer group to be the first to show their play. If none volunteer, based on what you saw of their preparation, choose one who you are confident will present a realistic and rich scenario with a range of stakeholders and a sense of conflict. Remind the performers to speak so that they can be heard (the most common suggestion is to "*slow down!*").

10. Run the first play and invite applause and celebration. Debrief the scene to identify:

   ■ *Who were the oppressed and the oppressors?*
   ■ *Were any silent or quiet stakeholders particularly impacted by the situation?*
   ■ *Might one of the lower status characters be able to influence or resolve the conflict (e.g. a person who decides who can make an appointment to see someone in a position of authority)?*

11. Set up a second performance of the first forum play by inviting a volunteer to take the part of one of the characters or give advice to the players on the stage, hoping to change the drama in a way which leads to a more productive outcome.

   If no one volunteers, invite the groups to discuss which character might make a difference and how (c3 minutes) and to share any good ideas. Emphasise again to the group as a whole the importance of respectful listening – not least as finding solutions to sustainability challenges is such a crucial, urgent issue for us all. Run the drama again, from a point in the drama that is most relevant to the volunteer's chosen character. Afterwards, invite the person who stepped forward to say what they hoped might happen and how it felt to be their character, and any comments from the other performers.

12. You can then run all or some of the remaining forum plays prepared by the small groups, depending on the size of the overall cohort and time constraints.

13. Close the workshop by relating the outcomes of the activity to your stated aims and learning outcomes and inviting their comments.

## Framing or pre-work

It is helpful to run the *Long lists and silent figures* icebreaker before this activity (see Chapter 6 in this volume) to identify the many stakeholders involved in sustainability scenarios and establish their hierarchy of status and power (from politicians and CEOs as high status, individual and local actors as medium or low status, to tomatoes, fish, and coral as the lowest status). Student discussions and experience in that activity may also enhance the issues and characters they choose for their forum plays.

Encourage your students to research examples of successful initiatives to address sustainability challenges, both to inform their own plays and to lessen the negative emotions, including overwhelm, hopelessness, and climate anxiety (see Chapter 15), which are so often evoked by climate change (see resources in Chapter 6 for examples of award-winning projects e.g. UNFCCC, 2024).

As an example of the potential power of applied drama, see the work of Natasha Cox (Actively Seeking, 2024), who is using Forum Theatre in social impact projects in London with school-aged boys from a variety of personal backgrounds, especially boys of black heritage.

## When to use and when not to use

For success, restrict your numbers to 20 for the first use of the activity. For larger groups, you could bring in another facilitator and consider spreading the debrief of the small groups' plays, for example, to run them through an afternoon interspersed with other activities and time to capture and deepen their reflections.

The activity's design assumes that all of the students can take part. You could invite a discussion about any individual learning needs which might prevent participation. If you identify students who are unable to join in group work or perform, you could invite them to capture and feedback to you on what they notice about each group's scenario, the status of the characters and who is oppressed, and about the impact of the intervention of the spect-actor. You can include them further by referring to their insights in your final debrief.

## Reflections from the field

You will enhance your own confidence in using drama by researching the aims and background of forum play, and its origins as a tool of activism (Boal, 2008; Österlind, 2011, Chapters 2, 3, and 13–16). For success, the students need to be in groups and feel comfortable with one another and with you. Before running this activity, establish your small groups using at least one icebreaker activity (e.g. the icebreaker in Chapter 6 was used prior to this forum play).

The master's students (all aged 25 to over 50) successfully planned and performed three forum plays, even though they did not complete the pre-work I assigned. Their scenarios included a conflict in an intergovernmental setting in which they played representatives of their own countries, a dispute in a food chain related to sustainable fishing, and a third story told from the perspective of tomatoes where only one of them had access to enough water to grow and reach the supermarket shelves. Some of these focused more successfully than others on both oppression and sustainability or identified characters with a clear hierarchy of status and potential for action.

When you have students with limited experience in participative and arts-based learning, allow more time to debrief the pre-work, and ensure that the proposed dramas include characters with a range of different status and potential for action. If your teaching context relates to summative assessment related to sustainability, provide scenarios for each small group which specify human characters with a range of status as well as considering non-human impacts. This would also work well with undergraduates and younger postgraduates, to ensure that the plays reflect the knowledge requirements of the learning outcomes.

## Things to consider

Depending on the number of small groups, you will need a large room with tables moved to the side and chairs which can safely be moved by the students. You will also need to plan spaces for each small group to prepare their short play without being overheard but where you can support them.

In order to run the activity, also decide where the stage will be, taking into account the confidence levels and skills of the group. Some participants may be daunted, for example, if asked to perform on a stage in an auditorium.

This forum play needs:

■ A flipchart roll of paper (or e-equivalent).
■ A marker board or flipchart stand.
■ Sticky notes and marker pens for each group.
■ Where the IT allows, slides to introduce key concepts and the briefing for the activity, or a summary handout (to be shared after the session to promote active listening in the room).

## Learning extensions

Depending on your target learning outcomes, other arts-based activities (Wall et al., 2019) can deepen the learning and allow the participants to create an artefact which is personally meaningful and powerful. Beyond the sense of fun and achievement that they are likely to feel after this forum play activity, personal journalling can also evoke a heightened sense of empathy for the planet and all of life (Talgorn & Ullerup, 2023). Depending on the context, your brief could also encourage the students to consider how to build on their insights in future assessments, or in their own personal learning, actions, or professional goals.

During the session, allowing a short time for reflection or paired discussion can help to settle the group if the fun of the experience and nerves around performances lead to laughter and chat which overwhelm the serious content and intention of the activity.

Similarly, if no one in the cohort volunteers, answers, or participates at any stage, you could ask them to work in pairs or trios to complete and post flipchart sheets or sticky notes and to nominate a single volunteer within each group to speak for the group.

## Integrating with assessment

This forum play was a formative experience towards a group performance assessment on a sustainability theme. The marking criteria for that assessment emphasised creative problem-solving, storytelling, integration with the themes of the programme as a whole, and participation – rather than skill in acting, which would be inappropriate. A reflective journal also formed part of the module assessment, with credit available for showing depth of reflection and engagement with the module, the programme and arts-informed practices.

If your context requires assessment, consider using the forum play as one of a series of activities related to sustainability, with assessment in the form of an individual reflective report appropriate to your target learning outcomes and discipline, and supported by critical sources on reflective practice and professional development (e.g. Bolton & Delderfield, 2018; Bassot, 2024) as well as appropriate scholarly or professional resources.

## Further reading

Nicholas, K. (2021). *Under the sky we make: How to be human in a warming world*. Putnam.
Boal, A. (2021). *Games for actors and non-actors* (3rd edition). Routledge.

## References

Actively Seeking. (2024). *Background*. https://activelyseeking.co.uk/home/background/
Bassot, B. (2024). *The reflective journal* (4th edition). Bloomsbury.
Boal, A. (2008). *Theatre of the oppressed* (3rd edition). Pluto Press.
Bolton, G., & Delderfield, R. (2018). *Reflective practice: Writing and professional development* (3rd edition). SAGE.
Freire, P. (2017). *Pedagogy of the oppressed* (17th edition). Penguin.
Österlind, E. (2011). Forum play. In S. Schonmann (Ed.), *Key concepts in theatre/drama education* (247–251). https://doi.org/10.1007/978-94-6091-332-7_40
Österlind, E. (2018). Drama in higher education for sustainability: Work-based learning through fiction? *Higher Education, Skills and Work-Based Learning*, 8(3), 337–52. https://doi.org/https://doi.org/10.1108/HESWBL-03-2018-0034
Österlind, E. (2022). Drama workshops as single events in higher education – what can we learn? In M. McAvoy & P. O'Connor (Eds.), *Routledge companion to drama in education* (324–37). Routledge.
Talgorn, E., & Ullerup, H. (2023). Invoking "empathy for the planet" through participatory ecological storytelling: From human-centered to planet-centered design. *Sustainability*, 15, 7794. https://doi.org/10.3390/su15107794
UNFCCC (United Nations Framework Convention on Climate Change). (2024). *Winning projects, UN global climate action awards*. UN Climate Change. https://unfccc.int/climate-action/un-global-climate-action-awards/winning-projects (12 June 2024).
Wall, T., Österlind, E., & Fries, J. (2019). Arts-based approaches for sustainability. In W. Leal Filho (Ed.), *Encyclopedia of sustainability in higher education*. Springer. https://doi.org/10.1007/978-3-319-63951-2_523-1

## Chapter 15

# Forum play

## Working with climate anxiety

Oleksandra Khalaim and Anna Lehtonen

### Learning outcomes and related terms

The drama processes in this chapter aim to:

- Reflect on your own personal experiences in managing climate-related emotions.
- Analyse and discuss different perceptions of eco/climate anxiety.
- Compare attitudes towards eco/climate anxiety in the group.
- Navigate through conflicting attitudes, seek and agreed solutions, and begin to embrace the complexity of climate change as a wicked problem.

Key terms and definitions:

- Climate anxiety (also referred as 'ecological' in some sources): is an adaptive response to the threat of climate change (Comtesse et al, 2021). An alternative definition by American Psychological Association (Clayton et al, 2017) says that eco-anxiety is the chronic fear of environmental cataclysm that comes from observing the seemingly irrevocable impact of climate change and the associated concern for one's future and that of the next generations.
- Climate-related emotions: are a core part of any kind of individual or collective response to climate change (Davidson & Kecinski, 2021).
- Forum play – see Chapter 2.

DOI: 10.4324/9781003496359-19

| Key sustainability-related outcomes |
| --- |
| **Embodying sustainability values** |
| Valuing sustainability/self-awareness and normative competencies |
| **Embracing complexity in sustainability** |
| Critical thinking |
| **Envisioning sustainable futures** |
| Adaptability |
| **Acting for sustainability** |
| Collective action/strategic/collaboration competence |

# Context of application

A workshop on climate anxiety using forum play was delivered for a mixed group from the Suderbyn Ecovillage community (in Sweden) and international students involved in sustainability-related study programmes at Uppsala University Campus Gotland (first-year master's students from two programmes: Sustainable Destination and Sustainable Management). The workshop took place in December 2022 in Visby (Sweden) with 15 participants. The participants were particularly interested in the topic of climate anxiety after being engaged in a small project on eco-emotions led by Suderbyn Ecovillage the same fall, so there was a warm and friendly atmosphere at the workshop.

# Step-by-step guidance

1. Introduction.

   ■ Re-organise the room so that there is enough space to walk around freely (warm-ups can also be conducted outdoors).
   ■ As an introduction, you may refer to research (e.g. Tyng et al., 2017) and explain why it is essential to acknowledge how emotions have a strong impact on learning and behaviour, how challenging emotions may interfere with cognitive reasoning, and how emotions could be considered in environmental and climate change education (Pihkala, 2020). In applied drama, emotions become naturally integrated and worked with (Lehtonen et al., 2020). Furthermore, the reason for using embodied warm-up is because emotions manifest in bodies.
   ■ Facilitate a joint discussion on what helps people feel safe to explore and express their emotions in a group. You may first ask the participants to talk in small groups with two or three others about what they need to feel safe to explore and express emotions in a group. Then collect and sum up these

reflections on the board. Another option is to prepare and present a slide of principles for a safe space (see below) and ask the participants to reflect on the principles and share their experiences.

■ Principles for a safe and creative space:

■ Listen to yourself and other participants.

■ Accept and respect all evolving ideas, attitudes, and emotions. There are no right or wrong attitudes or reactions.

■ Take part in the activity in a way that feels good for you today. It is acceptable to sit aside and only watch. However, encourage exploring all the challenging emotions it evokes and stepping into the uncomfortable zone.

■ Avoid unnecessary chat, especially during the warm-up.

2. Warm-up.

■ Here are detailed instructions to be read slowly with pauses.

■ Meditative music can be used as an inspiration for embodied reflection in the beginning.

■ *Find a comfortable spot in the room. You may stand, sit, or lie down.*

■ *Take some deep breaths. Close your eyes, if it feels ok. Let go of the experiences you had before you stepped in here, and let your thoughts flow.*

■ *Inhale and exhale. Focus on yourself, how you are today, focus on what you feel right now in your body and its different parts. Let your sensations flow, come and go…*

■ *Now begin to think about climate change and the current nested sustainability crises. How does climate change feel in your body? Listen to your body and start to move as you feel like.*

■ *Open your eyes, but still focus on yourself. Start to move, walk.*

■ *How does climate change make you move your feet and legs? How does it feel in the middle part of your body, in your belly, breast, what about your back? How does it feel to move your hands, shoulders, and neck? What kind of facial expressions evolve when thinking about climate change? What would be one sentence that describes your experience?*

■ *Now look around and meet other people in the space. Keep your bodily expression of emotional experience and share it with others. Move around in silence.*

■ Option: Working in small groups: *Express your emotional experiences in turn with embodied gestures and with a summarising verbal phrase. Others mirror how they see it. When it's your turn to show your emotions, you can ask the others in your group to respond all together at the same time either by 1) comforting, 2) strengthening or empowering your emotion, or 3) transforming your emotion by showing, for example, an opposite emotional gesture.* (These options should be made visible on a slide or board.) The one having the turn to express the emotion can show with fingers what kind of response they want.

3. Forum play

Stage 1: Preparation for a forum play.

Form an appropriate number of small groups out of all workshop partici-pants (four to six in each) and give them 20 minutes to prepare a five-minute performance about any conflict situation related to climate-related emotions and climate anxiety that can happen in the real world. The instructions are a) to create a scene that contains a problem, b) to escalate the problem and related tensions in the scene, and c) to end up in an open conflict. You may need to point out that their task is to present the problem and not solutions.

For example, during our workshop on Gotland, participants were divided into two groups and correspondingly they decided to pick two top-ics. The first group presented a tense situation between climate activists and oil industry workers, where the activists were blaming the oil industry for the climate impact and pushing workers to quit, while the latter disagreed as they needed their jobs to earn a living for themselves and their families. The second group presented a conflict between generations by enacting a scene during a family dinner, where the conversation was gradually growing into mutual blaming for the state of the Earth.

Stage 2: Performing.

After each play is performed to the audience, reflect with the audience how they perceived the conflict of the play. Ask the actors to play the conflict another time and tell the audience members about the opportunity to stop the play whenever they see a good moment where the situation could be changed. The audience may interrupt the play and step into it by trying out either the role of the oppressed or a by-stander and test different enactments. The goal for such an intervention is to try to solve the conflict situation or to manage it towards de-escalation. The intervening spect-actor says 'stop' to 'freeze' the action in the moment he/she wants to step in and substitute for one of the players. Encour-age the audience by telling them that even if the enactments do not resolve the conflict, they will help to understand the issue better. Several attempts to change the situation can be tried out, before moving on to the next play.

Stage 3: Reflections and discussions.

In general, the workshop facilitator ensures the flow of the whole process by 1) starting, 2) encouraging or even challenging the audience to step in and try to make change, 3) pausing, 4) moderating the discussions, and 5) ending performances and so on. After each original play and its alternative versions with the oppressed being replaced, the facilitator initiates a reflec-tion round. Some possible questions for discussion:

- What was the conflict about? What happened and why?
- How did the conflict situation escalate in the initial play and why?
- How did the conflict situation evolve after the interventions? Was it successful, promising or not? Why? How did the 'oppressor' experience the different attempts?

– What was your emotional response to the situation and its alternative developments before and after the intervention(s)?

Stage 4: Closing the workshop.

It is very important to ensure an emotional 'check-out' after the workshop. We recommend the following procedures:

1. Circle feedback. Participants and the facilitator form a circle and one by one shortly share two statements: (1) take-away from the workshop and (2) moment of gratitude (I am thankful for…).
2. Final relaxation round (inner work in silence). The facilitator asks all participants to sit comfortably, close their eyes, and gradually relax all parts of the body by naming them from top to bottom.
3. Hugs and good-bye!

# Framing or pre-work

A general recommendation is to look at other warm-ups (see Chapters 4–7) and consider whether they fit your teaching and facilitation style better. Read about and familiarise your students with forum play (see, for example, Österlind, 2011, and Chapters 13–16), and with Forum Theatre (Boal & Jackson, 2021).

Another recommendation is to pay attention to and emphasise mutual respect for different views and emotions. This needs to be reflected on together with the students as well, as it is important to form a safe and creative atmosphere for applied drama. Welcoming all the emerging emotions, accepting, and respecting without any judgements or questioning is an essential principle for exploring emotions.

It is encouraged to first focus on exploring and reflecting on your personal emotions. For the facilitator, it is good to practice and pay attention to your own emotions before conducting the workshop and emphasise the same principle for your students as well in case they are going to facilitate practices on emotional issues.

# When to use and when not to use

If the group is very diverse, with controversial views on climate change and/or climate-related emotions, this is not a problem as long as the facilitator emphasises that the variety of emotions and perspectives is respected.

At the same time, it should be mentioned that lack of eco-anxiety or any strong feelings towards climate change is also appropriate. The facilitator should be aware of climate deniers in the group or those who may neglect the importance of emotional work. Some students tend to follow the idea of not expressing emotions within university classrooms. If this is the case, the facilitator should take some time at the beginning of the workshop to discuss the different views on and reasons for emotional work, and the importance of accepting and respecting each other's emotions.

It might be better to not use the proposed workshop if there are problematic group dynamics known beforehand, and if the facilitator is not experienced or confident enough to deal with such challenges.

## Reflections from the field

During the warm-up, the participants reflected on the walking practice, e.g. they noted how they are strongly accustomed to thinking with mind and brain, and they had actually never paid that much attention to the expressiveness in their own bodies.

After the forum play, participants reflected on the difference between traditional teaching formats, like lectures and seminars, and embodied experiences of applied drama. The main conclusion here was focused on the potential of embodied practices to discuss complex, intertwined, and problematic topics, and to synthesise narratives into a more consolidated and holistic picture, even at the very beginning of the learning process. On the contrary, traditional formats often delivered separated components of the whole while pushing learners to find the synergy afterwards as 'homework'.

Another observation from the forum play process was related to the emotional side of it. A combination of forum play (as a method that aims to present, escalate, and solve a conflict) and climate anxiety (as content that is by its nature sensitive and can take different shapes) can be a bit more 'explosive' than traditional lectures as it evokes more emotions and connects personal experiences with theoretical concepts. This was the case in our workshop, but the emotional intensity apparently helped to reach learning outcomes in a clearer way. In other words, it was a constructive and helpful intensity.

## Things to consider

■ Make sure the group is comfortable to work with each other on this sensitive topic; be mentally prepared for this possibly 'emotionally explosive' combination of forum play as a method and climate anxiety as a topic.

■ Prepare yourself in advance with arguments for climate-change deniers and/ or those participants who neglect the importance of emotional work.

■ Collect some statistics on climate anxiety (e.g. regional or worldwide, among different age groups, and in higher education).

■ Read some additional material about forum play in order to get acquainted and comfortable with this method before you practise it with participants.

## Learning extensions

The walking warm-up is a good preparation for still-image practice, where all the emotions manifested can be watched and reflected on together. Forum play can be followed up with a lecture on related topics, for example, on climate emotions in higher education or climate anxiety among youth. Similarly, the facilitator can prepare in advance and propose some conflict situations for the play, keeping in mind corresponding lecture topics that can be brought up and presented to the workshop participants afterwards.

## Integrating with assessment

A reflective learning journal could work well as a tool for the assessment of this practice. To use a learning journal technique, it is good to schedule some time at the end of the workshop for writing some post-reflective notes straight after the practice that can be finalised afterwards. The focus of reflection could be on learning experiences related to the 'adaptability sustainability competence' of GreenComp or Inner Development Goals (Cooper & Gibson, 2022).

## Further reading

A newly developed workshop "Dealing with climate emotions" under the recently launched Climate Guide of Uppsala University: https://mp.uu.se/documents/432512/94660 6024/UU+Climate+Guide.pdf/

Boal, A., & Jackson, A. (2021). Forum Theatre: Doubts and certainties: Incorporating a new method of rehearsing and devising a Forum Theatre model. In A. Boal *Games for actors and non-actors* (253–276). Routledge. https://www.routledge.com/ Games-for-Actors-and-Non-Actors/Boal/p/book/9780367203542

Lehtonen, A., & Pihkala, P. (2021). Encounters with climate change and its psychosocial aspects through performance making among young people. *Environmental Education Research, 27*(5), 743–761. https://doi.org/10.1080/13504622.2021.1923663

Pihkala, P. (2022). Toward a taxonomy of climate emotions. *Frontiers in Climate, 3*, 738154. https://doi.org/10.3389/fclim.2021.738154

Zaremba, D., Kulesza, M., Herman, A. M., Marczak, M., Kossowski, B., Budziszewska, M., Michałowski, J. M., Klöckner, C. A., Marchewka, A., & Wierzba, M. (2023). A wise person plants a tree a day before the end of the world: Coping with the emotional experience of climate change in Poland. *Current Psychology, 42*, 27167–27185. https:// doi.org/10.1007/s12144-022-03807-3

## References

Clayton S., Manning C. M., Krygsman, K., & Speiser, M. (2017). *Mental health and our changing climate: Impacts, implications, and guidance.* APA and ecoAmerica. https:// www.apa.org/news/press/releases/2017/03/mental-health-climate.pdf

Comtesse, H., Ertl, V., Hengst, S.M.C., Rosner, R., & Smid, G.E. (2021). Ecological grief as a response to environmental change: A mental health risk or functional response? *International Journal of Environmental Research and Public Health, 18*(2), 734. https:// doi.org/10.3390/ijerph18020734

Cooper, K. J., & Gibson, R. B. (2022). A novel framework for inner-outer sustainability assessment. *Challenges, 13*(2), 64. https://doi.org/10.3390/challe13020064

Davidson, D. J., & Kecinski, M. (2021). Emotional pathways to climate change responses. *WIREs Climate Change, 13*(2). https://doi.org/10.1002/wcc.751

Lehtonen, A., Österlind, E., & Viirret, T. L. (2020). Drama in education for sustainability: Becoming connected through embodiment. *International Journal of Education & the Arts, 21*(19). https://doi.org/10.26209/ijea21n19

Österlind, E. (2011). Forum play: A Swedish mixture for consciousness and change. In S. Schonmann (Ed.), *Key concepts in theatre/drama education* (247–251). Brill.

Pihkala, P. (2020). Eco-anxiety and environmental education. *Sustainability, 12*(23), 10149. https://doi.org/10.3390/su122310149

Tyng, C. M., Amin, H. U., Saad, M. N., & Malik, A. S. (2017). The influences of emotion on learning and memory. *Frontiers in Psychology, 8*, 235933. https://doi.org/10.3389/fpsyg.2017.01454

## Chapter 16

# Forum play

## Exploring more-than-human perspectives

Anna Lehtonen and Viola Hakkarainen

### Learning outcomes and related terms

The drama processes in this chapter aim to develop:

- Understanding and empathy of multi-species perspectives.
- Critical awareness on conflicting needs and interests of more-than-human in urban planning.
- Creative collaboration skills in exploring diverse solution options for the conflict situations.

Key terms and definitions:

- Multi-species thinking emphasises the commitment to non-anthropocenic ways of thinking about nature and focuses on the political and ethical implications of human-centrism, thereby opening up thinking for the inclusion of other species.
- More-than-human refers to co-dwelling with other than human actors in the world.
- Forum play – see Chapter 2.

DOI: 10.4324/9781003496359-20

**129**

| Key sustainability-related outcomes |
| --- |
| **Embodying sustainability values** |
| Valuing sustainability/self-awareness and normative competencies |
| Supporting fairness |
| Promoting nature |
| **Embracing complexity in sustainability** |
| Systems thinking |
| Critical thinking |
| Problem framing/integrated problem-solving competence |
| **Envisioning sustainable futures** |
| Futures literacy/anticipatory competence |
| Adaptability |
| Exploratory thinking |
| **Acting for sustainability** |
| Political agency |
| Collective action/strategic/collaboration competence |
| Individual initiative |

## Context of application

The exercise was implemented as part of a two-day doctoral school focusing on embodied, creative, and applied drama methods in Helsinki (2023). The students were enrolled in the same doctoral programme in Interdisciplinary Environmental Sciences but had diverse disciplinary backgrounds, ranging from the natural sciences to social sciences and interdisciplinary sustainability science. The course comprised 20 students, and the forum play took place on the second day after they had already become familiar with other creative and embodied methods. For most, working with such methods was a new experience. The goal of the doctoral school was to introduce and explore how interdisciplinary sustainability scientists could apply such methods in their research and teaching.

## Step-by-step guidance

1. Setting the scene and warming up.

   ■ Begin the exercise by setting the scene with a question such as: 'Imagine a city designed from the perspective of more-than-human encounters. What if the space in the city prioritised the needs and interactions of animals and plants?' Explain the agenda for the day and the exercises you are going to use.

■ Use an icebreaker exercise (see Chapters 4–7). 'Person, House, Hurricane' (used as a warm-up in Chapter 13) can be adapted to fit the context of the forum play. In this instance, the roles in the game were modified to represent birds, nests, and the urban planning department.

2. More-than-human walk before the forum play.

Before delving into the main activity of forum play, conduct a 'More-than-human walk' as a precursor to the forum play.

a. Prior to the walk, engage the students in breathing exercises and 'mindful scanning' to ground oneself in the present moment and prepare for a shift in perspective. You can do this by suggesting everyone close their eyes (or look down) and go through the body from the feet and legs to the back, arms, neck, top of the head and face, by mentioning the body parts: '*Feel your feet and let them rest for a while… let your face became soft and relaxed*'. You may guide your students to take some deep breaths and focus for a moment in the sensation of their body and calm down (the same relaxation is used in Chapter 29).

b. Begin by asking students to step outdoors and observe the city through the lens of animals and plants. Encourage the students to envision themselves as more-than-human actors during the outdoor walk, allowing them the freedom to select their more specific roles. Prompt them to consider various senses, contemplating how the city environment might be perceived from a non-human perspective. Come back together at the designated meeting point after approximately 20 minutes.

c. After the walk, pair the students up, ask them to show each other some parts of their individual walk, and encourage them to share aspects of their experiences from different locations, selecting objects from the outdoor environment that symbolise their observations. Come back together at the meeting point after 20–30 minutes.

d. Upon returning indoors, arrange the students in a circle and invite everyone to briefly share insights gained from their experiences through the symbolic objects they have chosen.

e. Facilitate group discussions by dividing the students into smaller groups ideally consisting of four to five individuals, categorised according to their observational perspectives (e.g. those adopting a bird's perspective). Each group will collaboratively construct a scene for the upcoming forum play based on their shared experiences and perspectives.

3. Creating multi-species forum plays.

a. Ask students to brainstorm, plan, and later perform a conflict situation in urban planning that escalates. Students prepare a play consisting of scenes that manifest injustice or opposing relationships. This could be, for example, a planning conflict of building houses that threaten the habitats of endangered species or any conflict situation that arises from the interaction of human needs in relation to other beings. Students are likely to be inspired by the more-than-human walk. They will choose the roles within the group. Ask students to include at least one more-than-human role (e.g. a tree, a bee, a bird). Students can use in their play the materials that were collected outside.

A summary of instructions for a forum play:

- Choose a conflict situation that escalates.
- Choose actors and try to understand how and why the different parties (human, non-human) have differing views and needs in the situation. What do they think, how do they act, and why do they think so? At least one person should take a more-than-human role.
- Choose an object or material found outdoors that symbolises the conflict.
- Think about how to perform the situation.
- Prepare a performance about the conflict situation that does not get solved but keeps escalating. What is the situation and who is involved? How could you perform a conflict that escalates?
- Rehearse the play before performing. Be prepared to perform the play several times.

b. After preparations, each group plays their scene in front of the others. Ensure the flow of the whole process by moderating discussions, starting, pausing, and ending performances.

c. After each play is performed to the audience, reflect with the audience how they perceived the conflict of the play. *What was the conflict about? Why has it evolved?* Ask the actors to play the conflict another time.

d. Tell the audience about the opportunity to stop the play whenever they see a good moment where the situation could be changed. Then prompt one member of the audience at a time to interrupt the play and to join it to try out different enactments by taking the place of someone who is being oppressed or one of the bystanders.

e. Encourage them to test different ways of acting so even if the enactments do not resolve the conflict, they will help to better understand the issue. After the interventions in the play ask the audience, the spect-actors (a combination of spectators that has the power to act out/influence the scenes), what they think happened after the interventions, and what was the impact and outcome of the enactments. *Was it successful or promising or not? Why?*

f. Remember to thank all the performers and audience for their thought-provoking/inspiring performances.

4. Collective reflection and closure.

After such an intensive practice like a forum play, it is good to have a collective closure where people can share something about their experience with others. This can take place, for example, by 'marking the moment' with the following instruction:

*Reflect, what was the most impressive moment for you as a spectator or performer during this workshop? Place yourself on the stage where it happened.*

Ask each student in turn to share and express something about their experience to others.

## Framing or pre-work

It is crucial to apply a warm-up and icebreaking exercise before the actual forum play (see Chapter 4). It is also beneficial to familiarise yourself with the implementation of the forum-play method in general.

## When to use and when not to use

This workshop is useful for considering more-than-human perspectives in various settings. As a performative method, forum play can be demanding for students. Therefore, it is advisable to incorporate this exercise as part of a more extensive process involving other applied drama, creative, or performative methods. Especially if there are problematic group dynamics, strong social hierarchies, or poor group atmosphere, it is better to start with other simpler creative exercises and conduct several warm-ups.

This exercise requires sufficient time for preparations and post-reflection, so this might not be applicable during a normal 90-minute lecture. It is possible to divide the workshop into two or three parts. One option could be assigning the observation practice as a pre-homework. Then the first session (90 minutes) could include (1) a warm-up, (2) sharing the symbolising objects and photos of their experiences of the observation homework with the whole group, and (3) dividing the students into thematic groups for further reflective discussions and for setting the scene for the performance. The second session (90 minutes) then could include (1) a warm-up, (2) preparing and rehearsing the performances, and (3) the forum-play processes. The end reflection is essential but can also be postponed for another session.

## Reflections from the field

Based on the experiences of applying this method in the doctoral school, we found it potentially useful and applicable to various learning environments and groups to introduce multi-species thinking. From the cognitive perspective, the forum play particularly enables the exploration of complexity, plurality, and positionality in a fictive situation. At the same time, the experience of participating in the forum play fosters skills to cope with the anxiety, uncertainty, and ambiguity that conflicting situations may evoke. As one of the students reflected:

> Discovering that I was comfortable in a drama play setting was a pleasant surprise for me. Especially because it was about uncomfortable conflict situations. Yet, I felt like the exercise was in a way emancipatory by allowing escape from reality and picking imagined components for the play, and allowing for taking control of imagined, but realistic events... It was in a way empowering not only thinking about what could be, but actually acting the necessary steps out to achieve it.

The students appeared to thoroughly enjoy the workshop, which encouraged active participation in collective creation infused with joy and creativity. They reflected on how the observation practice and forum play facilitated a detachment from typical human-centric and mind-centred thinking.

Particularly, students without prior experience in drama had to navigate stepping out of their comfort zones when creating a play and performing in front of an audience. Despite facing their own struggles and psychological barriers to creative collaboration, all of the students expressed that the forum play was a positive experience. One wrote in her post-reflection:

> The forum play was an interesting experience... I had no experience of acting, improvising. Actually, some might say that this kind of experience is terrifying, as you need to be in front of a crowd without proper practising and not knowing what to expect. Nevertheless, it was surprisingly fun!.

## Things to consider

The application of forum plays benefits from students being familiar with embodied ways of working before the exercise. This is because acting in front of others takes courage and can be scary for many people if they do not have previous experience or if the members in the group are not very familiar with each other. It is important to gently encourage the students to step out of their comfort zone, to experience going beyond their own limits in a collaborative and supportive atmosphere. Encourage the students to listen to themselves and levels of comfort before the forum-play exercise and provide some time afterwards for collective and individual reflection.

## Learning extensions

If the group is new to forum play, it is good to ask students to familiarise themselves with the method and the topic before by, for example, recommending an article to read about the method (Österlind, 2011, Chapter 2).

The method could be used as an open-learning process to catalyse deeper understanding to be built in the future lectures or to continue to explore the topic through project work based on the exercise. It is possible to link the forum play to a specific case or context that is relevant to the course (such as urban planning in the example exercise of this chapter). Students can be asked to search for information to learn more about more-than-human in urban planning. Students could also get more deeply into how different species sense their environments through reading in prior, during, or after the exercise.

The process could be repeated after students have investigated the chosen topic during the course. Furthermore, the scenes could be performed to real-world actors or decision-makers as is done in Legislative Theatre (see Chapters 2 and 22) to formulate urban planning principles to be implemented in real-world settings.

## Integrating with assessment

The forum-play method could be assessed by using a learning diary as the course assessment. Time for free-associative or reflective writing could be scheduled after outdoors observing and after performing the forum plays. The reflection could be deepened by relating it to literature, or students could be asked to identify sustainability competences or the inner development goals (Cooper & Gibson, 2022) related to their learning experiences.

## Further reading

Aaltonen, H. (2015). Voice of the forest: Post-humanism and applied theatre practice. *Research in Drama Education: The Journal of Applied Theatre and Performance, 20*(3), 417–421. https://doi.org/10.1080/13569783.2015.1059263

Lehtonen, A. (2021). Drama as an interconnecting approach for climate change education. Thesis, *Helsinki Studies in Education Series*, 118. https://helda.helsinki.fi/server/api/core/bitstreams/2dce9f14-f567-4470-aca0-3dc3e4ce05ae/content.

Tschakert, P., Schlosberg, D., Celermajer, D., Rickards, L., Winter, C., Thaler, M., Stewart-Harawira, M., & Verlie, B. (2021). Multispecies justice: Climate-just futures with, for and beyond humans. *WIREs Climate Change, 12*(2), e699. https://doi.org/10.1002/wcc.699

## References

Cooper, K. J., & Gibson, R. B. (2022). A novel framework for inner-outer sustainability assessment. *Challenges, 13*(2), 64. https://doi.org/10.3390/challe13020064

Österlind, E. (2011). Forum play: A Swedish mixture for consciousness and change. In S. Schonmann (Ed.), *Key concepts in theatre/drama education* (247–51). Sense.

# PROVOKING INSIGHT THROUGH PERFORMANCE

5

## Chapter 17

# Provocation

## Co-creating a poem about the future

Katja Malmborg and Julia Fries

### Learning outcomes and related terms

The drama processes in this chapter aim to:

- Develop futures thinking and exploratory thinking.
- Explore creative writing as a tool in support of sustainability.
- Practice reflexivity.

Key terms and definitions:

- Reflexivity: in a higher education context, reflexivity relates to the students' self-awareness in how they learn, and use knowledge and act in the world.
- Futures thinking: a creative and exploratory process that uses divergent thinking, seeking many possible answers and acknowledging uncertainty when exploring various ideas about the future.

| Key sustainability-related outcomes |
| --- |
| Embodying sustainability values |
| Valuing sustainability/self-awareness and normative competencies |
| Supporting fairness |

DOI: 10.4324/9781003496359-22

| Envisioning sustainable futures |
| --- |
| Futures literacy/anticipatory competence |
| Exploratory thinking |
| **Acting for sustainability** |
| Collective action/strategic/collaboration competence |

## Context of application

This exercise comes out of work with young adults in projects run by the theatre group Teater K in Sweden, where role reversal with future persons and exploring future scenarios played key parts (also see Wall et al., 2019). The exercise was developed for online teaching during COVID-19 in the course *Sustainable Economic Futures – nature, equity and community* at Uppsala University in Sweden.

Approximately 30 students from different faculties, on both undergraduate and postgraduate level participated. The exercise was further developed into the form presented here in an elective course focusing on the Sustainable Development Goal 15 (life on land) at the Department of Biological Sciences at the University of Bergen, Norway.

This course is interdisciplinary in scope and covers both ecological and social science themes related to biodiversity loss and its causes. The course usually has approximately 25 enrolled students and is open to students at any faculty, but the proportion of undergraduate-level biology students tends to be higher than from other study programmes.

## Step-by-step guidance

1. Start the exercise with a brief individual meditation. Ask the participants to close their eyes and imagine that they are students 50 years into the future studying the same topics as today. In a calm voice, guide them through the meditation by asking:

   a. *What is your life like?*
   b. *How do you live?*
   c. *What do you eat?*
   d. *How do you transport yourself?*
   e. *What are your studies like?*
   f. *What has happened with the sustainability challenges that you are studying?*
   g. *Etc. (you might add your own questions).*

2. Ask the participants to organise themselves into pairs. Tell them to take turns interviewing each other about their imagined lives as students in 50 years.

Tell the interviewer to take notes of what they learned about their partner's imagined future.

3. When both partners in a pair have each been interviewer and interviewee, ask them to look at their notes from interviewing their partner. Tell them to pick a couple of words or phrases from their notes that pop out at them or that pique their interest.

4. Split up the pairs and ask the participants to form groups of four to six people. Tell them to present the words, phrases, or sentences that they picked out in the previous step to their other group members. Ask the groups to collectively reflect on how the words or phrases relate to each other: What kinds of futures could they be representing? Do they point towards similar futures? Or, could there be tensions between them?

5. Instruct the participants to write a poem about an imagined future, using the words and phrases from their interviews. If needed, they may add other words to make complete sentences. Suggest that the groups represent both the similarities and tensions in the imagined futures that were revealed through their selected words and phrases.

6. Distribute large papers and markers among the groups. Ask the students to write down their poems. Encourage them to include illustrations or other decorations on the paper if they wish.

7. Ask the groups to present or perform their poems to the class. Depending on the group, this may be done as a simple recitation, or they may choose to enact a more dramatic performance.

8. After the performance, arrange the poems from each group as posters on a wall in the classroom. Give the participants some time to silently read and reflect on the different poems about imagined futures.

9. Facilitate a discussion in the class, asking the students to reflect on questions such as: What similarities and tensions emerge between the visions of the future conveyed in the poems? What diversity in underlying values and ideas about the future among the students in the class do they reveal? Were they surprised by anything they experienced or heard in the meditation, their interviews with another student, the collaborative poetry writing or reading the other groups' poems? Have they gained any new perspectives?

## Framing or pre-work

Scenario development, future visioning, science fiction prototyping, and other types of futures methods are frequently used in sustainability science together with various groups of stakeholders and rightsholders. If a course includes lectures about various futures methods as examples of research approaches within sustainability science, this is a simple exercise that can be done in the classroom during a teaching session to give the students a taste of what a future visioning exercise can be like.

## When to use and when not to use

This exercise is easy to understand and generally engages most students. It has a clear output which is completed within the timeframe of an ordinary teaching session. Therefore, this is an exercise that can be used in a longer course about sustainability science or similar when the teacher wants to mix things up and include more interactive and creative components among more traditional teaching formats.

Beyond exploring approaches to futures methods, however, this exercise does not lend itself to teaching more specific topic-related subjects such as understanding the drivers of biodiversity loss or how to practice transdisciplinary research approaches. Therefore, this exercise may not be appropriate in a situation where teaching time is limited and aims for learning outcomes are very disciplinarily specific.

## Reflections from the field

Many students find this explorative and creative exercise engaging as well as a nice change to traditional teaching approaches in higher education. The combination of individual meditation, interviewing, collaborative poetry writing, illustration, and performance also provides a diverse range of creative expressions where students' combinations of various strengths tend to be expressed.

The process of articulating their own ideas about the future is valuable for the students, and they often express surprise at how different the emergent visions of the future in the class turn out to be (see examples of poems from students at the University of Bergen in Figure 17.1).

**Figure 17.1 Photographs of poems written by students.**

Figure text: Poems about various futures for life on land, co-created as part of this exercise by students at the University of Bergen. Source: Katja Malmorg, used with permission.

## Things to consider

This is an easy exercise to enact in various contexts; however, it might be difficult to manage in groups that are larger than 30 or more students. In that case, the class could be split into smaller groups, to make the number of students participating in the final step of performing and discussing the poems manageable.

## Learning extensions

This exercise may be broadened by delving deeper into other approaches to futures thinking, such as participatory scenario development, three horizons, Seeds of Good Anthropocenes, and science fiction prototyping.

## Integrating with assessment

This exercise is more exploratory and not suitable for assessment.

## Further reading

Hopkins, R. (2020). *From what is to what if: Unleashing the power of imagination to create the future we want.* Chelsea Green.
Seeds of Good Anthropocenes. (2024). https://goodanthropocenes.net/.
Radical Ocean Futures. (2024). https://radicaloceanfutures.earth/.

## Reference

Wall, T., Fries, J., Rowe, N., Malone, N., & Österlind, E. (2019). Drama and theatre for health and well-being. *Encyclopedia of the UN Sustainable Development Goals*, 130–142. https://doi.org/10.1007/978-3-319-95681-7_14

# Chapter 18

# Provocation

## The Farewell Falsterbo futurewalk

Mary Ann Kernan

### Learning outcomes and related terms

The drama processes in this chapter aim to develop:

- Embodied experience of a high-quality audio drama on a sustainability theme.
- Emotive engagement with the likely outcomes of the climate emergency.
- Engagement with the urgency of sustainability and the steps available to communities to address its impact.
- An embodied, private walk in a natural, external setting which invites reflection, empathy, and action related to sustainability.

| Key sustainability-related outcomes |
| --- |
| **Embodying sustainability values** |
| Valuing sustainability/self-awareness and normative competencies |
| Supporting fairness |
| Promoting nature |
| **Embracing complexity in sustainability** |
| Systems thinking |
| Critical thinking |
| Problem framing/integrated problem-solving competence |

DOI: 10.4324/9781003496359-23

| Envisioning sustainable futures |
|---|
| Futures literacy/anticipatory competence |
| Exploratory thinking |
| **Acting for sustainability** |
| Individual initiative |

## Context of application

This activity drew on the 'soundwalk' *Farewell Falsterbo: a soundwalk from the future*, which was developed and made freely available online by Climaginaries (Climaginaries, 2022). Part of their initiating aim was to '[explore] the transformative capacity of imaginaries; how compelling narratives are told, and how they can shape and enable efforts to confront climate change' (Climaginaries, 2024).

I used this soundwalk in 2023 as the basis of an activity with a group of 20 Bayes Business School students completing City's Masters in Innovation, Creativity and Leadership as part of a 15-credit capstone module called Creativity and the Creative Industries. This cohort consisted of primarily international students aged between 25 and 50, many of whom first encountered the nature and urgency of the UN's Sustainable Development Goals while studying for their programme (also see Chapters 6 and 14). All of the students were familiar with the process and disciplines of creative writing through a prior course.

## Step-by-step guidance

1. Brief the students before the event, as appropriate for your chosen space and time, including how to access the story and to bring a telephone and headphones to listen to it while walking, and to brief them on the Health and Safety, legal, and emergency guidance (eg through your virtual learning environment). Ask them to download the Climaginaries app and the storywalk audio file before they arrive (Climaginaries, 2022) and tell them where and when to meet, and what to bring in case of wet or cold weather.

2. When your group has gathered, brief them on your expectations for the time they will spend listening to the futurewalk. Tell them that they can choose a version in English or Swedish and choose a more or less negative outcome from the events described; and that this is an individual activity to be completed in silence. If appropriate, suggest that they stop and make notes in a journal about what they notice and experience (Baumard, 1994), especially if this experience is related to an assignment or other workshops.

3. Ensure that you also tell the participants where you will be, how they can reach you if they become separated from the group, what time the activity will end, and when and how you will debrief them on their experience (e.g. in the next session). Specify any limits in the space you want them to use for their walk, or whether they will walk together, to allow you to keep everyone in sight.

4. Debrief the experience with reference to sources appropriate to your students' context, as well as sources which emphasise the role of narrative in imagining climate futures (e.g. Kelsey, 2020; Nicholas, 2021); the effects of shared embodied experience; and the effects of listening to a dramatised account while walking (rather than reading or watching a film).

## Framing or pre-work

Before the session, ensure that you visit the space in which you will run the walk, to plan how you will manage the safety of your learners and your ability to see them while they complete the storywalk. The story is set near a beach, so if you can gain access to one that would work well (alternatively, it can be staged somewhere near water or in a park). The experience will have the most impact if delivered outdoors.

As required by my institution's Risk Assessment process, I included a Health and Safety and photography briefing in the outing handout. The wording included reference to the public information prepared by the UK Police relevant to London (e.g. how to respond in the unlikely but possible event of a terrorist incident). I also asked the students to remember not to take close pictures of members of the public in the park, especially any pictures of children.

## When to use and when not to use

The events that unfold within the narrative of the futurewalk are highly emotive, so with younger or vulnerable students it would be essential to brief them about this beforehand and be available to support any who become distressed, with an option to discontinue the story and return to it when they felt able to do so. Even with these mature adult students, several reported feelings of sadness (see below).

## Reflections from the field

In my experience of this activity, about half of the class actively engaged with the futurestory and therefore encountered an emotive narrative of a potential climate change future. The outdoor context also appeared, overall, to encourage them to relate the story to the physical impacts of sustainability events. The students provided feedback on this futurewalk as one of the arts-based activities in the module, and the words they offered were predominantly emotive, including 'calm', 'sad', 'scary', and 'reflective'. Two students found the immediate experience less engaging or productive than others, and one said 'I didn't connect with this as a walk. I listened to it again just sitting in my lounge'.

## Things to consider

The time of year and daylight should be considered for this kind of outdoor activity. In this case, the end of the walk coincided with sunset, which enhanced the drama of the story. The weather could also play a part in deciding when and where the activity is run: for example, my fallback plan was to run the activity inside a nearby museum.

I invited my students to complete the activity independently before they left the park, for debrief the following week. This allowed them to explore the park freely, but I cannot therefore be confident that they all listened to the whole of the audio. With younger or less disciplined groups, independent movement through a large public park at sunset would not allow oversight of their well-being.

The *Farewell Falsterbo* developers recommended a beach setting for the walk. If this was not practical, you could seek a safe riverside setting which allowed clear lines of sight to the group as they completed the activity. This would reinforce the context of the story for all participants but would also be needed to supervise a younger or unfamiliar group.

You should also establish a process for any students with physical restrictions or who found the emotive nature of the content difficult or triggering while the story progressed. I might, for example, designate a shared space where they could sit or walk with others as well as an agreed check-in process if they found they needed to pause the narrative.

## Learning extensions

You could prepare pre- and post-activities to debrief the constructive, hopeful aims and other projects run by the Climaginaries initiative, including to invite the participants to discuss whether they experienced the futurestory as a 'transformative… imaginar[y]… to shape and enable efforts to confront climate change' (Climaginaries, 2024). The students could also be encouraged to research and share other examples of hopeful and action-related climate change stories, films, cartoons, or music. Research about embodied audio storytelling which can support your own preparation as well as teaching towards analytical assessments include Talgorn and Ullerup (2023) on participatory ecological storytelling.

You could share recommended reading before the session (e.g. Nicholas, 2021), as well as preparing and circulating a series of questions related to your educational or informational context (e.g. to encourage self-reflection, see Bolton & Delderfield, 2018), for debrief after the walk in any related written or spoken assessments.

## Integration with assessment

These students were well prepared for this activity (from previous courses in Creative Writing and the Creativity and the Creative Industries modules). You could link this activity to the assessment of a substantial reflective portfolio which could encourage analysis of the aims and themes of the futurestory as well as of the experience itself. In this module's reflective journal assessment, some students commented directly on this activity. One said:

> The audio drama invited me to envision a future impacted by climate change, which was both captivating and unsettling. Listening to the story while walking through Regent's Park allowed me to connect more deeply with the narrative, as the natural surroundings served as a back-drop for the imagined future.

## Further reading

Kelsey, E. (2020). *Hope matters: Why changing the way we think is critical to solving the environmental crisis.* Greystone Books.

Lange, E. A. (2023). *Transformative sustainability education: Reimaging our future.* Routledge.

Nicholas, K. (2021). *Under the sky we make: How to be human in a warming world.* Putnam.

## References

Baumard, P. (1994). From noticing to making sense: Using intelligence to develop strategy. *International Journal of Intelligence and Counterintelligence, 7*(1), 29–73. https://doi.org/10.1080/08850609408435236

Bolton, G., & Delderfield, R. (2018). *Reflective practice: Writing and professional development* (3rd edition). Sage.

Climaginaries. (2022). *Farewell Falsterbo: A futurewalk set in Skanör-Falsterbo, Climaginaries.* https://www.climatefutures.lu.se/farewell-falsterbo

Climaginaries. (2024). *Who we are.* Climaginaries. www.climaginaries.org/our-impact

Talgorn, E., & Ullerup, H. (2023). Invoking "empathy for the planet" through participatory ecological storytelling: From human-centered to planet-centered design. *Sustainability, 15*(10), 7794. https://doi.org/10.3390/su15107794

## Chapter 19

---

# Provocation

---

## What a load of rubbish!

Maribel Blasco

### Learning outcomes and related terms

The drama processes in this chapter aim to:

- Connect sustainability theory with practical applications.
- Raise awareness about sustainability considerations in everyday behaviours.
- Connect sustainability issues with cultural self-reflexivity.

Key terms and definitions:

- Micro-behaviours: small, typically hidden behaviours which can be significant in terms of bigger issues such as sustainability, often referred to as '*hidden in plain sight*'.

| Key sustainability-related outcomes |
|---|
| Embodying sustainability values |
| Valuing sustainability/self-awareness and normative competencies |
| Embracing complexity in sustainability |
| Critical thinking |

DOI: 10.4324/9781003496359-24

| Envisioning sustainable futures |
| --- |
| Exploratory thinking |
| Acting for sustainability |
| Individual initiative |

# Context of application

This provocative intervention was applied at a Scandinavian business school which has purposefully integrated a values framework into its curricula which aims to inspire students to address societal challenges with compassion for themselves, others, and the planet. The course in question provides theoretical tools and exercises for students to reflect on their cultural assumptions, based on their overseas exchange experiences. Students are often surprised by other countries' excellent sustainability performance compared to Denmark, which challenges both their stereotypes and national pride.

Despite Denmark's strong international reputation for sustainability, internal challenges persist, such as high material consumption and a low circular economy metric (CGR Denmark, nd; Sustainable Development Report 2021, n.d.; The Danish Sustainability Indicators, n.d.). These factors highlight the need for sustainable consumer practices in Denmark, despite widespread environmental awareness and concern among the Danish population (European Investment Bank, 2021).

The specific intervention was applied in the sixth semester. The students had recently returned from a semester abroad and were pursuing a programme combining language, culture, and business. These students often refer to themselves as the school 'hippies', seemingly embracing this self-stereotype.

# Step-by-step guidance

1. Pre-intervention preparation.
   Seek any necessary permissions from the relevant governing bodies, such as Study Boards, for conducting the intervention, as there may be issues with waste handling and/or unsettling students in 'non-conventional' ways.
2. Setting the stage.
   Inform students that something unusual will happen: At the first lecture, show the slide such as Figure 19.1 to the students but without revealing the theme or goal of the experiment, as this might lessen its provocative value.
   Introduce the experiment: keeping a casual tone, announce that students' classroom rubbish will be collected at the end of class due to campus waste collection challenges.
3. Initiating the experiment.
   Collecting rubbish: stand at the exit after each class to collect the students' waste. Smile, and ask passing students if they have any classroom rubbish and if so to deposit it in the bag. Hold the bag open in front of you.

---

**Before we start - please read this in silence**

Dear Cultural Analysis students.

This is to inform you that I am participating in an experimental teaching project, run by Stockholm University Environmental Sciences and Drama departments.

In connection with the project, **you can expect an unusual, but harmless, classroom intervention during this course**, which we will discuss briefly at the end of the course.

The intervention has been approved by the BLC Study Leader.

Thank you so much for your cooperation and understanding.

I am really looking forward to the course with you!

---

**Figure 19.1 First slide introducing an 'unusual activity' at the start of the course.**

Observe student reactions: keep track of and note students' responses and interactions as they participate in the rubbish collection process over subsequent classes.

4. Follow-up and monitoring responses.
Maintain the routine: continue the rubbish collection process in subsequent classes to observe how students adapt to the routine and their evolving reactions.

Document observations: record students' responses and behaviours during the rubbish collection process. You can do this immediately afterwards, in a document made for this purpose.

5. Unveiling the experiment.
Recap the experiment: at the final lecture, present the slide from the first class to remind students of the 'unusual intervention' and explain the purpose behind the rubbish collection.

Engage students in discussion: facilitate a discussion on environmental awareness, self- and other cultural stereotypes, and collective action based on the rubbish collection experience. This could be done by, first, using a Slido or other poll software to collect national self-stereotypes about environmental friendliness (or whatever topic is relevant) (e.g. Figure 19.2), combined with other data regarding self-stereotypes (Figure 19.3 shows an excerpt from a student post to a course platform during her exchange semester, which illustrates such self-stereotypes – teachers who do not have such data could use scholarly literature or popular self-stereotypes instead) and ask students 'Do you think that this (e.g. poll results) represents reality'? Then teachers can follow up with statistics about the country's actual environmental friendliness.

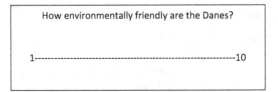

**Figure 19.2 Poll used to kick off student reflection about cultural self-stereotypes about environmentally friendly behaviour.**

> I am on exchange in Bordeaux in France. There is a lot of trash around the city, and there doesn't really seem to be a proper recycling system here. In the place where I live, the garbage truck comes three times a week to empty our trash. We only have two trashcans; one for non-recyclable items (like packaging for food) and one for everything else (paper, metal, plastic!). The trashcans are often overfilled on the streets. At my university here, however, there are a few more trashcans for sorting the trash.
>
> It doesn't seem like people are very focused on the environment as they are in Denmark. I have seen people just putting their old furniture, fridges, and other stuff out on the street, waiting for the garbage truck to pick it up. However, a positive thing is that sometimes people walking past take the stuff, if it is in good condition.
>
> In Denmark, I am used to recycling and sorting my trash. There is much more focus on the environment in Denmark. I am used to putting plastic, paper and metal in separate trashcans, so it is a bit strange to put all of the things in the same trashcan.

**Figure 19.3 Slide showing an excerpt from a student post uploaded to the course platform during her exchange semester abroad, used in class to discuss cultural self-stereotypes about environmentally friendly behaviour.**

6. Promoting reflection.

Encourage reflection: ask students (1) What do you think about the rubbish/collection? (2) What could we do collectively to avoid this? (3) What should I do with the rubbish?

Share statistics (Figure 19.4): present statistics about the estimated amount of rubbish generated based on the collected waste and foster reflection by discussing the upscaling implications ('this is how much rubbish will be generated if this is what is going on at every business school campus in the world').

7. Feedback and conclusion.

Gather student feedback: seek students' views about their own environmental friendliness and compare this with their experiences from their exchange country.

Conclude and discuss next steps: discuss the implications of the experiment, encouraging further reflection, and exploring potential next steps or

```
┌─────────────────────────────────┐
│          Upscaling              │
│                                 │
│  x 1300 classes x 52 weeks in a │
│  year                           │
│  x 10,000 business schools in the│
│  world (or 23,651 universities) │
│                                 │
│  = 202.800,000 m3 of rubbish    │
│                                 │
│                                 │
│                                 │
└─────────────────────────────────┘
```

**Figure 19.4 Slide showing the upscaling implications of students' waste gener-
ation, based on information gathered from the school campus and
Internet regarding the number of business schools and universities
globally.**

actions. For instance (i) place students in groups and task them with discussing
strategies that would be effective for their generation/social group students in
changing micro-behaviours such as classroom rubbish generation, (ii) the task
can be broadened out by asking groups to also think of other micro-behaviours
in their daily lives, and how they might be tackled, and (iii) students' strategies
should be gathered in plenum and used as a point of departure for 'micro-
behaviour experiments' where students implement their own strategies in their
daily lives for a limited time period, and report back to the class.

## Framing or pre-work

The pre-work for this activity is outlined above. This helps frame the activity and
ensure that students are expecting something will happen.

## When to use and when not to use

In hindsight, the 10 × large lecture series may have been too long for a first-time
foray into a drama-based teaching intervention. Even the minor practicality of
remembering to bring a rubbish bag to each lecture was surprisingly more difficult
than anticipated. I would recommend conducting the intervention over fewer sessions and with a smaller class, for easier manageability.

## Reflections from the field

Many students appeared to find the rubbish collection amusing, smiling while hand-
ing over their rubbish, and some even apologised for not having anything to give
me or joked that they were not going to give me personal items. The intervention

thus seemed to unsettle the teacher-student dynamic positively by disrupting the usual hierarchy and class 'normality'. Their responses to my questions in the final class were:

- 'The school should make it easier for us to avoid buying plastic' (*shifting responsibility onto the institution*).
- 'We should avoid single use utensils at the canteen' (*assuming personal responsibility as a consumer*).
- 'I tried to refill a water bottle at a campus building but the sinks were too small, so I had asked the janitor if there was somewhere else I could fill them up and he told me that I had to buy the bottles from the canteen – I think the canteen has a commercial interest in students buying as much as possible' (*showing agency but being met with no support from the institution*).

None of the students responded to my question about what I should do with the rubbish. I ended up sorting it myself in the school's bins. With hindsight, I could have used the 'disgusting' nature of the stored rubbish to draw students' attention more purposefully to the ugly sides of capitalism that are concealed from us and with which we normally do not have to deal. Perhaps I could have done this by insisting more that they dispose of the rubbish themselves.

I believe that positive student attitudes toward instructional activities should be a teaching priority (Simonsen, 1977: 167), but this exercise challenged me on this. Certainly, my intention was to challenge them, but I also wanted this to occur within a 'dignity safe' space (Callan, 2016). A colleague from the Stockholm drama group asked me 'does it matter if the students feel bad?' To me this remains a profound and unsettling question that should be at the heart of planning and conducting such interventions. No teacher or teaching context is alike and there will be different thresholds for what is appropriate here. I felt uncomfortable for effectively lying to the students about the reason for the rubbish collection. Future reiterations might simply omit an explanation, thereby avoiding compromising teacher/student integrity. Additionally, the rubbish intervention walked a fine line between awareness-raising and potential shaming, thereby raising the ethical dilemma of burdening students with a sense of personal responsibility for the climate crisis.

## Things to consider

Consider what infrastructure is needed for the intervention, such as moveable/sealable classroom dustbins in this case, or a backup plan if the classroom changes. If classroom dustbins are fixed, it may be challenging to move/conceal them, so alternatives should be considered, like arriving early and blocking or covering them. Alternatively, teachers could insert their own plastic bin bags within the existing classroom bins.

Consider what you do with the rubbish between lectures: storing it in my small office was awkward, especially as I used transparent bags. Disposing of the unsorted garbage after the intervention was also challenging and unpleasant, as it contained organic waste and was not sorted. I had not anticipated students depositing all types of rubbish, even liquids, resulting in a messy and unhygienic situation. Addressing this by collecting rubbish fewer times and sorting it immediately into different categories could solve this.

## Learning extensions

The students' responses illustrated a complex interplay of individual and institutional responsibility, showcasing the challenges they face in enacting environmentally conscious behaviours within institutional constraints. These responses could be used to prompt a deeper class discussion about the role of institutions in facilitating sustainable practices and the agency of individuals within these contexts. Their varied responses also underscored the need for a nuanced approach to sustainability learning interventions that takes account of the challenges that students encounter in practicing 'everyday sustainability'.

Students could also be asked to broaden the experiment to their other life contexts and to do the 'upscaling math' on all the waste they generate. They could also be asked to conduct research on how cultural self-stereotypes might impede sustainable micro-behaviours. Asking students to dispose of the rubbish at the end of the course could also offer a more radical denouement, possibly branding the intervention more vividly into students' memories and enhancing their sense of responsibility for own waste.

## Integrating with assessment

As part of a course assessment, students could write a reflective essay on their experience with the intervention, including concrete steps to act differently both in class and more broadly in their lives. They could also be tasked with conducting a research project related to the issues raised by the intervention, for instance, exploring institutional policies on waste management, student/consumer behaviours affecting the environment, or the impact (or otherwise) of sustainability awareness interventions/campaigns.

Students could also be encouraged to design and implement their own university sustainability intervention/ awareness campaign, drawing inspiration from the themes and ethical dilemmas highlighted by the initial teaching intervention, to encourage them to be proactive in promoting environmental responsibility. This could include offering suggestions to teachers about how sustainability awareness could be integrated into courses and assessments in a student- and generationally sensitive manner.

# Further reading

Argento, D., Einarson, D., Mårtensson, L., Persson, C., Wendin, K., & Westergren, A. (2020). Integrating sustainability in higher education: A Swedish case. *International Journal of Sustainability in Higher Education, 21*(6), 1131–1150.

Edwards, M., Brown, P., Benn, S., Bajada, C., Perey, R., Cotton, D., ... & Waite, K. (2020). Developing sustainability learning in business school curricula–productive boundary objects and participatory processes. *Environmental Education Research, 26*(2), 253–274.

Michaelson, C. (2021). How a catchy bass line might someday resonate beyond my business ethics classroom: Rock music in management learning. *Management Learning, 52*(2), 188–202.

# References

Callan, E. (2016). Education in safe and unsafe spaces. *Philosophical Inquiry in Education, 24*(1): 64–78.

CGR Denmark. (n.d.). www.circularity-Gap.world. https://www.circularity-gap.world/denmark Downloaded at https://www.circularity-gap.world/denmark on 24 January 2024.

European Investment Bank. (2021, November 11). 79% of Danish people think that climate change and its consequences are the biggest challenge for humanity in the 21st century. European Investment Bank. Downloaded at https://www.eib.org/en/press/all/2021-399-79-of-danish-people-think-that-climate-change-and-its-consequences-are-the-biggest-challenge-for-humanity-in-the-21st-century on 24 January 2024.

Simonson, M. R. (1977). Attitude change and achievement: Dissonance theory in education. *The Journal of Educational Research, 70*(3), 163–169.

Sustainable Development Report 2021. (n.d.). Dashboards.sdgindex.org. https://dashboards.sdgindex.org/profiles/denmark Downloaded on 24 January 2024.

The Danish sustainability indicators. (n.d.). Www.dst.dk. Downloaded at https://www.dst.dk/en/Statistik/temaer/SDG/danske-maalepunkter on 24 January 2024.

# Chapter 20

# Provocation

## Reflecting on biodiversity loss

Katja Malmborg

## Learning outcomes and related terms

The drama processes in this chapter aim to:

- Connect large-scale sustainability challenges to the students' everyday lives.
- Creatively explore and communicate a sustainability challenge.
- Practice inter- and trans-disciplinarity by connecting scientific insights with artistic expressions.

Key terms and definitions:

- Transdisciplinarity: a process of collaboration between scholars and non-scholars on specific real-world problems, often combining natural and social science approaches with practical, local, and/or indigenous knowledge as well as arts.
- Provocative performance: a performance or activity that gives attention to an everyday/societal (destructive) routine through a provocative twist, with the intention to inspire reflection in both the performer and the audience.

| Key sustainability-related outcomes |
| --- |
| Embodying sustainability values |
| Valuing sustainability/self-awareness and normative competencies |

DOI: 10.4324/9781003496359-25

| Promoting nature |
| --- |
| **Embracing complexity in sustainability** |
| Systems thinking |
| Critical thinking |
| **Envisioning sustainable futures** |
| Adaptability |
| Exploratory thinking |
| **Acting for sustainability** |
| Individual initiative |

# Context of application

This provocative performance exercise was developed for two elective courses at the Department of Biological Sciences at the University of Bergen, Norway. These courses focus on the Sustainable Development Goals 14 (life below water) and 15 (life on land), respectively. They are interdisciplinary in scope and cover both ecological and social science themes related to biodiversity loss and its causes. Various alternative teaching methods are used in these courses, including debates and natural resource games. Both courses culminate in a poster session, where students present a group project about a land- or sea-based biodiversity challenge. The courses usually have approximately 25 enrolled students. They are open to students in any faculty, but the proportion of bachelor-level biology students tends to be higher than from any other programmes of study.

# Step-by-step guidance

1. Organise the participants into groups of around three to six students. If the class is structured around a group project, use these groups. Ask each group to choose a sustainability challenge to focus on. Encourage them to pick a topic that is general, but not global. For example, "biodiversity loss" is too general, while "restoring a stream for an endangered river mussel" is too specific. A useful scope of the topic is, for example, "certification as a means to increase biodiversity in European production forests", "threats to biodiversity from Norwegian holiday home expansion", or "the causes and social implications of coral bleaching in the tropics".

2. Introduce what performance art or provocative performance is, and how it can be connected to a selected sustainability challenge through the framework in Figure 20.1.

   It is important to give the students several examples of performances with varying degrees of complexity. For students who are not practised in artistic

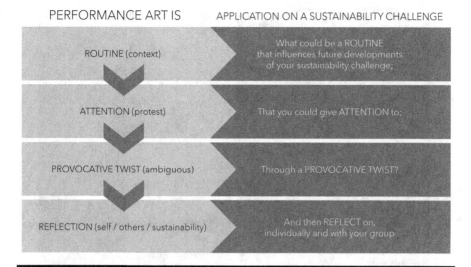

**Figure 20.1 A definition of performance art, and how it has been operationalised and connected to a sustainability challenge in this teaching tool.**

*Source:* Adapted from Tony Wall's workshop on 8th September 2023, based on Wall, 2022.

expressions, the idea of "provocative performance" can be intimidating. Therefore, including examples that are very simple and silly can make students more comfortable with approaching the exercise (see Ono, 1971).

In addition, providing an example of a piece performed by someone the students know, for example, the teacher, can bring the practice of provocative performance closer to the students' classroom experience and lower the threshold to engage in artistic expression (see example in Figure 20.2). As a teacher, it helps to introduce this exercise with humour and enthusiasm.

3. Explain to the students how engaging in the provocative performance exercise will support them in deepening their understanding of the course material. In the context where this exercise was developed, it was included in a module about sustainability science. To motivate the students, they were walked through a step-by-step framework of how sustainability science connects to core aspects of provocative performance (see Figure 20.3). In this way, the students are provided with an explanation for how engaging in the exercise will support them in meeting the learning goals of the course.

4. Over the course of a couple of short sessions, give the students time to develop ideas for different performances together in their groups. This could, for example, be done during the last 20 minutes of a couple of regular classes. Listen to the students and supervise them in how they can develop their ideas, connecting the performances to their chosen sustainability challenge and how to manage a potential audience.

Figure 20.2 Example of a performance that was shared with the students, performed by the teacher using scrap yarn from discarded clothes (a) as
well as knitting and crochet techniques in public spaces (b). The fibres
are shown to go through two cycles of making (c, f) and un-making
(d and e). The piece was framed around the sustainability challenge
of resource use in the textile industry and presented as a commentary
on fast fashion versus re-fashion. Printed with permission from artist:
Katja Malmborg; photos: Katja Malmborg (a and d–f) and Jan Malmborg (b and c).

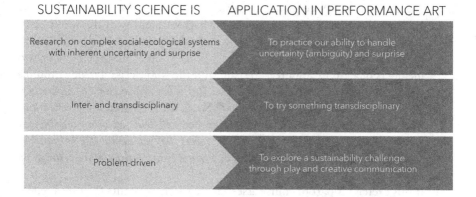

**Figure 20.3 A definition of sustainability science and how the students will explore sustainability science through this provocative performance tool.**

*Source:* Adapted from Clark, 2007 and Tony Wall's workshop on 8th September 2023, based on Wall, 2022.

Include instructions on the ethics, health, and safety of their performances. In addition to general ethical guidelines connected to good research practice, this may include that they should adjust the level of provocativeness to the type of audience they will have. This means that performances to strangers should be minimally invasive and easy to avoid as an audience member, whereas performances for friends or family may be more interactive. Encourage the students to also provoke themselves by potentially stepping outside of their comfort zone, but also that they should be careful not to cause themselves too much stress, discomfort, or any physical harm. The students should also be aware of the legal aspects of using public spaces and manage risks accordingly.

5. Give the students one to two weeks to perform their performances individually. The performances can be completely individual, done in collaboration with a classmate, or connect thematically with other group members' performances. A thematic connection could include students doing the same performance but in different places, to create emergent artistic effects from viewing multiple recorded performances when the pieces are presented in class later.

6. Before starting their performances, inform the students that they will be asked to present their work and reflect on their experiences in class after completing the exercise. Encourage them to take photos, to film, or in some other way record their performance, if this makes sense for the piece. However, instruct them that they need consent before taking and sharing any photographs or other recordings taken of identifiable people during their performances.

7. Once the performance period is over, organise a reflection session where the students share their experiences with their groups and with the whole class. Structure this sharing session in a way that makes sense for the class, for example, that all members of a group share with each other, and then one or two members of a group volunteer to share with the whole class. Provide prompts to help the students reflect, for example: *"(a) What did you do? (b) How did it go? (c) How did it make you feel/think?"* Similarly, for synthesising reflections with the whole class, useful prompts can be: *"(d) Did you or anyone in your group have any exciting or surprising experiences that you would like to share? (e) Were there any interesting or surprising differences or similarities between the group members?"*

8. If this exercise is part of course assessment, ask the students to write a reflection about their performance. Reflective writing can support reflexivity in students. Reflexivity in this context is understood as the students' self-awareness in how they learn, use knowledge, and act, in the world. The reflective text could answer questions such as: *"(a) What did you do and why? Explain how it connects to your chosen sustainability challenge; (b) How did your performance work out? (c) (If you had an audience) How did other people react to your performance? (d) How did it make you feel? Why did it make you feel this way? (e) After reflecting with your group and the others in class, what insights did you gain from the provocative performance exercise – from your own performance, and from listening to others' experiences? (f) What did you learn from this exercise about your chosen biodiversity challenge and sustainability more generally? What in the exercise supported your learning? (g) How did you like it?"*

## Framing or pre-work

This exercise was developed for an introductory module about sustainability science. The lectures leading up to the introduction of the exercise focused on defining sustainability science as a discipline: that it is research about social-ecological systems, often done through inter- and transdisciplinary approaches, and that it is problem-solving (Clark, 2007). See Chapter 1 in this book for further sustainability science information.

## When to use and when not to use

This tool requires time for the students to develop their ideas. Familiarity with other "alternative" forms of teaching, for example, active or experiential learning approaches or drama methods, also helps. Natural or social science students who lack experience of "alternative", more interactive forms of teaching, might require additional supervision and more time to prepare for the exercise.

# Reflections from the field

After some initial caution or even scepticism, most students happily engage in this exercise and express surprise at how fun it can be to experiment with something "artistic", even for those students who do not have an arts background. Through the support of the teacher, the reflection sessions following the students' performances often inspire deeper conversations in the class about conflicting values, ethics, the complexity and interconnectedness of sustainability challenges, and that there are many different approaches to act for sustainability. The students often make connections between science, activism, and art, collectively reflecting on when the different expressions are appropriate and most effective. See Figures 20.4–20.6 for examples of student performances.

In their written reflections, many students describe how they feel more aware of how decisions in their everyday lives are connected to larger sustainability challenges. They describe how even small performances instigate conversations among roommates, family, and friends. Many feel that these discussions are important to have, but that the ambiguity or strangeness of the performance actually makes it easier to start the conversation. For the audience, instigating conversation with a performance makes it funny or weird or surprising, inspiring curiosity, rather than directly being confronted with facts about the sustainability challenges we are facing

Figure 20.4 A student performance exploring biodiversity loss in the oceans due to dying corals, enabled by a personal interest in diving. Tin cans were used to build an artificial reef (a), which was left at the bottom of a fjord for 24 hours. After 24 hours, an underwater camera was placed in front of the reef to film an hour of fjord floor species interacting with the installation (b). The artist reflected: "it was surprising to see how fast sea life moved into their little temporary home. I think that points to how easily adaptable life is and how important reefs are, considering how fast someone moved in, even laid eggs!... Seeing the interactions for myself made me understand better how important the coral reefs actually are". Printed with permission from artist: Renate Løvlund Andersen.

Figure 20.5 A student performance about how humans are impacting our environment, focused on overconsumption, plastic pollution, and invasive species. The performance shows a person being choked by the plastic trash produced during a week in an average Norwegian family. She is surrounded by a production forest consisting of even-aged Sitka spruce, a species planted for its commercial value, but which has also started spreading on its own and become invasive in western Norwegian landscapes. In a way, the Sitka monocultures are choking native forest biodiversity, just like the plastic trash is choking the human. Printed with permission from artist: Lene Gramstad; photo: Bernt Eilef Gramstad.

as a society. This made the students realise that it is important to engage with a variety of communication strategies when it comes to sustainability issues, including ones that are artistic and humorous.

## Things to consider

This exercise requires time and support. Students who are not familiar with the arts need time to discuss with their peers about how to connect a sustainability challenge with a performance. These discussions are part of the exercise and should not be rushed. They are needed for effective learning. Some students might also need to be

Figure 20.6 A student performance focusing on the impacts of sea level rise on coastal communities. The piece shows a series of photos, where a sandcastle is built by the water's edge during low tide, and how it is partially and eventually completely gone after 12 and 24 hours, respectively. The experience brought fascination with the speed and rigour with which the force of water eliminated any trace of the sandcastle – but also sadness, that the experience and effort put into constructing it was completely lost within that short period of time. It made the student reflect on the dangers of not acknowledging and respecting the force of water, but also the importance of protecting and preserving the cultures, peoples, and knowledge that are under threat from sea level rise. Printed with permission from artist: Finn Corus.

supervised by a teacher in the idea-development phase, to encourage playfulness and to make the exercise be less intimidating. Many students tend to appreciate doing something different in class, however, this exercise is not for everyone. As a teacher, it is important to keep an eye on students who might feel too uncomfortable or pushed too far outside of their comfort zone through this exercise. For these students, it is enough to suggest that they try a small performance for themselves without an audience and then reflect on their own experience and feelings.

## Learning extensions

An extension of this tool could be to include an additional reflection session halfway through the performance period. This could specifically explore the students' own sense of self and place in the world, in terms of responsibility for sustainability, their own comfort zones, and how they inspire change in the world. This was not feasible timewise in the original context that the tool was developed for, but in a longer course, this could help students to further develop their performances or to be inspired by each other.

To broaden learning, this tool could be combined with explorations of other artistic expressions to communicate sustainability challenges. Such formats could include dramatised sketches, re-writing lyrics to famous songs, or bricolage. If the course is structured around a group project or final essay, the students could then choose which of the artistic expressions they want to use as part of a final presentation, to be assessed together with the academic content of the project or paper.

## Integrating with assessment

This exercise can be used to deepen learning about a sustainability-related topic that the students are writing an essay on or doing a group project about. It supports exploring creative and artistic ways to communicate about the topic and helps the students to connect it to their everyday lives in a playful rather than confrontational manner. One way to assess this exercise is to include a reflection section in the final essay or group project, where the students are encouraged to reflect on their performance piece, what it taught them about the sustainability topic, and how/if connecting the topic to their everyday lives broadened their understanding of how inter-connected sustainability challenges are. Suggestions for questions to include in such a reflection are listed above.

## Further reading

Tate. (n.d.). Performance art – Art term. Tate. https://www.tate.org.uk/art/art-terms/p/performance-art#:~:text=Artworks%20that%20are%20created%20through
Be inspired by visiting your local modern art museum and galleries with contemporary exhibitions. Encourage your students to do the same!

# References

Clark, W. C. (2007). Sustainability science: A room of its own. *Proceedings of the National Academy of Sciences, 104*(6), 1737–1738. https://doi.org/10.1073/pnas.0611291104

Ono, Y. (1971). *Grapefruit*. Simon and Schuster.

Wall, T. (2022). In corpore sano, acta non verba: Permanent performance under precariousness. Chesterrep.openrepository.com. https://chesterrep.openrepository.com/handle/10034/627440

*Chapter 21*

# Provocation

## Futuring at scale

Tony Wall, Sarah Jayne Williams, Laura Dixon, and Dave Soehren

### Learning outcomes and related terms

The drama processes in this chapter aim to:

■ Develop practical awareness of the different foresight practices under situations of uncertainty and ambiguity (with subsequent benefits in processing information, problem-solving, and handling stress in such circumstances).

Key terms and definitions (see Bennett & Lemoine, 2014; Bühren, Meier, & Pleßner, 2021; Minkkinen, Auffermann, & Ahokas, 2019):

■ Futuring – futuring is the act of implementing foresight practices, that is, practices which deal with the future in 'the now'.
■ Uncertainty – not knowing the likelihood of an event, but the response and outcomes are known (e.g. we don't know when a fire may happen, but we know how to put it out when it does).
■ Ambiguity – not having a clear view on likelihoods nor how a response might create outcomes, the realm of 'unknown unknowns'.
■ Provocation – an intentional experience which is unexpected within the context of its application.

DOI: 10.4324/9781003496359-26

| Key sustainability-related outcomes |
| --- |
| **Embodying sustainability values** |
| Valuing sustainability/self-awareness and normative competencies |
| **Embracing complexity in sustainability** |
| Critical thinking |
| **Envisioning sustainable futures** |
| Futures literacy/anticipatory competence |
| **Acting for sustainability** |
| Collective action/strategic/collaboration competence |

# Context of application

The 'futuring' provocative experience has been used as an immersive, experiential learning tool with managers and academics to explore and understand how we – as humans, managers, academics – operate in situations of ambiguity and uncertainty. To date, it has been used with over 600 participants to explore unfolding experience, including as part of an MBA, as part of post-experience professional development, and at academic conferences with teaching and research teams. Most applications have not been linked to academic assessment of learning.

# Step-by-step guidance

1. **Connect the provocative experience to learning outcomes**: the first step is to consider a meaningful conceptual/topical location for the immersive futuring experience, that is, where it might emphasise or connect to a broad learning point within the programme or course. This might be, for example, decisions specifically related to sustainability, related to one or more of the SDGs, or a more specific topic such as leadership, supply chain management, or disaster management. (Alternatively, the experience may be introduced (a) towards the start of a course as a highly interactive and engaging icebreaker and induction type experience or (b) towards the end of a programme or course as a kind of capstone immersive experience to help integrate and nuance the depth and complexity of the learning generated.) The futuring experience might be within a specific class (like a lecture or a seminar) or beyond the boundaries of a class in a course (like a module or unit), outside the curricula (open to students across an entire programme), or for an entire academic school.
2. **Framing the experience**: once you have decided on a focus and conceptual/topical location for the futuring experience, you will need to introduce it in a way which recognises and foregrounds ambiguity. One way of explaining this

to the students is to say that there is some element of emergence or unfolding, which means it is not possible for them to know the 'answer' at the start of the experience or indeed they may never know the 'answer'. It is important to state that this is intentional, to reflect real-world scenarios and is a way to develop experience and confidence in practically dealing with the complexities and uncertainties associated with the SDGs. This framing can be introduced and explained in both programme and/or course handbooks, as well as at the start of the futuring experience. An example from applications of the futuring experience includes:

■ Organise the larger group into their smaller group allocations.
■ Welcome the group in a way which draws attention to the learning content of the course or programme.
■ Ask the group if they want to know why we need the idea of 'sustainable development' beyond profit (they usually respond quite quickly). Explain that it is because humans are historically so poor at dealing with the future in the present, and specifically dealing with it practically in our diaries (this can be said provocatively and linked to a question of whether they would like evidence!).
■ This can be supplemented with a quick activity called 'predictive clapping' – here, you can ask the participants to mimic you, as a form of prediction (i.e. invite to clap with you at the same time). As the facilitator, start clapping and then stop at some random point (maybe 10 seconds). Draw attention to how many people keep on clapping. This can be repeated a couple of times to emphasise learning (if they generally stop clapping at the same time) or lack of attention, adaptation, and learning (if they continue clapping).

3. **Draw attention to uncertainty and ambiguity before, during, and after the experience**: the central feature of the futuring experience relates to the ambiguity and uncertainty that is experienced (in a safe environment). The ambiguities in the framing can be related to the **task-in-hand** (for example, mimicking the possible situation of receiving an instruction from a manager with competing demands and under pressure, or a new or unfamiliar work setting) or in terms of the **information available** (reflecting many work settings or crises settings). An example from applications of the futuring experience includes:

■ Whilst talking through the reflections, you can design your presentation slides so you are unexpectedly interrupted by an email alert sound and an email which pops up and displayed on the large screen (this can be activated by a presentation clicker, on your demand).
■ The email which pops up can introduce an emergency context, which requires the groups to respond quickly with task-in-hand and information

availability ambiguities. For example, it might be an email from a CEO of a national company which requires each of the groups to replace the local leadership teams across the country. Here it is useful to reinforce, there is no more information, but the single task is for the groups to plan their week to respond. There may be prompts in the email about where the groups should focus, for example, understanding who the local suppliers are, order updates, what else is outstanding. No more information is available.

■ At this point, you can provide a week-based diary printed on a large piece of paper for the group to record their plans for the week.

■ After the groups have had time to discuss and record their plans on the diaries, you can facilitate a whole group reflective plenary. Here, you might draw attention to the ambiguities and each group's response to them in terms of process (e.g. how they organised themselves) rather than content (e.g. the detail of the diary). Questions might include: What worked well in the group? What was not so effective? Was everyone included? What would you like to try as you move forward?

4. **Unfolding cycles of unexpected events and reflections**: depending on the time available, you can introduce more cycles of unexpected event and reflection (**this has been tested with three cycles in 90 minutes, with each cycle taking around 15 minutes of email alert, group planning, and then full group plenary**). You can plan these in advance so you can scaffold the experience and aspects of learning based on key points you want to raise or relevant news items. An example from applications of the futuring experience includes:

■ Again, when talking through the reflections (in each cycle), you can arrange for you to be interrupted by another email on the screen with an associated alert.

■ Each time it pops up, the email introduces a new level of complexity and ambiguity. For example, one email could be alerting the groups of a flood at their manufacturing plant and the need to respond quickly (with no extra information).

■ In mid-cycle activities, you can also introduce 'rumours' (as an explicit form of an uncertain or ambiguous message from somewhere). For example, it could be a rumour ('from the market') about a possible large-scale opportunity, or a rumour that the national government may be releasing a national opportunity in the next day or so. This is an opportunity, but the fictional company (that the student groups are now leading) can only produce 10% of the demand, so they need to re-organise their week to be able to respond. This can be followed up with the rumour coming true in the following cycle and asking the groups to respond quickly. Handling rumours of course requires a judgement of ambiguity, uncertainty, and risk.

■ In subsequent reflective cycles, it is useful to ask how groups reacted to the rumours (did they trust them or not?) and how they managed the flood that was introduced in the last round at the same time as the rumour of the opportunity. Other questions can relate to exploring or critically reflecting on the reflections shared in the group or indeed aspects not explored with the group. For example, you might explore the 'decent work' implications of outsourcing if mentioned, or you might explore why the whole group had not explored collaborating with other branches. It is very useful to reference theory that you know the group has studied during their programme or course (or which they might consider if the futuring experience is at the start of their studies). Good reference points here are ideas relating to cognitive biases, group or organisational dynamics (e.g. humans prefer to act on certain information and pay attention to areas we are more comfortable or familiar with).

5. **Consolidation around foresight practices**: the final reflective plenary involves asking the group which of the different futuring (foresight) practices they had applied in the experience, i.e. planning, predicting, visioning, scenario-exploring, transforming, and critical perspectives (see Minkkinen, Auffermann, & Ahokas, 2019). Again, it is useful to draw attention to the opportunities and limitations of the different strategies as emerging through the experience.

## Framing or prework

This tool has been applied with minimal framing or prework (e.g. just stating 'futuring' in the context of future work contexts). This is intentionally part of the way uncertainty and ambiguity is set up in the space.

## When to use and when not to use

This tool appears to be most effective when there are students in the group who have a general level of confidence to talk to others (e.g. have some work experience). This means they will be able to draw upon their experiences at work, and the possible managerial politics or constraints applicable to the unfolding scenario. The tool also works well when the participants do not know each other, as the pace of the experience encourages the rapid development of the group.

It might be less effective when most students in the group have very low confidence or are not familiar with working in a group or team environment (e.g. first-year students). Some students may benefit from additional framing or guidance before the experience, so they are able to interpret it in relation to the topic matter of their course or qualification. For example, within an MBA programme, this involved highlighting the reference to creative and innovative, responsible management, and systems thinking and practices (also see Chapter 1 for GreenComp).

## Reflections from the field

During the start of the experience, students can be seen to be 'disoriented', asking for clarifications around what the task is ('do you want us to…?') and what might be permissible ('are we allowed to…?'). This is typical and reflective of working with uncertainty and ambiguity in the learning context. This may well be the first time a participant has experienced this sensation within the educational environment. When the facilitator responds without further information, students can be seen to be reflecting and making sense of what this newfound ambiguous freedom means. The groups then progress and reflect on their progress as a team when invited to reflect.

Importantly, survey results (which will be available in a forthcoming publication) indicate that the experience impacts a range of motivational factors for behaviour change in relation to climate change (see van Valkengoed & Steg, 2019). The only area that it does not seem to change is 'feeling bad' about sustainability issues, which might be linked to the sense of autonomy the students felt in influencing the evolving experience and in the general positive feeling during it.

## Things to consider

There may be some contexts where some participants find the uncertainty and ambiguity unusually challenging (for example, especially for some students who have declared a neurodiversity which is impacted by such ambiguous scenarios). In these circumstances, it is useful to provide additional framing before the session or at the start of the session. Or, you might want to have a discrete conversation with those who you may think might be potentially challenged by the experience (preferably away from the main group). Such students may also enjoy becoming your learning partner in the scenario, supporting the evolving experience by distributing the 'diaries' or 'rumours'.

## Learning extensions

With large numbers, there may be a few facilitators involved in this experience. As an individual facilitator or team of facilitators, it can be helpful to walk around (literally or virtually) to help support the reflective processes of teams. Suggestions of prompts to facilitate or disrupt thinking might include:

■ How well did you handle ambiguity and uncertainty?
■ Has everyone's voice been shared and heard? How do you know?
■ What assumptions have you made?
■ How much are you trusting the information you have?
■ What are you noticing about your team processes?

■ What aspects of the 'flower' are you looking after, and which are you not? ('Flower' stands for the Framework for Long-Term, Whole-System, Equity-Based Reflection – this could be introduced between the experience or during (see further reading).

## Integrating with assessment

The experience can feature in assessment through:

*Reflection*: the futuring provocation can be used as a prompt for reflecting on own and others' behaviours, encouraging students to explore their own understanding and sensemaking of the practice. Here, prework to introduce single-, double-, and triple-loop learning may be useful to examine learning related to immediate action (single loop), learning related to learning process (double loop), and learning related to wider cultural systems or influences on our learning (triple loop).

*Peer review*: students could undertake peer review about individuals within their group, or come together to produce a jointly written, collective review for a group assignment. As with all peer review processes clear guidelines are needed to ensure students understand how to craft constructive comments. Students may use a reflective model or use a more appreciative approach, for example:

■ What went well in terms of single-, double-, or triple-loop learning?
■ What might you (the students) like to try in similar situations?

*Freeform creative, introspective pieces (including a short reflective component)*: students could be invited to produce a creative introspective piece which represents their learning through visual imagery, metaphors, stories, poems, short clips of video, and so on. Such forms of assessment not only build on the theme of uncertainty and ambiguity but also focus on the integration, interpretation, and presentation of knowledge, creativity, and depth of reflection. If choosing this method, care must be taken to have clear rubric for assessing a wide variety of submissions with some level of equity around the hours of learning effort.

## Further reading

FLOWER. (n.d.). Multisolving Institute. Retrieved March 1, 2024, from https://www.multisolving.org/flower/

## References

Bennett, N., & Lemoine, G. J. (2014). What VUCA really means for you. *Harvard Business Review*. https://hbr.org/2014/01/what-vuca-really-means-for-you

Bühren, C., Meier, F., & Pleßner, M. (2021). Ambiguity aversion: Bibliometric analysis and literature review of the last 60 years. *Management Review Quarterly*. https://doi.org/10.1007/s11301-021-00250-9

Minkkinen, M., Auffermann, B., & Ahokas, I. (2019). Six foresight frames: Classifying policy foresight processes in foresight systems according to perceived unpredictability and pursued change. *Technological Forecasting and Social Change, 149*, 119753. https://doi.org/10.1016/j.techfore.2019.119753

van Valkengoed, A. M., & Steg, L. (2019). Meta-analyses of factors motivating climate change adaptation behaviour. *Nature Climate Change, 9*(2), 158–163. https://doi.org/10.1038/s41558-018-0371-y

# Chapter 22

# Provocation

## Rights of the river

Tony Wall, Richard Ridyard, Alison Lui,
and Kenneth Kang

### Learning outcomes and related terms

The drama processes in this chapter aim to:

- Explore human- and non-human perspectives involved in the rights of rivers.
- Generate and integrate human- and non-human perspectives.

Key terms and definitions:

- Rights of the river – specifically refers to the Universal Declaration of the Rights of Rivers, a movement to foreground the personhood of rivers.
- Legislative Theatre – see Chapter 2. This workshop is not a strict form of Legislative Theatre.

| Key sustainability-related outcomes |
| --- |
| Embodying sustainability values |
| Supporting fairness |
| Promoting nature |

DOI: 10.4324/9781003496359-27

| Embracing complexity in sustainability |
|---|
| Problem framing/integrated problem-solving competence |
| **Envisioning sustainable futures** |
| Adaptability |
| Exploratory thinking |
| **Acting for sustainability** |
| Political agency |
| Collective action/strategic/collaboration competence |

# Context of application

This process has been delivered in the UK as part of a non-accredited experience connecting the themes of creativity and climate change. It was performed with 5 higher education teachers from business and law schools with around 25 participants, for 90 minutes. The participants were from across disciplines and some were senior leaders within social mission organisations.

This is a process that can be applied in any discipline, particularly those that interact with legal systems, processes, or practices. This piece is based in the UK and the fictional River Yesrem (Mersey spelt backwards). Currently, in the UK, there is a serious problem regarding raw sewage spills into rivers. Discharges of untreated sewage by water companies doubled from 1.8 million hours in 2022 to 3.6 million in 2023. Only 14% of UK rivers have good ecological status (House of Lords Library, 2024). In the UK, there is increased public anger over water pollution. Questions have been raised as to what the government has done to regulate water companies and enforce Environmental Law. The topic is thus contemporary and calls for urgent action and is examined under Environmental Law (see for example Kang, 2019, 2023a, 2023b).

Although performed in the UK, the Universal Declaration of the Rights of Rivers is not currently active there, but the performance invites participants to engage in the possibility of considering the rights of rivers in decision-making or law-making.

# Step-by-step guidance

1. Preparation: Organise participants into tables/groups with approximately four to six people per table (we assume three tables in this setup which would take circa 90 minutes, but there could be 25 students in the class, organised across four to five tables).
2. Brief participants about the focus of the session and its expectations of interaction. This should be done out of role, as the facilitator of the session. It is useful to use a prop to differentiate between facilitator of the session and a role which is performed as part of the role play – e.g. a pair of glasses or a formal jacket can be put on when in role and taken off when playing the facilitator. This is

then followed by an introduction of the scenario in broad terms (e.g. upholding the rights of rivers in modern society). The following steps relate to what we delivered based on our chosen topics, the rights of rivers, and scenario, the expansion of a private water company into the local town. However, this can be something more locally based. There may be other possible contextualisations made to the subject learning.

An example contextualisation for a class: In Athens, Pericles claimed 'everyone is equal before the law'. It is a sentiment around which there appears to be consensus. Probe a little deeper, however, and issues emerge. One problem is that the meaning of equality can radically differ depending on who you ask. And the fragility of this consensus becomes graphically clear when specific proposals are advanced. This is especially apt within our context: the rights of rivers. We challenge our understanding of this ideal of equality before the law when it comes to harms to rivers.

3. After the initial briefing, the performance commences. For the performance below, five actors are required (in our case, five higher education teachers), but you can reduce this number depending on the roles you want to include. The roles are as follows:

MS. ANNA VAVANCE, CEO of Trussty Rivers – a private water company
MR. H. J. RIMMONS, In-house Lawyer at Trussty Rivers
The Right Honourable Mr. Tony Marsters MP (Member of Parliament), local politician, and low-level government minister
MS. ELIZABETH BILLING, assistant to (and gatekeeper of) Mr. Tony Marsters MP
DR. FRANCIS STOCKMANN, concerned local resident and convenor of the local Thriving Nature task group

*Scene 1*: The role play begins by the CEO and Lawyer of the water company Trussty Rivers being warmly welcomed by the assistant to Mr. Tony Marsters MP who takes them straight through to meet with the local MP. During their meeting, the CEO and Lawyer set about convincing the MP to hand over the management of the local waters to their company. Partway through their meeting, the concerned local resident approaches the MP's assistant wishing to meet with the MP to discuss possible issues with the proposed deal with Trussty Rivers. The MP's assistant dismisses the resident and claims the MP is too busy to discuss their concerns. Back in the meeting, and the CEO and Lawyer offer to donate to the MP's upcoming re-election campaign. This seals the deal and Trussty Rivers take over the local rivers, much to the distress of the local resident.

*Scene 2*: Once the scene concludes, there is then a transition to a newsroom. We jump forward in time. Six months have passed since Trussty Rivers took over the management of local waters. One actor presents the following breaking news item.

*News Broadcast*

Good evening and welcome to the Tonight News programme. We start with a breaking story. Raging sewage spillages – that's the headline. After the expansion of Trussty Rivers, there are alarming reports emerging on the number of possible dry sewage spills into our local rivers. Reports also suggest there has been a significant deterioration in the quality of local water – *it is getting worse [emphasised]*. According to a Tonight News investigation, there have been 118 potential dry spills by Trussty Rivers in the last four months alone. This refers to when untreated wastewater spills straight into our rivers and seas when there is no rain. Such spills are illegal and Trussty Rivers faces possible prosecution and unlimited fines. Swimmers are warned to stay away, whilst untreated sewage is being discharged into the sea. The contaminated water could lead to serious illnesses. Risks include gastrointestinal illnesses, or stomach bugs, which may cause diarrhoea and or vomiting, as well as respiratory, skin, ear and eye infections. Rowers taking part in the upcoming boat race have been warned not to enter the river after high levels of E. coli were found. This comes off the back of recent findings by the Environment Agency which states that only approximately 8% of the surface water in the area reaches 'good' ecological status. This is below the 2023 national average of 16%. We have contacted Trussty Rivers and local MP Tony Marsters for comment. We are still waiting for a response. Local residents are increasingly angry with this situation. Whilst local task group Thriving Nature have threatened to launch legal action against Trussty Rivers. In the meantime, Tonight News understands that a local consultation is being arranged to try to resolve these issues.

4. Ask the participants to imagine themselves as local residents engaging with an open consultation with Trussty Rivers and the local Thriving Nature task group. One actor, still in their original role, will be assigned per table/group to facilitate the discussion. The roles used are Ms. Anna Vavance (CEO, representing her own organisation despite conflicts of interest), Mr. H.J. Rimmons (lawyer, representing his own organisation, who tries to negotiate silence with a donation to charity groups), and Dr. Francis Stockmann (representing wider environmental concerns). Ten minutes are allocated to this discussion. Experience tells us this can range from calm discussion through to quite demanding conversations and frustrations.

5. Once time elapses, have the actor from each table openly feedback to the local MP on what their table discussed and concluded, e.g. whether a resolution was reached. Highlight the different perspectives, conflicts of interest, practices used to silence groups – all of which have been found to be prevalent in real-world cases.

6. Out of role, ask the groups to reflect on what they would change if they could pause, step into a role, and replay the scenes. In a more direct Legislative Theatre approach, with more time, you may take longer to physically stop and start the play with alternative voices being played out.

7. The performance moves to scene 3, the courtroom, where a judge (in role) summarises 'we are here today the failed attempts at consulting different stakeholder groups in resolving the damage that has occurred'. The judge then asks the jurors (3 groups) to then consider the evidence in line with the rights of rivers – the Universal Declaration of the Rights of Rivers is shown on the screen and printed out for immediate reference (see details here: Rights of Rivers, n.d.).

8. The judge provides the options of penalties (as would normally happen within a court), and the jurors (in their groups) are asked to for a judgment (this can be altered based on the particular learning insights you want to create). In our case, an example set of options is as follows. Each option has wider implications on economics and so demonstrates the interconnectedness of a jury's decision on economics and society.

**Option 1: Penalty by Strict Liability on Water Company:**

Profit: Significant penalties could directly impact profits and threaten the company's stability.

Economic: If the company is a key local employer, financial difficulties could lead to job losses or reduced economic activity.

Social: Could increase pressure on other companies to prevent similar incidents.

**Option 2: Penalty by Water Usage Restrictions:**

Profit: Lower water usage by consumers could reduce the company's revenue and impact its financial health.

Economic: Water usage restrictions could increase costs, reduce output, and lead to job losses in water-intensive sectors.

Social: Restrictions could impact consumers' daily lives, potentially leading to public outcry and increased inequality. However, they could also raise awareness and promote water conservation.

**Option 3: Penalty by Increased Water Tariffs:**

Profit: The company may pass penalty costs to consumers via higher water tariffs, maintaining profit margins but at consumers' expense.

Economic: Higher water tariffs could ripple through the economy, raising living and business costs, especially for water-dependent industries.

Social: Increased tariffs could spark public outcry if consumers feel unfairly penalised, potentially leading to protests and exacerbated inequality for low-income households.

9. Stepping out of character, again, the groups are asked to reflect on what they would change if they could pause, step into a role, and replay the scenes (within Legislative Theatre you may take longer here to physically stop and start the play with alternative voices being played out – see the further reading section). Each reflection or frustration is a strong learning point and invitation as to what to do from the wider group, for example:

■ How do we practically represent the views of the river in the decision-making and law-making practices?

■ How do we practically represent the views of the wildlife and other life around the river in the decision-making and law-making practices?

- What can we learn from other cases about how this was handled in the past – what worked, what had unintended consequences?
- What aspects of the system can change behaviour, e.g. the governance of organisations, executive pay (e.g. Ridyard, 2019; Kang, 2023a, 2023b)?

## Framing or pre-work

Given the context of our process, we were not able to provide detailed framing or pre-work. It was important to frame the session with our expectations of interaction and share own thinking and emotions as this is part of the power of the approach. It is important also to note whether or not the Universal Declaration of the Rights of Rivers is currently active in the country of application: if it is not, then the exercise becomes anticipatory and exploratory in terms of what issues are raised if we acted 'as if it was true'. If the Declaration is active, then the session becomes exploratory in terms of implementation locally. This helps contextualise the process in the local context.

It is also possible to keep the details of the pollution and legal issue ambiguous. Here, the audience is invited to associate their own experiences and perspectives with the situation. This can lead to a richer discussion and a wider range of solutions. It also encourages personal investment and ownership of potential solutions.

## When to use and when not to use

This is a positive and productive process for exploring situations for learning outcomes. Its origins were from participatory law and policy-making, so it is useful to consider wider applications there, too. However, it is useful not to suggest that this (or wider Legislative Theatre) process will easily and quickly resolve complex sustainability problems and challenges, given the power and stability of wider legal or economic systems which sustain the status quo. The process is useful in an educational context to highlight leverage points or points of access for change.

## Reflections from the field

Participants enthusiastically immersed themselves into the workshop and its Legislative Theatre inspired mode of delivery and interaction. By design, part of the object was to provoke and frustrate. The success became strikingly clear: participants were quick to signal their dismay over the way in which the initial deal between the local MP and the water company was conducted. In particular, the absence of a meaningful consultation and the failure to account for the rights of the river, were targeted. During the open consultation and jury deliberation, discussion was wonderfully rich and animated. Actors playing the local MP and water company representatives were especially scrutinised for their perceived lack of consideration for the health of the river. The participants provided very interesting and thought-provoking comments, such as the call to consider the perspectives of wildlife in the rivers and hear their voices in the play in legal contexts. For us, this was precisely the role of a provocative process.

## Things to consider

Participants can sometimes focus on the quality of the performance or perceived gaps in it – these are rich moments to encourage a shift from 'what is missing' to 'what precisely, concretely' can be done. Here, welcome the comment and ask questions about who exactly in 'the scenes' can do what? Here, explore the possibilities of specific people or roles that can champion or be an ally for those who are missing, and the possibilities of who or what else could be collaborated with to enact something different. Try to keep the focus on agency, on action, or lines of inquiry for those areas that are more complex and difficult to articulate in the moment. This ongoing reflection, as an option, should be welcomed.

## Learning extensions

The process could also conclude with some participatory voting. To extend the learning and engagement, you could consider a follow-up activity where participants generate ideas about concrete actions they can take to advocate for the river's rights beyond the workshop setting. This could involve contacting local representatives, organising clean-up efforts, or spreading awareness through social media campaigns.

More broadly, the process can be used particularly to explore certain aspects such as the importance of scientific evidence for activists (e.g. the scene with politician) and how activists can challenge misleading information (e.g. in the public consultation). The workshop portrays power imbalances (e.g. CEO vs. politician) and challenges of getting a fair hearing (e.g. a 'framed' consultation). These can be examined in more depth outside of the process, backed up with readings such as classic texts or contemporary news websites. This may take a historical perspective, a contemporary perspective, or oscillating between the two to examine how such difficulties have been tackled (and perhaps not solved) in the past.

In addition, instead of focusing solely on immediate solutions, you might want to explore the long-term consequences of the pollution and potential penalties. Participants could create long lists of future scenarios and the impact these have on their choices. This broadens the scope of the exercise, encouraging participants to consider the ripple effects of environmental decisions. It fosters a sense of long-term responsibility for the health of the river.

## Integration with assessment

Legislative Theatre approaches could be integrated into a portfolio type of assessment. Students could be asked to consider the question: *'If you have the power to change the law in the area of X* [an area of your/learner choice], *what would it be?'* The question could incorporate the relevant module learning objectives.

The assessment could consist of two parts:

1. The practical part where the students – in small groups – are asked to write a script for part of the drama, perform it and invite the audience to contribute their ideas. The script will incorporate some of the learning objectives and aims of the module.
2. After the performance, the students could write an individual essay as to how the Legislative Theatre experience enabled them to understand the topic better, how the audience has impacted on their views on the relevant topic, and how Legislative Theatre helps with finding solutions to real-life problems and changing the status quo.

## Further reading

Boal, A. (1998/2005). *Legislative Theatre – using performance to make politics*. Routledge.

Maher, R., Pedemonte-Rojas, N., Gálvez, D., & Banerjee, S.B. (2023). The role of multistakeholder initiatives in the radicalization of resistance: The Forestry Stewardship Council and the Mapuche Conflict in Chile. *Journal of Management Studies*. https://doi.org/10.1111/joms.13015

## References

House of Lords Library. River pollution and the regulation of private water companies, 19 February 2024. [Online] Available at: https://lordslibrary.parliament.uk/river-pollution-and-the-regulation-of-private-water-companies/ [Accessed 4 June 2024].

Kang, K. (2019). On the problem of the justification of river rights. *Water International*, 44(6–7), 667–683. https://doi.org/10.1080/02508060.2019.1643523. [Accessed 4 June 2024].

Kang, K. (2023a). On contingency, confidence and trust: How international water law stabilizes expectations under conditions of uncertainty. *Water International*, 48(6), 688–706. https://doi.org/10.1080/02508060.2023.2257557. [Accessed 4 June 2024].

Kang, K. (2023b). Navigating international water law: A systems theory approach. [online] Available at: https://www.globalwaterforum.org/2023/11/16/navigating-international-water-law-a-systems-theory-approach. [Accessed 4 June 2024].

Ridyard, R. (2019). Carrots and sticks in bank governance: Time for a bigger stick? *Journal of Financial Regulation and Compliance*. https://doi.org/10.1108/jfrc-05-2018-0084. [Accessed 4 June 2024].

Rights of Rivers. (n.d.). [online]. https://www.rightsofrivers.org/

# Chapter 23

# Provocation

## The manifold orchard

Kerstin Bragby

### Learning outcomes and related terms

Scharmer and Pomeroy (2024, p. 20) tell us that the main challenge in the crises of the world "is our sense that we are powerless to change any of it". They argue that "if we are going to serve societal transformation in the face of this collapse, as we believe is fully possible, we need to draw on a new form of knowing—knowing for transformative action". This knowing is invited here to generate explorative thinking powered by interconnected human-and-natural-world-awareness. This chapter uses the term "transcontextual" (see Bateson, 2016, 2020) to describe this relational complexity. One of the outcomes is a much deeper orientation towards transformative action in relation to concrete issues.

Key terms and definitions:

- Transcontextual – "refers to the intricate web of interactions and interdependencies that span across multiple contexts in any system. It captures the essence of how various domains – be they personal, social, ecological, or technological – intersect and influence one another in a dynamic, co-evolving dance of complexity" (Reid, 2024, n.p.)

| Key sustainability-related outcomes |
| --- |
| Embodying sustainability values |
| Promoting nature |

DOI: 10.4324/9781003496359-28

| Embracing complexity in sustainability |
| --- |
| Systems thinking |
| **Envisioning sustainable futures** |
| Exploratory thinking |
| **Acting for sustainability** |
| Collective action/strategic/collaboration competence |

## Context of application

This exercise was born in a master course with 15 students in applied theatre and drama (who were training to be drama teachers), at a university in Sweden. They were challenged as drama teachers to face didactic approaches to process issues of ecological, environmental as well as sociocultural dimensions of sustainability and in writing an essay to integrate theory and practice, as part of their professional cultivation. They were invited to do so through a deeply sensed interconnection with nature and the field of research and practice as a living web of life. As such, they were invited to be critically aware of their own preconceptions, and yet go beyond that and be creatively confident in their own curiosities and in their awareness of how knowledge can be created. They were exploring how their own human nature can be experienced as embedded in a transcontextual, real-imagined dialogue with nature as a resource for deeper understandings.

## Step-by-step guidance

1. Preparations and setting the stage.
   Invite your participants to open their focus of inquiry and connect to their personal understandings of how sustainability and challenges in the context of their professional learning can be linked. For example, you might ask *how can your context of learning be related to a core aspect of ecological as well as sociocultural sustainable adaptation, where keeping alive complexity and alternative pathways of thinking, acting, and living gives you a resilient mindset and robustness to change in the face of shifting circumstances?* Or frame the session with relevant questions for your purpose.

   Let them talk in pairs, and find one or two chosen focuses, challenges, or inquiries from their professional learning and applications of pedagogies which link with some dimension of sustainability.

   Place in front of everyone a sheet of white paper with access to coloured pens. Ask them to write 3 keywords or meanings from their conversation. Everyone briefly shares their own focuses in the whole group. Let them know they will return to their paper as part of the exercise.

Describe how this process will now be staged as a combined inside-and-out-door-process (if possible). Invite them to step into a conversation with their relationship with "nature/trees", to explore their issues/questions/challenges – evoking the nature of the intertwined sociocultural and ecological field. Explain that they will be exploring a transcontextual capacity of presence and how that can make a difference in exploring their issues, embodying sustainability values.

Ideally, you will have access to an outdoor environment, with real trees for the participants to seek out. If so, you can lead the explorative inquiry and inner journey ahead on the site, in a way that everyone can still hear you, when leaning their back to a "collective body of individual trees", maybe in an orchard.

If you do not have access to an outdoor environment, you can do an indoor fictionally staged version of contact with nature. You can also let the indoor version be a warm-up exercise, to be combined with an outdoor collective interaction with trees in situ, in a forest/orchard environment. You can also let the indoor version lead up to the individuals finding their own encounter with a tree at a later moment after the class.

2. Indoor/outdoor preparation.

For staging the indoor experience, you can find an image of trees (preferably an orchard of apple trees) that is inviting, and project it in the room together with some forest sounds/music (e.g. Wingbeats with Hidden Orchestra). You then ask the participants to find a partner and sit down in pairs, first so that they can see the image of trees, and later so they can easily move into a position of back-to-back (as comfortable as requested by the participants on the floor or on chairs, but with body contact).

Ask them to hold their issues alive in the background of their minds and lead them into an inner conversation between themselves and nature – dreaming that the trees become a communicative partner with the sound/music. Below is a way of blurring the separation between a person and nature to make awareness transcontextual. You can amend it to reflect your own context.

Let them sink into the ambience that is created by the image and the sounds/music. Then start a guided inner journey with a slow pace and pauses (indicated by … below). You can say: *Contemplate the relationship between you and nature… ask yourself like Nora Bateson does… where are the edges of me… I live in a body that internally requires co-existence with more than 10 trillion organisms, while externally my survival is ecological, emotional, and cultural. I am not an isolated species … rather I live in a transcontextuality with all forms of life, over time and space… and as Nora's father Gregory Bateson said… what if it is in our nature to think and create like nature and learn together with all living relations, and that there is absolutely no real separation between the internal and external... something that seems to come at me from outside, a bird flying towards sight, turn up in my dream and internal thoughts... where it speaks to me ... and I can, the next day, project those thoughts outside of me, by telling a friend the story... who then carries it on in the world through her... the intimate relationship between the imagined and the real... is real...*

*Let yourself relax, and breathe deeply into the image and sounds for a little while... give space to this...*

Then you can ask: "*What do the trees evoke in you? Let yourself step into this image, sense the smells, and hear the sounds as if entering the "living room" of your best friends ... what if you evoke something in them, and they have been longing to see and meet you, what does that feel like?*

Ask the participants to find their position, back-to-back to their partner, and then say *close their eyes and lean onto and into each other... as if you could sense the other as a representation of both a tree and a human friend... imagining the reality of growth, of seasons, of moments over time and space that have made this tree evolve, and thrive... embodying rings of experiences in its uniqueness, living in an interconnected field with other trees and the environment... ask yourself what your "rings of experiences" are made of... which where or are the grounds and invisible soils of encounters and learnings in life that carries you?*

*With which other trees or practitioners, in your professional or extended field, are you interconnected over time and space, right now... what are your joint field of awareness and knowledge that you can draw from as a drama (or other) practitioner? Feel the tree as your true companion and friend in this. Ask the whole orchard (or forest if relevant) - as a field of knowledge - to support you and your field of practitioners to meet the issues and challenges at hand.*

*Communicate with the tree about your own dilemmas inside and ask for help and listen... what wants to come through you? Imagine picking an (or pick a real) apple, and as you eat it, imagine that you can taste the knowing of how to orient yourself in this issue you are investigating... and see what comes... images, answers, leads... a sense of insight...*

You can guide them to keep asking and imagining using the interconnected metaphors of human and ecological co-realities, or a format that is adapted to the purpose of your course.

3. Harvesting reflections.

After 5–10 minutes, go indoors or let the participants open their eyes and come back into the room. Ask the participant to draw, write and gather their impressions in silence on the paper. Then let each participant share their impressions with the help of the drawings. Ask them, in a new round, where they are now, in relation to moving forward with their issues?

## Framing or pre-work

All the framing is in the activity above. If the facilitators are not used to use fiction or aesthetic expressions in learning, any icebreaker exercises linked thematically to your learning focus' can be used (see Chapters 4–7).

## When to use and when not to use

This process can help provide seriously playful ways to experience and explore what systemic thinking in action for change could be and how to source a new sense of orientation in relation to a higher degree of complexity and interspecies interdependency. Many different learning focuses can be explored in this process, indirectly embodying sustainability values, as well as addressing more factual information. It is appropriate when exploring deep awareness, communication, and transcontextual co-creativity. It is less appropriate to use before learners have developed experiential openness and a foundational understanding of why to use more imaginative methods addressing dilemmas.

## Reflections from the field

One of the strongest outcomes of this exercise has been a powerful sense of motivation in the participants. Expressed, for example, in gratitude for being emotionally touched, engaged, and invited to participate with an authentic and expanded sense of self. This elicits a motivation anchored in the full range of existential and everyday practical issues. To experience life as a holistic co-creative human being, where imagination can actualise new realities as real, seems to lift some of the anxiety and powerlessness in relation to sustainability issues, as well as personal dilemmas.

An important observation has been a shift into resourcefulness and agency. When the participants experience this expanded self – in a tension in between "what is" and "what if" – they also see more clearly and can discern the conventions in thinking, doing, and relating, in relation to be able to influence all levels of the systemic complexity. They seem to perceive that they can embody sustainability values through which they can act.

Even if just small or ground-breaking novel opportunities for alternative action are emerging in participants, the premises for how to move in difficult dilemmas have shifted radically. The participants speak about a sense of "new accountability", because "all that they are" (which includes their pains and joys, doubts and uncertainties, their deepest longings and fears) all "count" and are included as an influential resource.

## Things to consider

It is important to consider the learning context's and participants' intentional, theoretical, and imaginative framing and wording in this process. Preferably take the framing of the process from your own course content so that the implications of the insights are contextually valid for the teaching situation. This assures that a concrete, subjective, and intersubjective relevance is present in the sense- and meaning-making. Leading and guiding the process requires an incorporated understanding of what is aspired for, or at least an openness to discover it. If you are uncertain, practice first with someone you feel safe with, to become comfortable in your own guided journey and connection to your context. A patient and relaxed pace that invite the seriousness and lightness through a wide and deep receptive listening and curiosity, helps the participant to immerse into a more existentially vulnerable and expanded space. Humour and sometimes staying with what is strongly felt can be necessary to grow a balanced social carrying capacity in the collective space.

## Learning extensions

The ability to grasp, cultivate, and make real use of a transcontextual mode of awareness for sustainability purposes will grow over time and with contrasting learning cultures. The differences between how conventional or predetermined thinking in problem-solving and a more creative and intertwined openness impact your ability to act and co-create in an engaged way will be perceivable. To combine the expanded conscious engagement with reflection is crucial and requires you to have observed from a meta-position to make connections between the course and the live experience. To help participants frame ways of applying new suggestions that emerge is also very helpful to be able to practice these co-creative transformative interactions and build trust in how transcontextual competence can be applied to concrete dilemmas.

## Integration with assessment

This process can align with most learning goals and can support formative and iterative feedback through the opportunity to explore topics in divergent ways and through gathering convergent insights documented in collective reflexivity and reflecting (e.g. words, images, metaphors which can be captured for essays or portfolios). As such, the process can give you concrete materials for assessing the development of both content knowledge and transcontextual awareness, especially if you thematically link the process to these. This material can give evidence of deep critical and creative thinking and the capacity to learn how to learn, often expressed as a capacity to problematise, and hold nuanced and deepened ways of reasoning in complex and individually authentic ways.

## Further reading

Bateson, N. (2022). *Nora Bateson: "Complexity between the lines"* | The Great Simplification #10, https://www.youtube.com/watch?v=d2f_0myyEeE

Bateson, N. (2023a). *Combining.* Triarchy Press.

Bateson, N. (2023b). *Nora Bateson for the re-imagining education conference.* https://www.youtube.com/watch?v=KV0fH_iBQZk

## References

Bateson, N. (2016). *Small arcs of larger circles: Framing through other patterns.* Triarchy Press.

Bateson, N. (2020). *Preparing for a confusing future, complexity, warm data and education.* https://norabateson.wordpress.com/2020/03/20/preparing-for-a-confusing-future-complexity-warm-data-and-education/

Reid, S. (2024). *Transcontextual· Nora Bateson's knowledgegraph.* Retrieved June 19, 2024, from https://stephenreid.net/k/nora/terms/transcontextual?page=2webpage

Scharmer, O., & Pomeroy, E. (2024). Fourth person: The knowing of the field. *Journal of Awareness-Based Systems Change, 4*(1), 19–48. https://doi.org/10.47061/jasc.v4i1.7909

# DEEPENING INSIGHT THROUGH DRAMA PROCESSES

6

# Chapter 24

---

# Drama workshop

---

## Papperssnö

Shelley Piasecka

### Learning outcomes and related terms

The drama processes in this chapter aim to:

- Apply creative and imaginative modes of non-verbal expression and self-reflection.
- Develop adaptive and exploratory thinking to envisage alternative futures.
- Appreciate the value of collective action to enact positive change.

Key terms and definitions:

- Climate anxiety – as extreme distress and/or anxiety about the impact of climate change. Clayton (2020, p. 2) says 'almost everyone… could be affected by climate anxiety regardless of their own personal vulnerability or relative safety'. For this reason, it is important to recognise that students may experience climate anxiety even when they are not directly affected.
- Futures literacy – allows 'people to better understand the role of the future in what they see and do. Being futures literate empowers the imagination, enhances our ability to prepare, recover and invent as changes occur' (UNESCO, 2023, n.p.). This drama workshop invites participants to imagine alternative visions of the future in order to facilitate conversation, debate, and the possibility to create long-term change.

DOI: 10.4324/9781003496359-30

■ Papperssnö: Swedish for paper snow. Also known as paperilumi (Finnish), papirsnø (Norwegian), and pappírssnjór (Icelandic).

| Key sustainability-related outcomes |
| --- |
| **Embodying sustainability values** |
| Valuing sustainability/self-awareness and normative competencies |
| Supporting fairness |
| **Embracing complexity in sustainability** |
| Critical thinking |
| **Envisioning sustainable futures** |
| Futures literacy/anticipatory competence |
| Adaptability |
| Exploratory thinking |
| **Acting for sustainability** |
| Political agency |
| Collective action/strategic/collaboration competence |
| Individual initiative |

# Context of application

This activity has been undertaken in UK higher education and has been running in some form or another for over 20 years. It should be stressed that the idea for paper snow is not original. The author first encountered a drama workshop using ripped-up newspapers to make snow in the early 2000s and, like many drama games and exercises, it is difficult to trace who first came up with the idea. In the years since, the author has gratefully borrowed, adapted, and re-adapted the idea for different groups and purposes. The climate theme and storytelling futures aspect is the author's addition and has been running in this format since 2022. Sessions are typically comprised of between 20 and 30 undergraduate students. The author invites teachers and students to adapt Papperssnö and to make it their own.

# Step-by-step guidance

This activity takes 60 minutes to complete.

1. Preparation.

■ Check the suitability of the teaching room because this activity requires space to move around in freely and to lie on the floor.
■ You will need access to a basic sound system to play music.

- Select music for the activity. Classical or relaxing instrumental music is preferable.
- You need 25 minutes of music.
- The activity requires you to tell a story. Feel free to add personal touches and embellishments.
- Collect <u>used</u> paper for recycling. It doesn't need to be white paper. Any used paper will do.
- You need enough paper to fill the room with snow, so collect over a few weeks if necessary. Remove metal staples or bindings.
- Print out or digitally show images of an attic room full of junk. This will help participants who struggle to visualise images in their mind's eye.
- You will need a box of pens or pencils, a broom, a dustpan and brush, and refuse sacks.

2. Warm-up game. 10 minutes.

- Play a short warm-up game (see Chapters 4–7).

3. Introduce the main activity. 5 minutes.

- Tell participants that the activity will involve them using their imaginations and to follow certain commands.
- They will imagine that they are in an attic room full of junk.
- Show pictures of attics room to aid imagination.
- The participants will also need to imagine the future in 100 years' time.
- Other than the teacher's voice and background music, the activity is to be conducted in silence.
- Participants are free to leave the activity at any point if they do so quietly.

4. Making the paper snow. 5 minutes.

- Hand out the paper and ask participants to rip it into small pieces.
- Encourage the participant to throw the paper snow into the air.
- Play in the snow.
- Throw snowballs.
- Make snow angels.

5. Papperssnö. 25 minutes.

- Ask participants to lie on the floor in amongst the paper snow. Make sure there is enough space for them to lie down without touching each other.
- Ask them to close their eyes.
- Play music softly in the background, not so loud that they can't hear your voice.
- Tell this story:

It's winter and you're back home for the holidays. While the rest of the family are downstairs cooking supper, you've decided to explore the attic room.

> The attic is full of old junk: dusty furniture, discarded objects and forgotten toys. The room smells like childhood.
> Through a window you can see an old-fashioned streetlamp. The room is warm and inviting and so you decide to stay a while looking out of the window.
> It begins to snow.
> Earlier that week, you had a lesson on the climate emergency. You wonder what the world will look like in 100 hundred years' time. You worry about the future.
> But then, you realise the attic is a magical room. Because, somewhere, hidden amongst the junk, is the solution to the climate emergency.

◼ Tell the participants that when they are ready, they should search for the solution.
◼ This requires them to move and search amongst the paper snow.
◼ Tell them to do it without talking.
◼ Tell them that while they do not find the solution, they are to keep on looking.
◼ After a few minutes, ask them to lie back down and close their eyes.
◼ Continue the story:

> Disheartened, you look through the window. Outside, the wind has picked up. The falling snow dances in the light of the streetlamp.
> The smell of wonderful home-cooked food drifts up into the room. You should go downstairs but choose to stay a little longer.
> The swirling snow makes shapes and patterns in front of the window. Again, you wonder what the world will look like in 100 years' time.
> The solution is in the attic. You must find it!

◼ Tell the participants that this time they will search with increased urgency. They really want to find it!
◼ This should be done with care for others in the space.
◼ Once, again, they do not find the solution.
◼ After a few minutes of searching, ask them to lie back down and close their eyes.
◼ Ask them to imagine the world in 100 years' time.
◼ Continue the story:

> Somewhere is one solution to save the world, only you cannot find it. You watch the falling snow, wondering and hoping.
> Downstairs, a door opens, and you hear footsteps crunching on ice, the clinking of bottles, the gentle thump of a bin lid.

You realise that you had the solution all along. It is not in the attic, hidden out of sight.

■ Tell the participants to open their eyes and to sit up.
■ Ask them to think of one small act of behavioural change that they could do to support the planet. For example, conserving energy, reducing food waste, recycling, eating less meat, etc.
■ The acts must be doable and achievable.
■ Tell them to write it down on a piece of the paper snow.
■ Ask them to fold it in half and store somewhere safe, such as in a pocket or bag.

6. Reflection activity. 15 minutes.

■ Turn off the music.
■ Invite the participants to discuss the activity.
■ Ask them what childhood smells like (to stimulate alternative thinking).
■ Ask them to reflect on how they felt looking for the solution to the climate emergency and not finding it.
■ Ask them to reflect on the power of small acts of behavioural change when undertaken as a collective action.
■ Invite them to share their vision of a sustainable future.
■ Leave enough time to sweep up the remaining paper and recycle.

## Framing or pre-work

You may want to consider complementary climate-themed drama games (see Chapter 9), poetry-themed drama workshops (see Chapter 17), or other creative approaches to developing futures literacy (see Chapter 18).

## When to use and when not to use

This activity is most effective when used alongside lessons on sustainability and climate issues. Try running the session after core themes are established and so that students are comfortable with the notion of envisioning alternative futures.

Avoid running the activity at times of heightened emotional risk, such as instances of flooding, earthquakes, or wildfires, and particularly if participant's countries, homes, and/or families are likely to be affected.

## Reflections from the field

This activity can create strong responses from participants, which can be a powerful learning and teaching tool for developing exploratory thinking and envisaging alternative futures. However, some participants, particularly those who feel anxious about climate change and the future of the planet, may find the activity overwhelming (research indicates between 20% and 40% are 'very worried', see Clayton, 2020). Albeit very low numbers, there have been occasions when some participants have become visually emotional during the searching section of the activity and in one instance, a student asked not to participate due to extreme feelings of climate anxiety.

This said, as Clayton notes, 'active engagement in addressing climate change may itself have positive effects on the mental health of those who are involved' (2020, p. 5). For this reason, the task actively encourages participants to look for small behavioural changes that are doable and achievable. Moreover, when seen through the perspective of collection action, small acts are magnified.

## Things to consider

Managing the emotional well-being of all participants is a priority. When implementing the process:

- Work in the light, preferably daylight, and avoid closing the curtains or dimming the lights. This will help participants to transition from the imaginary world to their real selves.
- Look for and play music that lends itself to the story but not too sad or depressing. *Hoppipolla* by Sigur Rós is a favourite track, as well as *Metamorphosis*, by Philip Glass.
- Remind participants that they can leave the session at any point. Ensure you have a backup lesson that students can do in their own time.
- Keep an eye on the clock so that you leave enough time for discussion and reflection.

## Learning extensions

To extend knowledge of futures literacy, it is well worth engaging with similar creative projects (see Chapter 18). For other creative responses, consider reading poetry with students, such as Franny Choi's *The World Keeps Ending, and the World Goes On* (2023).

An extension task may also help participants manage their emotional response to the activity. Activities like these offer space for participants to talk and laugh with each other while making and creating and reinforce the underpinning theme of the main activity; that of the value of collective action.

Examples of other extension tasks include:

Paper Snow Sculptures. 30 minutes.

- Divide the class into smaller groups.
- Ask them to create floor-based paper sculptures from the paper snow. Suggest that these are part of an art exhibition on climate action.

- Encourage humorous, silly, and imaginative responses to the task.
- Discourage the use of cello tape or paper tape as this cannot be recycled.
- Walk through the exhibition.
- Sweep up and recycle.

Paper Snow Poetry. 45 minutes.

For this activity, you will need a poem (for example, from Franny Choi's collection) and bundles of old newspapers.

1. Sit in a circle and invite your students to read the poem aloud.
2. Discuss the poem's themes, choice of words, and rhythm.
3. Tear sheets of newspaper into long strips.
4. Divide the class into smaller groups
5. Ask them to sort through the strips and to look for words, sentences, and phrases.
6. Tell them to create their own poem.
7. Using the poem as a stimulus, create still images, actions, and dialogue.
8. Discuss and reflect on the activity.

## Integrating with assessment

Activity as a workshop exercise does not lend itself directly to assessment, so it is not suitable to assess students on their participation. However, you could use it as a creative and embodied illustration of the value of deep and exploratory thinking for envisioning alternative futures and the role of individual and collective action. If used in this context, there are clear and demonstrable links to GreenComp (see Chapter 2) which could be integrated into further reflections and discussion with students.

## References

Choi, F. (2022). *The world keeps ending, and the world goes on.* HarperCollins.

Clayton, S. (2020). Climate anxiety: Psychological responses to climate change. *Journal of Anxiety Disorders, 74*, 102263.

*Farewell Falsterbo | Narrating Climate Futures. www.climatefutures.lu.se.* Retrieved April 15, 2024, from https://www.climatefutures.lu.se/farewell-falsterbo

*Metamorphosis: One.* (n.d.). www.youtube.com. Retrieved April 15, 2024, from https://www.youtube.com/watch?v=8l9Lr9loHG4&list=OLAK5uy_mHrQHy6ZPWPqr-gIszqgSQrTGbxi6in-UQ&index=2

Sigur Rós – *Hoppípolla [Official Music Video - 4K].* (n.d.). www.youtube.com. Retrieved April 15, 2024, from https://www.youtube.com/watch?v=JAYb8ZyjzD0

UNESCO. (2023). *Futures Literacy.* UNESCO.org. https://www.unesco.org/en/futures-literacy

# Chapter 25

# Process drama

## The River

Eva Hallgren

## Learning outcomes and related terms

The drama processes in this chapter aim to:

- Develop a capability to shift/transgress between human and non-human perspectives.
- Explore how *historying* and *futuring* may be keys to sustainable life.
- Develop knowledge about the concept of *nature as a legal entity.*

Key terms and definitions:

- *Non-human perspective* – A way of understanding the world where humans are not at the centre but more equal to vegetation, natural phenomena and animals, and where we are all entangled, related to, and dependent on each other (Haraway, 2016).
- *Historying* and *futuring* – Using temporality and moving between past, present, and the future may provide students with a more holistic experience of exploring sustainability issues, facilitating transformative learning.
- *Nature as a legal entity* – Here, elements in nature, rivers, mountains, and tress, are given legal rights and this allows people, often indigenous groups living in the area, to represent them in court. This is a movement inspired by the

DOI: 10.4324/9781003496359-31

holistic approach to nature of many indigenous peoples where we reconsider alternative ways of relating to the world we live in (see Local and Indigenous Knowledge Systems, 2021).

| Key sustainability-related outcomes |
| --- |
| **Embodying sustainability values** |
| Valuing sustainability/self-awareness and normative competencies |
| Supporting fairness |
| Promoting nature |
| **Embracing complexity in sustainability** |
| Systems thinking |
| Critical thinking |
| **Envisioning sustainable futures** |
| Futures literacy/anticipatory competence |
| Exploratory thinking |
| **Acting for sustainability** |
| Political agency |
| Collective action/strategic/collaboration competence |
| Individual initiative |

# Context of application

The River has been applied in different courses in higher education in Sweden, in groups with a special interest in sustainability and in teacher education/drama courses learning about drama as a tool for education. It has been applied in groups of between 8 and 30 students. Whatever the discipline area, The River has opened up new questions among participants. The process drama is used to develop possibilities of imagination to explore more forms of existence, how we are all entangled, related to, and dependent on, each other.

# Step-by-step guidance

Each step below contains a description of what to do and suggestions of what the facilitator might say to the participants (these are written in *italics*). These suggestions might be used to model a way of speaking before you let the participants talk or as suggestions as to what can be said with a narrator's voice to summarise or move the drama forward.

**Figure 25.1 Verbs written in Swedish connected with the movement of water.**

*Source:* Author, used with permission.

### 1. Get to know the River

a. **Word collection with movement.** Gather everyone at the 'marker board' and ask them to write at least one verb they connect with the movement of water. Talk about the different qualities of the movements and whereabouts in a river or sea you could notice that movement (Figure 25.1).

b. **Name presentation in circle.** One person at a time says their name and chooses one of the water-verbs that describe the mood they are in right now. Choose from the words on the marker board.

c. **Movement with fabric.** Give each participant a piece of fabric in the colours of a river. Say each verb aloud and ask the participants to find movements to illustrate the words. Put on music with a water theme and tell them to explore the movements and the words. The fabric will enhance the movements. Encourage them: *Feel like you are the river!*

d. **I am the River.** Gather in a circle. Ask the participants to imagine that the river is flowing through your space from its beginning in the mountains (from one corner of the room) and all the way down to the sea (the other corner of the room). Ask them, one at a time, to step on to the diagonal of the room and put down the fabric on the floor and say: *I'm the river and I ...* describe how the river is moving through the landscape (*swirl down the mountains, flow still between the fields*). The fabrics may remain on the floor like a river through a landscape. You can, as a narrator, summarise what was said (Figures 25.2 and 25.3).

e. **Role on the wall** – What if... ...the river was a human being? How would you describe it? Draw an outline of a human body symbolising the river as

**Figure 25.2 The River flows through the landscape... or the floor.**

*Source:* Author, used with permission.

a person on a marker board or on a big piece of paper. On the outside of the outline, let the participants write the river's actions, or just use the verbs you have already collected and place them in relation to the relevant part of the body. Inside the outline you write the feelings and thoughts of the river when it is moving through the landscape. Let the participants consider how big a normal-sized person would be if you were to draw one person each living along the river? Reflect about the difference in size, power, and possibility to affect their surroundings. Leave a piece of fabric on a chair to symbolise the River. The fabric can be draped over the shoulders if or when someone wants to take on the role of the River (Figure 25.4).

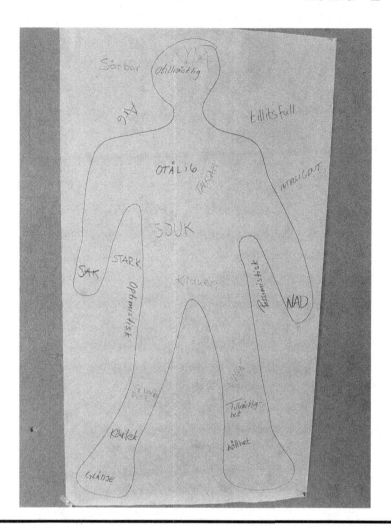

**Figure 25.3 What if the river was a human being?**

*Source:* Author, used with permission.

## 2. Living along the River

   **a. Narrate:** People have lived along the river since ancient times. What do you think the first people who lived along this river did in relation to the river? Suggestions? Ask those who make suggestions to represent their ideas, and then the whole group imitates. Sum up the suggestions by narrating something like this:

   *They lived with the river*
   *They lived off the river*
   *They had taken care of the river*

**Figure 25.4 A piece of fabric on a chair to symbolise The River and can be used by anyone who wants to step into role as the river.**

*Source:* author, used with permission.

> *Been dependent on the river*
> *Been empowered by the river*
> *The river has not only given life to people but also to the surrounding nature and animals.*

(You may want to expand and let the participants to go into role as phenomenon in nature. This strand is not included in the outline here but is both possible and fruitful to explore.)

**b. Going into role.** Divide the group into pairs where one is A and the other is B.

Tell them they are the people who lived by the river a long time ago. Person A is a young person and person B is an old member of the family.

**Narrate:** *Your family have, since ancient times, been responsible for and taken care of a special thing in nature in relation to the river.* (Kaitiaki is the Māori for being a guardian of something in nature.)

- Decide in the pairs what the pair will become a guardian for (guardians of clams, of fish, of water, of irrigation, etc.).
- Agree on where the pair's special place along the river is, and what their family has done there (i.e. this will become the ritual which is enacted along the river).
- Mark the place along the river with an object that symbolises what the river gives. The object can be any ordinary thing lying around in the room or in participants' bags, but there is a choice to be made in relation to what it symbolises. (Maybe the pair can write a few lines about the significance of the place. Then place the note under the object.)
- Ask the pairs to create a ritual that has been performed next to the river since ancient times. Something that can be easily repeated. It can be a movement with the hands, a bending of the neck... Each ritual ends with the words that the people along the river have always said: *I'm the river, the river is me.*
- Ask the older person to show the younger person the ritual. The younger may be somewhat reluctant, wondering or supportive with questions.

**c.** Share with each other: Once a year the people take a walk along the river and watch each group perform their rituals.

The facilitator goes into role as *The Oldest* leading the group along the river where the pairs have chosen their special places. Each pair performs their ritual in front of the others.

**d.** Reflection out of role. Sit down in a circle: *What did we experience? What do we know now? What does it tell us about life along the river for these people?*

3. **Sounds from the future.** Ask the participants to go back into role as those who have just completed the ritual walk. *Thank each other and now go home to bed.* On the way back home, they hear sounds that are unfamiliar (play sounds in the background from engines, tractors, big machines). Ask the participants to reflect on *What can it be? What are these sounds from the future... but the sound fades away so there is nothing to worry about.* The sounds from the engines will symbolise that time is changing; we are moving towards the future but still not paying that much attention to it.

4. **Written reflection in role.**

**a.** Sit or lie down in a place close to your ritual place which is home.

Invite participants to write a few lines in their (fictional) diary about the day and what might come ahead – say *Write so someone else can read the text. It will be read anonymously. Remember that you write as if you are the older or the younger person.*

**b.** The facilitator collects and reads the lines out loud while the group is sleeping.

**c.** Reflection out of role: Invite the participants to reflect on What did the people along the river bring with them to sleep? What kind of thoughts did we hear?

**5. Populating the River.**

**a.** Narrate as the group still relaxes: *Years pass... Word of the river's wealth spreads, and more and more people settle along the river.*

Then tell the group that you all are going to change perspective and go into role as someone else.

**b.** The teacher-in-role as an official representative from a municipality close by. The representative's mission is to attract new investors to the place and talk to the participants as if they are developers wanting to invest in the river area. Narrate:

*Welcome! There are opportunities to get energy, fantastic rocks, tributaries can be diverted, the riverbeds can be used for filling masses for railway construction... The river is amazing! It carries away everything you throw in it! You probably have your own ideas about what to use the River and the surrounding area for. You're welcome to ask questions!"*

Now, the facilitator out-of-role asks:

*What do you need the river for? What does modern society require?"*

**c. Pairs in role.** Divide the group into new pairs as investors and developers. Tell them to walk along the river and find a good place for their business. Ask them to explore the place and see if they find anything interesting, such as objects or text fragments from old times. What do these fragments tell the investors? The facilitator, as teacher-in-role as the municipal representative again, moves around, listens to ideas, encourages, and supports ideas.

**d. Eavesdropping.** The facilitator steps out of role and asks the group to freeze in their talk. The facilitator moves from pair to pair and when passing one pair she 'overhears' what they are talking about. The rest of the group is quiet when each pair improvises their talk about investing in something along the river.

**e. Change of perspective and reflection in role.** Tell the participants to take a step to the side, out of the role of the investor, and step back into the role of the person (young/old) who still lives along the river and is hiding in the forest along the riverbank. Invite reflections about *How do you feel right now, hiding among the trees? What do you think about this?* The facilitator walks among the group and puts a hand on the shoulder of each participant as a sign that she/he can say her/his inner thoughts out loud. Each one can contribute a reflection or choose to be quiet.

**f. Reflection out of role.** Invite the participants to step out of role and reflect from their own perspective as well: *What is happening? What do we know now? What do we know by history that might happen next?*

Reflecting from both different perspectives in role and also out of role adds layers to the drama and to the content being explored and is one of the didactic potentials when using drama as a learning medium.

**6. Building factories.**

    **a. Movement exercise.** Pair the investors into groups of four and let them decide for a place along the river. Each group agrees on what kind of factory they are and what they are producing. They are invited to identify movements and a word each that symbolises the production line and can be repeated.

    **b.** The movements and words are repeated calmly and clearly. Start one factory at a time and make the movements flow from one factory to the next along the river. Gradually the facilitator increases the pace by saying, e.g. *Work harder! Faster!* Finally, the facilitator shouts *STOP!*

    **c.** The facilitator tells everyone to step out of role and opens for a reflection:

    *Now it was me, the facilitator, who said stop. But in reality, who says stop? When will it come to a halt? How will that happen?*

    **d.** Go back into production, into the movement of the different factories again. Try out the different ideas of saying *Stop!* that appeared in the reflection. Be careful to try out one suggestion at a time so you can notice the difference after every attempt. Reflect again out of role – the facilitator can ask questions like the following:

    *Can this be dealt with in another way?*
    *Who has a right to say something about using the river and its surroundings? The indigenous population, the settlers, the municipality?*

    **If the group has not suggested setting up a legal trial the facilitator can do that by asking these questions:**

    *Why not set up a legal trial?*
    *What does the river say?*
    *Who can speak for the river in court?*

**7. A Legal Trial: Who has the right to the river?**

    **a.** The facilitator rounds them all up for a legal trial. Ask the participants what they think is at stake and who needs to attend the trial. If they do not mention the River the facilitator does. It might be now the facilitator tells the facts about that phenomena in nature can become a 'legal entity' (see below).

    When the group has decided on who will attend the trial the facilitator distributes the roles so that everyone is involved:

    – Judge – 2–3 participants and maybe with assistance of teacher-in-role as 'assistant'
    – People who have lived along the river for generations/group of Indigenous people

- Factory owners
- The River (2–3 participants)
- If there are other roles mentioned by the group, they need to be represented too.

Let each group prepare their arguments for who has the right to the river and in what way. The Judge and assistants prepare the procedures.

**b.** Organise the room together so it looks like a courtroom and stage the trial. If the facilitator is using teacher-in-role as assistant, she/he can remind everybody about procedures and the issues to be addressed. Remind the participants to keep a formal tone in the courtroom.

Let each group raise their arguments.

This is a wicked problem and there is no easy or right answer. The facilitator can suggest the judge to ask a question like: *What would happen if each team backed on one of their points?*

Another question to ponder is: *When during history could we have chosen another path?*

How it all ends and what they agree on, no one knows in advance. The judges' team summaries and concludes when appropriate.

**c.** A reflective ending in role. The facilitator goes out of role as assistant and asks everybody to stand up and turn away from each other. The facilitator goes around and puts a hand on each one's shoulder and in role everyone gets to say what they think and feel as they leave the courtroom.

8. **a.** Step out of role and gather for reflection.

The facilitator invites reflection: What did you experience during the process drama? What questions do you bring with you? Connect to the outside world, to the more-than-human relation and think about if the drama might have any implications 'out there'.

If the facilitator has not talked about the fact that phenomena in nature can become a 'legal entity' do so and exemplify by talking about, e.g. the Whanganui River in New Zeeland which is portrayed in an article in National Geographic and in a presentation: https://www.nationalgeographic.com/culture/graphics/maori-river-in-new-zealand-is-a-legal-person and in this presentation https://riversymposium.com/wp-content/uploads/2017/09/Gerrard-Albert.pdf

# Framing or pre-work

It might be useful to:

■ Create an oral drama contract (or 'ground rules') proposing a learning environment for safety, exploration, and ethics, as presented in Chapter 3.

■ Explain that you are going to use teacher-in-role during the process drama and that the participants also will be going in and out of different roles. A description of and how to use teacher-in-role is presented in Chapter 2.

■ Reinforce and emphasise the role and importance of reflection for learning, which will take place both in and out of role.

## When to use and when not to use

The process drama can be applied in any course where it is appropriate to open up thinking and acting for the more-than-human and questions about when and where in history another way of living could have been taken. It is a chance to explore a more holistic approach to nature inspired by many indigenous peoples' ways of relating to the world we live in (Local and Indigenous Knowledge Systems, 2021).

This process drama requires time, at least two hours, so that participants will get a chance to identify with the different roles and perspectives that are offered in the outline. However, the drama can be split up and carried out over several occasions. When doing that, other materials like texts on the subject matter or films can be fed into the process in between the drama sessions.

## Reflections from the field

In previous applications, participants have been fully engaged in the process drama and in the life of the river and its environment. Participants have explored history and into present time with a gaze into the future. Questions have been posed about how we could change our perception of the environment around us, how we became conquerors of the world, and if and how we can now change again and act differently. Interest in *nature as a legal entity* has also been evoked and further explored.

## Things to consider

For an enriched performance of The River, you will need:

■ An empty floor with chairs placed in a circle.

■ Pieces of fabric (as big as possible) for each participant preferably in the colour of water. If you cannot get hold of fabric, use bigger pieces of different kinds of paper – e.g. thin/thick paper, tissue paper, newspaper.

■ A big piece or role of paper is needed to draw the outline of a body.

■ Papers and thick pens enough for each participant.

■ Possibility to play music – sound of water, music about water (e.g. *River flows in you by Yiruma, River by Bishop Briggs)*, sound of engines.

## Learning extensions

After finishing the process drama – or in between each section – you can add other material like texts on the subject matter or films. It is useful to listen out for questions from the students since that is where their interest to dig deeper is – student interests might take you in another direction and you can account for that through the structure presented here.

## Integrating with assessment

While being in the drama your students are in a 'safe zone', in a playful fictional activity, and should not be graded on their subject content knowledge. Formative assessment takes place here so that the coming steps in the drama can be fine-tuned and participants are being both supported and challenged. It is useful to see the process drama as a way to explore, to open up perspectives, and as a possibility to step into not only someone else's shoes but also into water and maybe other phenomena in nature and experience from different perspectives. Coming out of role, you (and others) have emotionally charged experiences and have created plenty of material to reflect on and continue working around in your ordinary educational and assessment activity.

## Further reading

Bowell, P., & S. Heap, B. (2013). *Planning Process Drama: Enriching teaching and learning* (expanded 2nd edition). Taylor and Francis.

Any book by Patrice Baldwin which are very "user friendly" for non-drama-specialists. The titles indicate a special year group or subject area, but they are easy to adapt to your interest. For example: Baldwin, P., & Galazka, A. (2021). *Process Drama for second language teaching and learning: a toolkit for developing language and life skills.* Bloomsbury Publishing.

Magallanes, C. I. (2017). Reframing rights and responsibilities to prioritize nature [Review of *Reframing Rights and Responsibilities to Prioritize Nature*]. In M. Scanlon (Ed.), *Law and policy for a new economy: sustainable, just, and democratic* (pp. 70–96). Edward Elgar.

## References

Albert, G. (2017). *Tupua Te Kawa – The Journey to Return the Whanganui River to the Whanganui River. Chair of Nga Tangata Tiaki o Whanganui Trust.* Retrieved February 23, 2024, from https://riversymposium.com/wp-content/uploads/2017/09/Gerrard-Albert.pdf.

Haraway, D. J. (2016). *Staying with the trouble. Makin Kin in the Chthulucene.* Duke University Press

*Local and Indigenous Knowledge Systems (LINKS).* (2021). Unesco.org. https://www.unesco.org/en/links?hub=66750.

Warne, K. (n.d.). *This River in New Zealand is a Legal Person. How Will It Use Its Voice?.* National Geographic. Retrieved March 5, 2021, from https://www.nationalgeographic.com/culture/graphics/maori-river-in-new-zealand-is-a-legal-person.

## Chapter 26

# Drama workshop

## Flood!

Charlotte Gottfries

### Learning outcomes and related terms

The drama processes in this chapter aim to:

- Develop both intellectual and emotional knowledge about the consequences of climate change in the lives of people in countries strongly affected.
- Deepen the understanding of the experience of solastalgia (existential distress caused by environmental change) when livelihoods and nearly everything in a person's life disappear.
- Expand empathy and solidarity to inspire the participants to think critically, take responsibility, and contribute to more sustainable daily living.

Key terms and definitions:

- Climate change witness: a person who has personally experienced strong negative consequences of climate change.
- Solastalgia: the feelings of pain and longing that people experience when their environment changes in a destructive way.

DOI: 10.4324/9781003496359-32

| Key sustainability-related outcomes |
| --- |
| **Embodying sustainability values** |
| Valuing sustainability/self-awareness and normative competencies |
| Supporting fairness |
| **Embracing complexity in sustainability** |
| Systems thinking |
| Critical thinking |
| Problem framing/integrated problem-solving competence |
| **Envisioning sustainable futures** |
| Adaptability |
| Exploratory thinking |
| **Acting for sustainability** |
| Political agency |
| Collective action/strategic/collaboration competence |
| Individual initiative |

## Context of application

This process drama was written and conducted with students by Charlotte Gottfries, inspired by conversations with David Kronlid, associate professor in ethics and senior lecturer in pedagogy at Mittuniversitetet. It was conducted at Uppsala University in an optional course with the name 'Drama in education, Theatre and Communication' open to students training to be teachers. There were students of different genders and ages, but the majority of the students were women 20–30 years old. The process drama was also conducted in an optional course on climate didactics, conducted in English. In that course half of the group were male students. The process drama was carried out in a drama studio with 20 students at a time and takes around three hours but can be divided into two units with a break in between. In the Nordic countries, there are not yet such strong consequences of climate change, in India people already live with strong consequences of climate change and try to survive.

## Step-by-step guidance

1. Preparation – before the session.
   At least one week before this activity, instruct the participants to read about the thoughts of Tulsi Khara, a climate witness (see *Climate witness* in the references section).

Choose a room with enough chairs for the participants. The chairs must be movable so you can put them in a circle (if there are tables, just move them to the sides). Bring:

■ Pens and papers.
■ An Indian sari or shawl.
■ Three pieces of long blue fabric.
■ A microphone (just a prop).
■ A small loudspeaker connected to a mobile phone (if there are no loud-speakers in the room).
■ Some soft music with water as a theme (freely available on the web).

2. Brief the participants about the warm-up exercises.
Brief the participants about how warm-up exercises at the beginning of a session can establish a positive, relaxed, and open group climate which can prepare them to open up to an embodied experience when proceeding into the serious process drama. Explain that all of the participants will activate their bodies, senses, and intellect which can allow a deeper understanding than only reading a text.

Tell the group that there will be very short time for preparations, so they will not have time to become nervous or try too hard to perform something that is great. The participants are allowed to just come up with something spontaneously.

3. Water and name – a warm-up exercise.
Organise the room so there is a large circle of chairs with an empty space in the middle.

Invite the participants to stand in a circle, with you included inside the circle of chairs, and to think of water (give them around one minute).

Ask the students to, one at a time, say their name and make one movement with their hand or whole body what they associate with water (e.g. the movements or use of water).

The first person starts with name and a movement. The rest of the group repeats the name of that person and imitates the movement. The next person says his/her name and makes a new movement and the rest of the group repeat the name and imitate the movement and so it continues around the circle.

Now put on the water music and ask all the participants to try to make all the movements linked together so it becomes like a kind of dance with everyone included.

4. Personal memory of water.
Put the three pieces of long blue fabric (symbolic of water) on the floor within the circle. Tell the participants that they can use the fabrics if they want to, when they show their scenes.

Put the chairs in groups of four and tell the participants to sit in groups of four. There can be one group of five if needed.

Ask the participants to silently reflect approximately for 3 minutes on both a positive and a negative personal experience in relation to water or lack of water.

Invite the participants to share their experiences in their small groups, if it feels ok to do so. After that, ask the students to choose one of the stories that they are willing to show to the rest of the group in a small scene.

Ask each group to create a small scene from their chosen memory and rehearse it for 5–10 minutes and then they show their scenes to each other. Encourage them to use the blue fabric as water.

It is important that the groups play the scenes exactly where they are in the room so everyone very rapidly can change between acting and watching and every part of the room is both an area for performing and for watching.

Now first ask the participants who were watching – and then those who were acting – to reflect, using open questions like '*How did you experience this?*' or '*What did you see/hear/feel?*'. This should be voluntary, without pressure.

5. Interview with a fictive climate change witness.

Remind the participants of the pre-reading (Tulsi Khara's account of her experience of a climate change disaster, a flood).

Invite the whole group to use Tulsi Khara's story as a starting point and to use their imagination to build a broader picture and a fictive continuation of the story.

Now change the name of the main character to Shanti (fictive) instead of Tulsi Khara. Ask for a volunteer to play Shanti (gender does not matter as long as the person is serious and willing to play the role). Tell the participants that the person playing Shanti just has to sit down, be in touch with the Tulsi Khara's story and improvise answers to the questions. Shanti (person-in-role) can just say what comes to her mind, and responses do not need to be aligned with the story (Bolton & Heathcote, 1999).

After the volunteer is ready, invite anyone who wants to act as a 'shadow voice', there can be one or two. Those who act as a shadow voice place themselves behind Shanti and whisper words into her ears if she feels unsure of what to say.

Help Shanti to put on a sari or Indian shawl and invite her to sit on a chair facing the rest of the group. This marks the role of the Indian woman.

Ask the rest of the group to bring their chairs and sit in a semi-circle close to her.

Ask the person acting to relax, try to just be Shanti inside, and improvise spontaneous answers to the questions. Say that knowledge about India is not necessary.

Invite every participant to ask Shanti a question. Let the group ask 20–30 curious specific questions about her personal history, children, farming, economy, life, the disaster, and so on. The questions are created in the moment, through improvisation.

Break – Take a break for 20 minutes before the panel debate (or when you feel necessary).

6. Panel debate.

Write the different roles in the debate on a whiteboard or paper: social worker, lawyer, UN climate expert, climate activist, feminist, manager for a multi-national clothing company, left-wing politician, conservative politician, representatives from different religions, the Indian climate minister, the Indian enterprise minister, Shanti, and Shanti's son/daughter.

Put five chairs in a semicircle as a debate panel in front of the rest of the group.

Tell the participants that there is deliberately very little time for preparation and the reason is to let the people who act be spontaneous, emotional, and just say what comes to their minds.

Invite five new volunteers to play different roles in a fictive panel debate on television. Every role has a different perspective on the situation. The volunteers can choose which roles they want to play.

Ask for another volunteer who wants to play the journalist leading the debate.

Brief the journalist to bring the debate to a close when the debate is fading.

Tell the audience that the people on the panel have just seen the interview with Shanti on a screen and will have this panel debate to discuss what they have seen.

Ask the journalist to use the microphone to start the debate by asking five questions:

What has happened?
Why has this happened?
Who is responsible?
What can be done so that this will not happen again?
What can you on the panel do about it?

The journalist lets everyone on the panel have space to speak and take turns. It is perfectly acceptable if the debate becomes heated. If time allows, you can run another round of debate with new volunteers.

7. Meta reflection.

Ask all the participants to stand up and shake their shoulders to get out of their roles and the fiction, then to sit down in pairs in the circle and share thoughts and feelings about what they have experienced.

Invite every pair to share what they want to tell the whole group. Encourage the participants to search for more knowledge about this and think about their own choices in their lives when it comes to sustainability.

End by thanking everybody for their participation and interesting reflections.

## Framing or pre-work

Pre-work includes reading (*Climate Witness*, 2024, see references) and can include icebreakers (see Chapters 2 and 3), or other readings (see further reading below). You may also want to connect this process drama with the context of your curriculum.

## When to use and when not to use

This process drama can be used with a group which knows very little about climate change issues or a group that knows a lot. There will be slightly different but valuable outcomes.

## Reflections from the field

The process drama has received positive oral evaluations from the students in the two different courses, saying it was interesting and valuable. All the students participated actively and showed a lot of energy and curiosity.

In the structure of this process drama students can choose to participate on different levels. Some of them like being 'on stage' in front of the others and often choose more exposed roles, and some prefer to do a small amount of role playing but might bring very interesting observations and thoughts into the reflections.

## Things to consider

You should be the one who creates the smaller groups by counting so the participants mix in new ways. Avoid small groups of friends with their own agenda, as they appear and exclude others (Bolton & Heathcote, 1999).

Before the activity about creating scenes of personal memories, advise the participants not to play themselves or take the role of Shanti if they have experienced strong traumas in relation to water. A person with this experience has very interesting and important experience to tell at the beginning of the small group work but do not take the risk that s/he goes deep into a role, e.g. as somebody drowning. Instead, that person can instruct somebody else how to play that role.

However, if a participant becomes strongly emotionally triggered during the activity, you need to be ready to handle the situation in a caring way and bring what happened in as a part of the process drama. You might say '*Thank you for sharing your feelings. This was how many, many human beings, and animals as well, experienced the disaster*'. This is unlikely to happen because of the precautions mentioned above.

# Learning extensions

If running this process drama in a more research-based context, you may choose to allow more time for pre-reading and fact-finding for every role in this process drama (see further reading and references below). Then the debate might be more fact-based, and the students could spend more time preparing different critical perspectives and arguments (Rudberg, 2014). This might be less emotionally connected and spontaneous.

Within the same process above, you could also encourage the participants to study all kinds of climate change effects before they join the process drama. This can give a deeper grounding and more content to explore. Similarly, you could ask the participants to study more examples of process drama (e.g. Bowell & Heap, 2013).

An activity that should only be conducted in a group of grown-ups (because of sensitive content), is writing a letter from Shanti and her children. Here, students imagine being five years in the future. The journalist who held the debate has just contacted Shanti and her children and wants to make a follow-up on television. The journalist asks how life has developed for them and if they want to join the program. Here, you ask the students to write a short letter to the journalist from Shanti or one of Shanti´s children. Has life developed well or badly after the disaster? If you do this in the class, this can be done in a circle, followed by inviting one or two volunteers to share their letters.

In each of the extensions above, you can invite students to make lists about what they can change in their lives to live more sustainably, and then create scenes or frozen pictures of their ideas.

# Integrating with assessment

In any assessment, active participation should be the main criterion rather than an evaluation of acting skills. If it is necessary to evaluate the activity formally, consider asking students to write reflective essays where they connect their experiences in the process drama with relevant literature on climate change.

# Further reading

Hallgren, E., & Jacquet, E. (2023). *Stärk pedagogiken med estetiken (Strengthen pedagogy with aesthetic processes - drama, art and storytelling in thematic education)*. Studentlitteratur AB.
van Poeck, K., Östman, L., & Öhman, J. (2019). *Sustainable development teaching*. Routledge.

# References

Boal, A. (1980). *Förtrollad, förvandlad, förstenad. (Stop! E magico)*. Gidlunds.
Bolton, G., & Heathcote, D. (1999). *So you want to use roleplay?* Trentham Book Ltd.

Bowell, P., & Heap, B. S. (2013). *Planning process drama: Enriching teaching and learning.* Routledge.

*Climate witness: Tulsi Khara, India.* (2024). wwf.panda.org. Retrieved July 4, 2024, from https://wwf.panda.org/es/?22345/Climate-Witness-Tulsi-Khara-India.

Rudberg, K. (2014). *Elevers lärande i argumentativa diskussioner om hållbar utveckling. (Student´s learning in argumentative discussions about sustainable development).* [Doctoral dissertation, Acta Universitatis Upsaliensis. Uppsala Studies in Education].

## Chapter 27

# Drama workshop

## The journey to Dystoplastica

Kerstin Danckwardt-Lillieström

### Learning outcomes and related terms

The drama processes in this chapter aim to:

- Participate in explorations of the plastic issue combining science with values and societal perspectives.
- Frame the plastic problem as a complex sustainability issue understood as wicked problems, integrating problem-solving competence.
- Explore imaginary transitions through time, and how transitions back and forth may afford more nuanced understandings of wicked sustainability problems, promoting anticipatory competence.

Key terms and definitions:

- *Wicked problems* concern sustainability issues that are characterised by a problem that "is unclear, undefinable, or that there is a lack of agreement on whether the 'problem' is a problem or what the problem is" and solutions that "are not well defined, not agreed upon or require transformation of the system structure" (Glasser, 2018, p. 37).
- *Problem-solving competence-* "To formulate current or potential challenges as a sustainability problem in terms of difficulty, people involved, time and

DOI: 10.4324/9781003496359-33

geographical scope, in order to identify suitable approaches to anticipating and preventing problems, and to mitigating and adapting to already existing problems" (European Commission, 2022, p. 14).

■ *Anticipatory competence* - "the ability to understand and evaluate multiple futures – possible, probable and desirable – and to create one's own visions for the future, to apply the precautionary principle, to assess the consequences of actions, and to deal with risks and changes" (Rieckmann, 2018, p. 44).

| Key sustainability-related outcomes |
| :--- |
| **Embodying sustainability values** |
| Valuing sustainability/self-awareness and normative competencies |
| Supporting fairness |
| **Embracing complexity in sustainability** |
| Problem framing/integrated problem-solving competence |
| **Envisioning sustainable futures** |
| Futures literacy/anticipatory competence |
| Exploratory thinking |
| **Acting for sustainability** |
| Collective action/strategic/collaboration competence |

# Context of application

The process drama has been applied in the ongoing teaching of organic chemistry, within the discipline area of chemistry (at an upper secondary school in Sweden) but is suitable to be performed in undergraduate courses in chemistry (or other natural science subjects) in higher education. The process drama described lasted 3 hours and involved 17 students (without previous experience of drama in teaching) in their second year of the Natural Science program (also see Danckwardt-Lillieström, Andrée & Rundgren, 2024). The students' chemistry and biology teachers participated as teachers in role and the author participated as a drama facilitator.

# Step-by-step guidance

1. Prepare roles that serve the context of the plastic sustainability issue from different perspectives. For example, journalists, politicians, and scientists. Develop fictional brief descriptions of the role or develop more detailed role descriptions based on inquiries to authentic stakeholders (see Figure 27.1). Place the role descriptions on chairs in groups of four people along with name tags. Arrange the room so that there is plenty of space to move around in whole class activities.

# Role card

## Process drama about plastics

| Name: Björn Beakersson |
|---|
| Age: 52 |
| Education: Doctorate in Environmental Science from MIT |
| Profession: Professor of Environmental Science at Stockholm University |

| Motto: Plastic is everywhere in the environment and will be for a long time. And that's a problem! |
|---|

**Skills**

*Enter 0-3 per row and a maximum of 12 points in total*

| | |
|---|---|
| 3 | Material knowledge |
| 2 | Large scale manufacturing |
| 0 | Business economics |
| 0 | Marketing |
| 1 | Communication |
| 3 | Sustainability |
| 3 | Global perspective |

**Special skills**

- Measuring plastic in the environment

- Modeling plastic pollution of water, soil and sediments now and in the future

- Experience with other persistent global pollutants, like PCBs and DDT

**Questions for you as a specialist**

1. *Which plastics should we focus on producing in order to achieve a sustainable future?*

   Plastic escapes into the environment from many types of uses, and stays there for a long time. To avoid further increasing the levels of plastic in the global environment, new "virgin" plastic made from fossil fuels should only be produced for functions where there are no possible substitutes. We should avoid producing new "virgin" plastic from fossil fuels because transitioning away from fossil fuels as an energy source to confront climate change risks could otherwise flood the market with vast amounts of cheap virgin plastic due to technical production systems that are "locked-in".
   (https://www.sciencedirect.com/science/article/pii/S0301421521002883)

2. *Which ones should we avoid?*

   Currently, plastic is poorly recyclable and recycling rates are low. Restricting production of virgin plastic will incentivize research and development of infrastructure to improve recycling, and stimulate a transition to circular economy by making used plastic into a valuable commodity.

**Figure 27.1** Example of role card from authentic plastic scientist used in The Journey to "Dystoplastica". Developed in collaboration with Jenny Olander at Chemistry Teachers' Resource Center (Kemilärarnas resurscentrum, KRC), based on enquiries to plastics scientists and chemical engineers. Used with permission.

2. Invite the students to sit or lie on the floor and encourage them to close their eyes, imagine driving their car while listening to the radio. As a radio newscaster, tell them a story and build up a dilemma about polluted seas in their neighbourhood. Then tell them that they are suddenly interrupted and called to an important meeting with an authority, e.g. the Public Health Authority.

3. When the students enter the meeting, the teacher-in-role acts as the representative of the Authority and welcomes and encourages the students to choose roles and place themselves in groups. Ask students to read the role descriptions, decide names for their characters, and then write them on their name tags. Encourage the students to introduce themselves to each other and individualise the roles, for example, according to their research interests, where they work, and so on. When the students have had enough time to introduce themselves to each other, the teacher-in-role interrupts to provide information about plastic pollution, and the background to why the teams had been called to the meeting. Here is an opportunity to connect to the Sustainable Development Goals and current research. Encourage students in role to interact and comment on the information by asking questions directed at different stakeholders. Give students plenty of time to improvise in their groups and encourage them to comment on the information according to their characters' opinions. To promote further interaction in the groups, the teacher-in-role may walk around in the room, listen in and ask provocative questions.

4. Then inform the students about the mission to find out how to deal with the wicked plastic problem in society, by taking on the authoritarian teacher-in-role as Space Agency Chief, for example, wearing a military hat. Ask the students to sit in teams in a time machine and travel 100 years back in time.

5. Back in time, the teams are met by a teacher-in-role as Hermann Staudinger, plastic chemist and Nobel laureate, who talks about the first plastic materials and how they were made. Here, in the improvisation with the students, the opportunity is given to reinforce the image of the possibilities of plastics from a historical perspective and bring in chemistry content that the students could connect to their own experiences with organic chemistry. For example, ask about the team-members' materials in their clothes and shoes, as well as "happening to find" a plastic bag in one of the students' pockets and ask how it is made. Here students can help Staudinger make an advertising jingle for plastics through online software (e.g. Tableau).

6. Show clearly that the teacher is stepping out of role, for example, by taking off goggles and a coat that have been worn as Hermann Staudinger. Tell the students that they will now step out of their role and invite students and teachers to sit in a ring on the floor, to discuss what they have experienced in the drama. Allow students to ask questions and share their thoughts. End the activity by asking the students how far into the future they want to go and invite them to get back into the time machine and travel into the future.

7. Use storytelling and ask the students to step out of the time machine, look around and imagine the dystopian polluted landscape, walking on huge

plastic graves in a gloomy and dark environment. Have students gather around an imaginary polluted smelly lake. Ask them to think of something they see in this lake. Then ask the first student to step into the lake and "be this thing" while saying what he/she is (I am…). Then instruct the student to "freeze" and for the next student to build on the previous one – so, through collective imagination, students together create a tableau (a still or motionless sculture using their bodies) of the future "Dystoplastica".

8. Have a teacher-in-role suddenly appear as a villager, wearing a torn blanket, gas mask, and safety goggles, throwing out and kicking old plastic items and bottles around on the floor, while asking the students who they are. Create space for improvisation and interaction with and between the students where students' own reflections on the consequences of plastic use, as well as chemical content, could be explored.

9. Tell the students to go back to their time machine. Ask the students, still in role, to reflect on the experiences thus far, by writing in their diary, to the glow of candles that are set up in the room (writing-in-role). Tell the students to underline the most important sentence, which is then read aloud, to get a collective experience. Then ask the students to go into the time machine and travel back to the representative of the Authority.

10. Once there, the students are met by teacher-in-role as the representative of the Authority, giving students, still in role, the task to prepare and present three important proposals to reduce the negative impact of plastic on the environment. They must also state and justify which plastic materials should be developed and which plastics should be avoided. Instruct the students to present their proposals to the other team members, still in role.

11. Clearly step out of role and tell students to do so as well. Invite students to ask questions and share their thoughts about their experiences in the process drama.

## Framing or pre-work

If the students have no experience of drama in teaching, it is important to make clear that the students are in a "safe zone" and what is expected from students and teachers during the drama activity (for example, in the form of an "oral drama contract", see Chapter 3). After that, it is good to start with one or more warm-up exercises or icebreakers (see Chapters 4–9) before entering the process drama. When performing the described process drama, it is important to understand how to use the drama convention teacher-in-role and reflections in and out of role (see below).

## When to use and when not to use

The process drama can be useful as an introduction to organic chemistry as well as during the course. As an introduction, the process can be used to pique interest and to find out more about plastics and its consequences for the environment. This helps motivate, make it meaningful, and create interest in studying the subject further during the course. If the focus is on students being able to use and learn disciplinary chemistry whilst also exploring the value and social implications of plastics, it is appropriate to perform the drama during the course, as the students have more chemistry knowledge to weave into the drama.

## Reflections from the field

Spaces were created for the students' agentic participation in an interplay between societal, values, and scientific perspectives, both on a personal and social level whilst considering their global responsibility. The process enabled students to bring the context of reality into chemistry teaching to tackle wicked plastic problems and gave students the opportunity to express themselves in ways that are not common in traditional chemistry teaching. Further, the students' transition through time enabled them to explore the plastic issue from a time perspective. This enabled them to understand the present based on the past which can give the students a readiness to act for the future (see Seixas, 2006).

A student in the role of a journalist reflected that: "I have changed my mind on the climate issue… after traveling into the future, I now understand that everyone has their own responsibility to take care of the environment, we can't just rely on technological development as the solution… if you don't experience the consequences of our daily lives, I think it's hard to change your mind". Further, some students were so inspired that they wanted to do their final year project (gymnasiearbete) on plastics and successfully used university equipment to develop bioplastics from algae.

## Things to consider

As teacher in role, be aware of the position towards the students, as this has a big impact on the ways in which students can participate in the process, which in turn affects learning. For example, let teacher-in-role as "Hermann Staudinger" and the "villager in Dystoplastica" assume a *low-status or middle-status position* (see Chapters 2 and 29) to support students in their roles, and give the students' space to ask their own questions. For an inexperienced teacher, it can be easy to ask questions that expect correct answers, and the drama instead takes on the character of a "regular lesson" where the teacher becomes a *teacher-in-disguise* (see Chapter 2). Further, it is important that the teacher clearly shows when they are in role (or not) because then the probability that the students are also in role increases.

It is also pivotal to give the students time for reflection both in role and out of role - enable students to perceive a connection between the drama and one's own life

(Hallgren, 2018), and experience the plastic issue from different perspectives, which can increase the opportunities for learning the wicked problems of plastics.

## Learning extensions

A suggestion to deepen the learning (if time allows) is to continue the process drama or introduce another lesson, where the students can imagine a future scenario in groups that is not a "Dystoplastica", where they show how the past/present has changed to achieve this future scenario. The students can then perform this together with their peers. The students could also come up with stakeholders themselves before the drama is performed (see Chapter 2). Appropriate music can also be played as an introduction/during the episodes to enhance the surrounding atmosphere.

In this chapter, a framework for moving backwards and forwards in time has been described, and there is a lot that can be put into this framework. Focusing more on the chemistry content, the teams could meet several different types of historical figures from the past, related to the topic at hand. The students could also help someone in the future or the past to carry out lab work, e.g. in the production of some plastic material in role. Focusing more on the value and societal perspective, planning and performing the process drama together with several subjects, such as biology, social studies, and history, could be a way to broaden the learning.

## Integrating with assessment

It is not appropriate to assess the students' subject knowledge during the drama. Instead, assessment aspects can take place after the process has been conducted, and consider experiences, knowledge, and the interest that the drama has generated. For example, students may submit a reflective task in which they individually describe the issues raised in the drama. Another assessment can be a task that takes its starting point from the performed process drama in the upcoming exam in organic chemistry - where the students have the opportunity to show both knowledge of chemistry linked to social implications of chemistry, and knowledge involving the wicked problems of plastics in a sustainability perspective.

## Further reading

Bowell, P., & S. Heap, B. (2013). *Planning process drama: Enriching teaching and learning* (expanded 2nd Edition). Taylor and Francis. https://doi.org/10.4324/9780203125335.

Ødegaard, M. (2023). Using drama in science education in and for sustainability issues. In D. McGregor & D. Anderson (Eds.), *Learning science through drama. Exploring international perspectives* (pp. 69–86). Springer. https://doi.org.ezp.sub.su.se/10.1007/978-3-031-17350-9_5.

# References

Danckwardt-Lillieström, K., Andrée, M., & Rundgren, C-J. (2024). Process drama as a tool for participation in explorations of 'wicked problems' in upper secondary chemistry education. *LUMAT: International Journal on Math, Science and Technology Education, 12*(2), 50–79. https://doi.org/10.31129/LUMAT.12.2.2132

European Commission, Joint Research Centre. (2022). *GreenComp, the European sustainability competence framework.* Publications Office of the European Union. https://data.europa.eu/doi/10.2760/13286

Glasser, H. (2019). Toward robust foundations for sustainable well-being societies: Learning to change by changing how we learn. In J. W. Cook (Ed.), *Sustainability, human well-being, and the future of education* (p. 31). Palgrave Macmillan.

Hallgren, E. (2018). *Ledtrådar till estetiskt engagemang i processdrama. Samspel i roll i en fiktiv verksamhet* [Clues to aesthetic engagement in process drama: Joint action in a fictional activity] [Doctoral dissertation]. Stockholm University.

Rieckmann, M. (2018). Learning to transform the world: Key competencies in education for sustainable development. *Issues and Trends in Education for Sustainable Development, 39*(1), 39–59. https://unesdoc.unesco.org/ark:/48223/pf0000261802.

Seixas, P. (2006). *Theorizing historical consciousness.* University of Toronto Press.

## Chapter 28

# Drama workshop

## Climate activists

Aysel Korkmaz

### Learning outcomes and related terms

The drama processes in this chapter aim to:

- Relate global goals for sustainability with climate change.
- Develop awareness and foresight regarding climate change, exhibit appropriate attitudes, and take action.
- Analyse and evaluate the reasons behind climate activists' actions against climate change.

Keywords and definitions:

- Climate change is the significant and long-term alteration of average weather conditions, such as increased warmth, coldness, precipitation, and aridity (United Nations, 2024).
- A climate activist is an individual who protests about the unjust and unsustainable use of nature, aiming to enhance the planet's well-being (Scheidel et al., 2020).
- Global goals (or the Sustainable Development Goals) represent a universal call to action by member countries of the United Nations to achieve environmental conservation, addressing the climate change crisis, eliminating poverty,

DOI: 10.4324/9781003496359-34

ensuring equitable distribution of prosperity, and promoting peace by 2030 (United Nations Development Programme [UNDP], 2024).

■ Process drama – see Chapter 2.

| Key sustainability-related outcomes |
|---|
| **Embodying sustainability values** |
| Valuing sustainability/self-awareness and normative competencies |
| Supporting fairness |
| Promoting nature |
| **Embracing complexity in sustainability** |
| Systems thinking |
| Critical thinking |
| Problem framing/integrated problem-solving competence |
| **Envisioning sustainable futures** |
| Futures literacy/anticipatory competence |
| Adaptability |
| **Acting for sustainability** |
| Political agency |
| Collective action/strategic/collaboration competence |
| Individual initiative |

# Context of application

This chapter describes a process drama workshop aimed at deeply exploring the role of climate activists in addressing the global issues arising from climate change and gaining activist experience. The group comprised 25 students training to be pre-school teachers at a university in Türkiye. Utilising process drama, the study calls for action activists to think globally and act locally to draw attention to the climate change issues occurring in the Greenland region through the portrayal of a fictional character, Alice. Throughout the process, a variety of drama techniques were employed to enable the participants to assume diverse roles and to encourage multidimensional and flexible thinking about the topic. The participants were encouraged to communicate with others in the group, express their emotions, develop confidence, and remain motivated.

# Step-by-step guidance

1. Pre-intervention preparation.

   ■ You may need to obtain ethical approval from the university's Ethics Committee if you undertake this as a research study.

- Activity 1: Show the students Luisa Neubauer's TEDx talk entitled (Neubauer, 2019) – Neubauer discusses the importance of climate activism in the video.
- Following the video, explain how the coming process drama sessions relate to activist movements against climate change. Linked to ethical approval, collect voluntary consent forms from students who wish to participate in the sessions.

2. Warming-up.

- Organise the participants in a large circle for a warm-up activity. One participant throws the ball to anyone in the circle while stating something about them (such as the last book they read, their favourite food, or their favourite sport). This activity can continue with different statements. Once you are certain that all participants have joined the icebreaking activity, transition to the preparatory activity.
- In the preparatory activity, play Ludovico Einaudi's piece *Elegy for the Arctic* to draw attention to global warming and climate change (Einaudi, 2016). Encourage the participants to move their bodies according to the rhythm of the piece.
- Then, blindfold a volunteer in the group and hide a bag containing global goals. The blindfolded individual finds the bag with the group's guidance of "warmer–colder". Discuss the potential global goals that could be in the bag (Figure 28.1).
- Now divide the students into groups of four to five. In each group, have the students select three global goals from the bag. Prompt: "*What kind of relationship exists between global goals and climate change?*" The groups conduct quick research (e.g. on their phones) and take notes to associate their chosen global goals with climate change (Figure 28.2).
- Subsequently, each group then introduces their global goal, displays it on a bulletin board, and shares a key effect of climate change related to their chosen global goals (Figure 28.3).

3. High Sea Warming.

- Instruct students to move into circles, made from fabric placed on the floor, representing the ice of a glacier, when they hear the term "high sea". Only when "sea" is mentioned, they are directed to move outside the circle. The circle shrinks gradually, allowing the game to continue. Eventually, when it becomes difficult to move within the circle, the game is ended.
- After the game is over, ask questions like, "*If you lived on a glacier, how would you feel?*" and "*Why do glaciers melt and what kind of changes happen on our planet when glaciers melt?*". Students might emphasise that it would be very difficult for them to live when the glaciers melted due to global warming (Figures 28.4 and 28.5).

**Figure 28.1 Finding the pouch in the warmer–colder play.**

*Source:* The author, used with permission.

4. The Letter.

   Assume the role of a postman or postwoman, and enter the classroom stating, "*We have a letter from the land of icebergs, Greenland*". In the letter, a fictional character named Alice calls upon young activists to take action regarding climate change occurring in the Greenland region. In this context, stressing the importance of thinking globally and acting locally, Alice urges young activists to take action. Proceed to read the letter from Alice. The letter positions the participants as climate activists.

**Figure 28.2 Relating global goals to climate change.**

*Source:* The author, used with permission.

*Dear Young Climate Activists,*

*Thank you for joining our climate activism initiative. Despite our diverse locations, we share one planet impacted by local issues with global consequences. Greenland, my homeland, epitomises this. As the world's largest island, it boasts vast glaciers and tundras. With 81% covered by glaciers, agriculture is limited, and drinking water is sourced from glacier mountains. Dog sleds and snowmobiles facilitate transportation. Yet, Greenland faces rapid climate change, impacting its traditional lifestyle, wildlife, and economy. We urge action to raise global awareness of Greenland's plight. Let's plan climate activism events, create banners, and share our concerns. Hand in hand for a sustainable planet.*

*Yours sincerely*

5. Role on the Wall.

   ■ In "Role on the Wall" technique, detailed information about the character's environment is gathered and developed continuously (Sandercoe, 2021).
   ■ Divide the students into small groups of five to six participants and in the role of teacher ask *"Who lives in the Greenland region where Alice was*

**Figure 28.3 Placing global goals on the board.**

*Source:* The author, used with permission.

*born and raised? How do they sustain their lives in such an environment?"*. All participants share their knowledge and thoughts about Greenland with the whole group, using sticky notes.

■ Now ask *"What was Greenland like before the problems caused by climate change? How did the problems start to arise?"*. Here, you can invite the participants to create still images of the answers, or if they are more confident, improvise a scene of their answers with their small group.

**Figure 28.4 Circles created for the high above the sea play.**

*Source:* The author, used with permission.

6. Climate activists.

■ Express the need for everyone to take action for climate change.

■ This time, divide the group into groups of four to organise actions against the adverse effects of climate change in the Greenland region. Ask, "*Who is a climate activist? Where, how, when, and why do they engage in climate actions?*". The participants conduct research on climate activism for 10 minutes and discuss their findings within their groups. Each group then shares their findings.

**Figure 28.5 Play the game high above the sea.**

*Source*: The author, used with permission.

■ At the same time, teacher-in-role as a climate activist walks around the classroom, loudly proclaiming *"Hands off my air, my water, my soil!"*. This allows participants to sense what climate activism is for themselves, drawing attention to climate change, internalising the emotion, arousing dramatic tension, and assuming a role in the process. This process prepares participants for their own transition in the next step.

■ Each group devises slogans for Greenland protests, like *"Let the climate remain stable, and the glaciers not melt"*, *"Preserve the lives of sled dogs:*

*safeguard against abandonment and demise*", and "*Don't reduce glaciers, reduce carbon footprint*". The students then prepare protest signs, ready for the protest in the next step.

■ Now within the classroom, ask the students to march as activists, chanting slogans, and carrying their protest signs. Some students might laugh, noting surprise, and enjoyment. You now act as a reporter, filming the protest, and highlighting global participation (Figures 28.6 and 28.7).

7. Reflection.

■ At the end of the activity, ask the students to reflect (Figure 28.8):

■ What are your thoughts on climate change now?
■ What kind of actions can we plan to raise awareness about climate change?
■ What are your thoughts on climate activist actions for a sustainable planet?

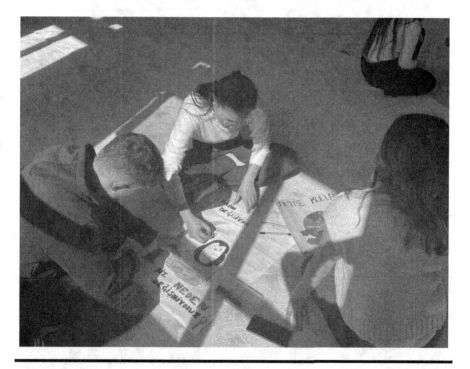

**Figure 28.6 Poster preparation 1.**

*Source:* The author, used with permission.

**Figure 28.7 Poster preparation 2.**

*Source:* The author, used with permission.

**Figure 28.8 Climate activists and their posters.**

*Source:* The author, used with permission.

## Framing or pre-work

Depending on the context and students, you will need to determine which warm-up exercises to use to prepare students for the activity (see Chapters 4–7). You will need to plan and rehearse your own role playing in the activity to maintain its dramatic structure, facilitate classroom management, provide information, and guide the process.

## When to use and when not to use

These workshop activities can be conducted in indoor or outdoor environments where the group can easily communicate. However, process drama activities like this are often challenging to implement in 50- or 60-minute lessons, and with such timing constraints the topics to be addressed should be spread over several sessions.

Additionally, participants may experience a sense of helplessness during the session as they realise the negative impact of climate change on various aspects of their lives. Here, it is useful to advise participants about the topic before they engage in the process and provide opportunities for "time out" if needed.

## Reflections from the field

In their discussions and reflective journals, participants indicated that sustainability-related topics addressed through the process drama method contributed more to their sustainable learning and personal development compared to traditional teaching methods. Additionally, participants emphasised the development of communication, teamwork, problem-solving, creative thinking, and the ability to see different perspectives, for example:

> *"We don't live alone on the planet. I realized that many of our behaviours affect the lives of people living in other countries."* (Taking responsibility for behaviours)

> *"Climate change is the biggest problem on our planet, and this issue made me feel helpless."* (Awareness of personal feelings)

> *"I saw the power of acting together to create awareness of the problems causing the disappearance of living beings and elements in nature, and to take action for solutions. This showed how powerful we are for change if we want to be."* (Importance of acting together)

> *"Climate activism isn't such a bad thing after all."* (Change in perception)

These findings highlight process drama's efficacy in fostering emotional awareness, collaborative action, perceptual shifts, and accountability, thus serving its purpose effectively. However, one participant expressed scepticism in their journal, suggesting that real climate issues require serious policy changes rather than light-hearted approaches.

## Things to consider

Adapt this activity to reflect the age, developmental characteristics, and interests of the group members to manage group dynamics. Plan your session according to group's existing knowledge on climate change and activism, as it is a sensitive and potentially misunderstood topic, to ensure relevance and clarity. Also consider the 12 competency areas identified by GreenComp (2022) as learning outcomes (Bianchi, Pisiotis & Cabrera Giralde, 2022) and how this links to your own curriculum context.

It is worth anticipating the possibility of encountering participants with negative attitudes towards climate activism and change and prepare arguments in advance after reading relevant literature. Gain knowledge about the groups and activities created by activist movements and their effectiveness.

## Learning extensions

If participants are new to process drama games and sustainability, provide readings to familiarise them with the method and topic. You may also want to encourage participants to identify local issues in their own communities related to climate change and provide opportunities for them to determine the causes of these issues and engage in efforts to raise awareness with relevant authorities. Doing this might – with careful consideration, risk management, and ethical approval – provide real world, experiential learning opportunities to change local circumstances.

## Integrating with assessment

Process drama method can be evaluated using various tools such as improvisation observation forms, interviews, journals, and project portfolios. Especially through journals, participants have the opportunity to evaluate their own feelings and responses. This activity could be linked to responsible consumption so students could be encouraged to compile newspaper articles about their negative impacts on life and write projects aimed at reducing consumption, carbon footprint, pollution, noise, and so on.

## Further reading

Lehtonen, A., Österlind, E., & Vierre, T.L. (2020). Drama in education for sustainability: Becoming connected through embodiment. *International Journal of Education & the Arts, 21*(19). https://doi.org/10.26209/ijea21n19

Österlind, E. (2018). Drama in higher education for sustainability: Work-based learning through fiction? *Higher Education, Skills and Work-Based Learning, 8*(3), 337–352. https://doi.org/10.1108/HESWBL-03-2018-0034

Wall, T., Österlind, E., & Fries, J. (2018). Arts based approaches for sustainability. In W. L. Leal Filho (Ed.), *Encyclopedia of sustainability in higher education* (1–7). Springer.

# References

Bianchi, G., Pisiotis, U., & Cabrera Giraldez, M. (2022). Executive summary. In Punie, Y. & Bacigalupo, M. (Eds.), *GreenComp – The European sustainability competence framework* (pp. 17–27). Publications Office of the European Union.

Einaud, L. (2016, June). *Elegy for the Arctic* [Music]. https://www.youtube.com/watch?v=2DLnhdnSUVs

Neubauer, L. (2019, August). *Why I became a climate activist -- and you should, too* [Video]. TED Konferansları. https://www.youtube.com/watch?v=WsfacjPOBIw

Sandercoe, H. (2021). "I wish I could fly": A process drama based on "Circle" by Jeannie Baker. In J. Raphael & D. Hradsky (Eds.), *Drama and sustainability 2021* (27–35). Drama Australia.

Scheidel, A., Del Bene, D., Liu, J., Navas, G., Mingorría, S., Demaria, F., Avila, S., Roy, B., Ertör, I., Temper, L., & Martínez-Alier, J. (2020). Environmental conflicts and defenders: A global overview. *Global Environmental Change, 63.* https://doi.org/10.1016/j.gloenvcha.2020.102104

United Nations. (2024). *Climate action.* https://www.un.org/en/climatechange/what-is-climate-change

United Nations Development Programme [UNDP]. (2024). *The global goals for sustainable development.* https://www.globalgoals.org/

# Chapter 29

# Drama workshop

## The climate conference

Eva Österlind

### Learning outcomes and key terms

The drama processes in this chapter aim to:

- Deepen understanding of how the complexity, based on different perspectives, agendas, and stakeholders, affects efforts towards sustainable development.
- Develop a more integrated view of sustainability issues at all levels.
- Provide an experience of applied drama in learning for sustainability, using body language, improvisation, relaxation, and visualisation, as a resource for (academic) teaching.

| Key sustainability-related outcomes |
| --- |
| **Embodying sustainability values** |
| Valuing sustainability/self-awareness and normative competencies |
| Supporting fairness |
| Promoting nature |
| **Embracing complexity in sustainability** |
| Critical thinking |
| Problem framing/integrated problem-solving competence |

DOI: 10.4324/9781003496359-35

| Envisioning sustainable futures |
| --- |
| Exploratory thinking |
| **Acting for sustainability** |
| Political agency |
| Individual initiative |

## Context of application

The core idea of this drama workshop is to address the big issue of sustainability with open eyes and mind without diminishing the scale of the problem – and avoiding feelings of hopelessness and psychological defence. Another purpose is to explore the global–individual dimension and begin to sort out questions of accountability; what is possible for a single person to do, and what requires decisions on a corporate or political level? The intention is that all participants acknowledge the global threats, stay open to individual responses in terms of thoughts and feelings, become more aware of systemic challenges, and still find energy and motivation to consider choices and actions within their own reach.

This explorative drama process was originally designed for students training to be teachers. Over the years it has been applied in various academic settings to teacher students aiming for primary or secondary level and drama students at undergraduate and postgraduate levels. It has also been part of continuing professional development for in-service school teachers, academic teachers, and applied theatre practitioners. The workshop has been given in Finland, France, Greece, Iceland, New Zealand, Sweden, and the UK, which means it has been applied in various contexts, but always with adult participants (see published research about it here: Österlind, 2018, 2020, 2022; Lehtonen et al, 2020).

The workshop has been carried out with as many as 60+ students, but such large groups are quite challenging and not recommended. Very small groups can also be challenging, not least for participants unfamiliar to drama, as each person becomes more visible and may feel exposed. From 12 to 24 participants is fine, up to 30 is acceptable as long as the space is big enough, while 15–18 would be an ideal group size.

## Step-by-step guidance

Prepare an open space and place chairs for all participants in a circle. A marker board is also needed and a sign for when the teacher/facilitator is in role (e.g. a scarf). The whole process takes 2.5–3 hours including a break, but it is also possible to do the process in 2 or 3 parts, or to choose a single activity and try it out for a few minutes.

1. Introduction.

    a. Stand in a circle (push back the chairs) and introduce yourself.
    b. Ask everyone to say their first name and something they appreciate in nature. Do this round twice if the group is new to each other (and not too large).
    c. Introduce a playful *icebreaker* (see Chapters 4–7 and 13).

2. Facing global challenges.

    a. Let the students sit down in a half circle, facing the marker board. Draw a circle to symbolise the earth and ask them to *brainstorm* challenges to the planet. Note all suggestions on the board (e.g. rising sea levels, loss of species, etc.).
    b. Ask the students to look at what is written. Then offer a brief *relaxation*. Suggest everyone close their eyes (or look down) and go through the body from the feet and legs to the back, arms, neck, top of the head and face, by mentioning the body parts: "*Feel your feet and let them rest for a while… let your face became soft and relaxed*".
    c. When you have talked through the body, ask the students to recall what is written on the board, and ask "*What do you feel in front of these problems?*". Let them ponder this for a little while, identifying one or several emotions. Ask them to "*focus on one feeling and visualise "an object" which symbolises this feeling. It can be a natural object or a man-made artefact*". Ask specific questions, for example, "*What colour is it? What size? What is the surface like – take a close look*". Then ask them to "*store your object in a place where you can find it again*", and finally "*focus on your body again, sitting on the chair, start to move your hands and feet, stretch your arms and legs, and when you are ready – open your eyes*".
    d. Then say "*Talk to the person sitting next to you and tell them about your object.*" Please note, in this case the wording is significant. Explicitly asking the students to talk about their *object* is a strategy to "protect into emotion", as the participants are free to choose if they also want to talk about the feeling the object symbolises, or just talk about the object.

3. Creating still images about the causes.

    a. Ask each pair of students to join another pair, creating groups of four. The task is to talk about "*What are the causes of these global challenges, at a human level?*". Here, you are not asking for scientific reasons like carbon emissions, but, e.g. greed, lack of legislation, and so forth. Check that every group has found some causes.
    b. Ask each group to form a *still image* showing one or several of the identified causes. Encourage them to get on their feet and try out how to show this with their bodies. Suggest they also use gaze, facial expression, and perhaps add chairs, bags, or phones, to clarify and strengthen their message.

    c. Look at the still images one by one. Invite the "audience" to walk around to see better, and ask them "*What do you see?*", "*What are your interpretations?*" "*Anyone else?*". At this point, it is possible to add "*voice buttons*". The teacher touches each person in the still image one by one, in their position, as a sign to say a single word or sentence from a first-person perspective (e.g. "*I'm hungry!*", "*I'm in charge!*"). Finally, ask the performing group what they wanted to put forward. Repeat this process until all groups have presented their images. You may note the causes on the marker board and allow the groups a short debrief.

4. Mingle.

    a. Introduce *mingle* by asking the whole group to stand up and walk around in the open space. When they meet someone, start to talk. After a while others may join, and someone leaves and finds a new person to talk to. Based on the still images, the question for the conversations is "*What needs to be done, and by whom?*".

    b. After some discussions in varying constellations, ask the group to literally stop where they are, and introduce *eavesdropping*. This technique is an alternative to asking each cluster what they have been talking about, which can be a bit "stiff" and repetitive. Eavesdropping means the teacher moves around the space in silence, and when being close to one cluster, they pick up their conversation and continue (as if no one is listening). When the teacher moves on, that cluster is supposed to be silent (this is usually the hardest part). This gives everyone an idea of the topics and issues, and adds an element of unpredictability, as nobody knows where the teacher will go next or how long s/he will let each conversation go on.

Break – with the question "*What needs to be done, and by whom?*" in mind.

5. Preparing a role play.

    a. Prepare for a *role play* about a fictional environmental conference. Together with the students, start by making a list of possible stakeholders on the board (e.g. activists, farmers, CEOs, politicians, researchers, etc.). Then ask everyone to individually choose which *perspective* they want to explore and represent. Create groups (or at least pairs) with the same or similar interests. Ask them to briefly prepare by stating why they will join this conference and what they want to achieve (e.g. a group of politicians or CEOs need to decide if they represent one or several parties or companies, real or fictive, and why they spend time/money to attend the conference). If time allows, ask them also to briefly "interview" each other in pairs about "who they are" (e.g. *Do you like your work, do you have a family/hobby, or what is your view on "climate"?*). Each group also needs to agree on how they, as a group, will to and from the conference (e.g. by metro, canoe, private jet).

    b. When the groups are ready, ask them to leave the room for a minute and explain that when you open the door again, everyone will be in role – even you.

Arrange the chairs in a circle with some space between each group of stake-holders. Put on your "scarf" to signal that you are someone else and pre-pare yourself for a few seconds. The *teacher* will be *in role* as the host/ess, a stressed substitute for the formal chair. The conference, which has been prepared carefully for a long time, is facing a problem. With short notice, you had to change to a less fancy venue.

6. The Climate Conference.

a. Open the door and welcome everybody. Thank them a lot for travelling, especially long-distance guests, and apologise for the changed venue (refer to a local high-end place). Mention that instead you will be at your univer-sity (or what suits your context), "*and it will be nice too*". Then announce that "*as you already know, this conference has no keynote speaker, because it is so important to provide open spaces like this for extended dialogues. You are the main speakers!*"

b. Let the conference participants in and invite them to sit down (in their groups). Ask them to briefly introduce themselves (who they are, where they come from, why they are here) and say something like "*Thrilled to have you here*" to each group before moving on to the next.

c. After this round of presentations, announce that "*It is time for a coffee break! You'll find the tables over here, and of course everything is ecologi-cal and fairtrade, there are all kinds of milk...*". Invite the participants to "*make use of the time to expand your network and talk to persons who are new to you*". While they *mingle in-role*, you may walk around and offer "*More coffee?*".

d. After the "break" ask everyone to sit down again, but now in mixed groups (turn the chairs to form small groups). Let the groups discuss whatever is on the agenda. After a while you may feed in some material, like a graph of carbon emissions (a blue line for the curve turning downwards and a red line for the sky-rocketing curve – also see information in Chapter 1). This diagram can be handed out with or without text (Y for temperature, X for time, or more technical details). Say something like "*Take a look at this diagram and see if it may add anything to your ongoing discussion*".

e. Finish the group discussions by announcing that a delicious lunch will soon be served "*on the terrace*".

f. Invite everybody back to the big circle, to sit in their original groups of stakeholders. Still in-role as the conference host/ess, ask the groups to sum up and say a few words about what they learned or achieved during the conference. After this round, thank everybody for coming, appreciate what has been done (e.g. more insight, new contacts, business deals, etc.), and wish everyone a safe journey back home. Then take off your scarf/sign and step out of role – but ask the students to remain in their roles.

g. Now, it is time for the conference participants to travel back home. Ask the students to arrange the chairs to indicate *how* they will travel, according to their earlier decision (see 5a). Then invite each group to *"get into their vehicle"* and openly share their "true" impressions of the conference, whatever they are, spoken out loud as if nobody is listening. Let all groups talk at the same time to get started, then listen to each group in turn by *eavesdropping* (see above, 4b).

h. When all groups are being heard, ask the students to step out of role and sit down in a circle. Give space for some reflections connected to the role play experience. At this point, you may end this sequence or continue as follows.

7. Observations from a distance.

a. Here, you may introduce a *more-than-human perspective*. Ask the participants to individually choose an animal that lives not too far from the conference venue. Imagine that this particular animal has somehow observed the humans at this conference, and other conferences as well. Ask *"What is being noticed? Tasty food in the garbage bins? The risk of being killed by a taxi?"*. Ask the students to stand up and talk briefly in small groups. Let them share some observations (in first person) from their animals' perspective: *"What have you seen? What is going on?"*.

b. Now, arrange a *conscious alley*. Let all students, still in-role as the animals, line up in two rows facing each other. Encourage the animals to use the opportunity to express what really worries them and give short messages to the humans passing by. Then let one person at a time (or maybe two) slowly walk along the alley, as themselves, while the animals whisper. When all students have walked down the alley and listened to the animals' voices, give them some time to reflect on the experience, rather quietly, with only a few words.

8. Silent introspection.

a. Finally, ask the students to sit down again. Expand the circle a bit (if possible). It is time for another guided relaxation. Start as before (see 2 b), by talking through the body. When this is done, mention that they have been doing a lot during this workshop, sometimes rather intense, like the first game and the role play, sometimes quieter like the conscious alley, the still images, and the brainstorm.

b. Now, ask them to *"go back to their (fictive) object and look closely at it again, see the colour, perhaps touch it… and remember the feeling it symbolises"*. Then ask them to think of something they are able to do, in one way or another, to address these challenges. Say, *"It can be tiny, like changing something when buying food, or making one phone call to a politician. Or it can be a bit more, like reading a book or joining an organisation. The important thing is to think about something that is possible for you to do."* Give some time to think about this and add that it will not be shared, it is private. And ask the final question, *"Are you ready to actually do it?"*.

c. Then, ask them to focus on their body again, sitting on a chair in this room, begin to move and stretch, and open their eyes.

d. Declare that the workshop is over and thank them for their participation. If relevant, as for teacher students, this is the time to go through the activities and point out the various drama techniques. If the workshop is done in another context, just end here, without any deconstruction or educational explanation.

e. Another option is to open for a discussion on possible *joint actions* to address these challenges. This might be more relevant in a course dedicated to sustainability.

This workshop is carefully organised to allow participants with no drama experience to actively take part in drama work. Some techniques which appear in the first part, before the break, are used again in the second part. The still image is the first time the participants use bodily expression and say something in role (one word or sentence), while the teacher pays a lot of attention to the audience. In the first mingle, people talk as themselves, and in the second mingle, they talk in role as conference participants but all at once. Even the teacher is in role as conference host/ess, busy serving coffee, and by doing so also builds belief in the fiction. During the role play everybody is active at the same time, often in smaller groups, meaning still no one is watching. It is not until the improvised "travel back home" that they are asked to act (move and talk) in role, in front of their peers. By that time, usually no one seems to care much about it.

## Framing or pre-work

To prepare for the drama process, a warm-up activity will be useful (see Chapters 4–7). Trying some of these will make drama work more familiar to both the facilitator and the participants. Icebreakers will give the students a hint of what to expect, and their playful character is usually highly appreciated. Role play is a wide concept (see Chapter 2, and for examples of different kinds of role play, see Chapters 8–12 and 21). When it comes to applying teacher-in-role, see Chapters 2 and 25.

## When to use and when not to use

The workshop is designed for university students with varying knowledge about climate change and other challenges to the planet, and without previous drama experience. This is usually the case for a large majority of the participants, but not for all.

The suggested drama process works best for groups with limited, general, or mixed levels of knowledge about global challenges. Students who know little about these problems will learn from other students during the process, thus considerable variations in previous knowledge will not be a problem. Instead, this can be discussed afterwards as it reflects the current situation in society. For students with more qualified knowledge about climate change, the workshop and especially the role play may be seen as superficial.

Students with some drama experience may also find the role play superficial or simplistic. The minimal time for preparation and the imprecise group roles defining the fictive conference participants may lead to stereotypical characters holding predictable views, instead of complex characters exploring dilemmas in a more nuanced way.

The workshop does not require any drama experience, but being familiar with drama work may allow the participants to focus more on the topic (see below).

# Reflections from the field

Applied drama is often seen as a teaching resource to be utilised in other subjects, and put forward as a creative form of learning at all levels. There is increasing evidence to support this claim, although contextual aspects may affect the outcomes. In Swedish higher education drama is often organised as single workshops, which implies some limitations. For instance, students' level of previous studies seems to have an impact on learning for sustainability.

Evaluative questionnaires on how this workshop was received in varying contexts have been answered by university students in Athens, Helsinki, and Stockholm. The respondents represent (a) teacher students for primary level, early in their studies, (b) teacher students for secondary level, final part of their studies, (c) in-service teachers, interested in drama and sustainability, (d) drama students at bachelor level, and (e) drama students at advanced level, experienced drama teachers. A preliminary, comparative analysis (Österlind, 2022) shows considerable differences between these groups in terms of their learning experiences. The differences are connected to previous drama experience and level of teacher training/teaching experience.

Most relevant here is the notion that beginning teacher students were extremely enthusiastic during the workshop (Österlind, 2022). The energy level was very high, and their written responses were very appreciative. But when asked if they had learned something about sustainability, their response was almost non-existent. My interpretation is that these students had not really got to know each other, thus they were absorbed by the playful, interactive drama work as such, which allowed them to get in touch in a less formal way, and as a consequence the topic of sustainability disappeared into the background. Conversely, there is evidence that in-service teachers who took part in three connected drama workshops had clear memories one year later, and some reported changing habits in their daily life as an effect of the drama workshops (Österlind, 2018; Lehtonen et al., 2020). There is also evidence clearly indicating considerable learning experiences both in relation to sustainability and to drama as a resource for teaching (Österlind, 2020, 2022).

## Things to consider

A general piece of advice is to avoid all kinds of costumes and props, like wigs, for the role play. It adds very little but may easily lead to over-acting, turning the role play into a parody. To laugh and have fun while doing drama is perfectly fine, but not all the time. Too much "fooling around" will disturb others and water down the learning experience. The only time to add something (e.g. a scarf, a jacket) is to clearly indicate when you as teacher act as teacher-in-role (and remove it when you step out of role). In the example above, the teacher-in-role as host/ess takes a *low-status position*, making many excuses and working hard to keep everyone happy, in order to be able to encourage and put forward the students-in-role as conference participants in a supportive way.

It might be worth mentioning that the role play is not going to be performed for the others, it happens only once, and the point is to gain experiences. Encourage the students to choose a role or perspective that is far from their own, in order to explore and find out more. This role play can be characterised as rather superficial, so one aspect to discuss afterwards could be the complexity generated by multiple perspectives, dilemmas, and conflicts of interest, and how this reflects why international climate negotiations often seem to be unsuccessful.

## Learning extensions

To address the content, no specialist knowledge is needed, although it is possible to qualify the discussions by asking the students to prepare by readings and lectures on the topic.

If used as an introduction to issues like climate change, this workshop gives the teacher a hint about the students' level of pre-understanding, what they already know. The process touches on the complexity of sustainability, sustainability, from global threats to individual choices, and addresses questions of political and corporate responsibility (and challenges), and issues of social (in)justice like poverty and famine. It also invites a non-human perspective. Any of these aspects can serve as starting points for extended learning in more specific areas, connecting to research/literature in various academic disciplines (e.g. Chapter 12).

## Integrating with assessment

The workshop is designed as a broad, explorative introduction to sustainability, thus assessment is not at the forefront in this context. Instead, you may choose to hand out a couple of open-ended questions about the participants' experiences, what they learned, what they take with them. This gives the participants a moment to reflect, and the facilitator gains valuable insight into how the workshop was received.

# Further reading

For a theoretical framework related to drama workshops for sustainability in higher education, see Lehtonen et al (2020).

For an example of how to combine scientific knowledge, arts-based outdoor experiences, and applied drama work, see Davis and Tarrant (2014).

For an evaluative study on how the current workshop was received by teacher students, see Österlind (2020).

For a comparative analysis on how the current workshop was received by different groups of students, see Österlind (2022).

# References

Davis, S., & Tarrant, M. (2014). Environmentalism, stories and science: Exploring applied theatre processes for sustainability education. *Research in Drama Education: The Journal of Applied Theatre and Performance, 19*(2), 190–194. https://doi.org/10.1080/135697 83.2014.895613

Lehtonen, A., Österlind, E., & Viirret, T. J. (2020). Drama in education for sustainability: Becoming connected through embodiment. *International Journal of Education & the Arts, 21*(19). https://doi.org/10.26209/ijea21n19

Österlind, E. (2018). Drama in higher education for sustainability: Work-based learning through fiction? *Higher Education, Skills and Work-Based Learning, 8*(3), 337–352.

Österlind, E. (2020). "I can be the beginning of what i want to see in the world": Outcomes of a drama workshop on sustainability in teacher education. In V. Brinia & J. Paolo Davim (Eds.), *Designing an innovative pedagogy for sustainable development in higher education* (49–68). Taylor & Francis CRC Press.

Österlind, E. (2022). Drama workshops as single events in higher education – what can we learn? In M. McAvoy & P. O'Connor (Eds.), *The Routledge companion to drama in education* (324–337). Routledge.

# SUSTAINING FUTURE PRACTICE

## Chapter 30

# Rehearsing for change together with colleagues

Radhika Mittal

## Learning outcomes and related terms

The drama processes in this chapter aim to:

- Develop insight into the use of dramatic techniques to engage with 'wicked problems' (Rittel & Webber, 1973).
- Integrate the fields of communication science and environmental communication to promote active, experiential learning.

Key terms and definitions:

- Forum Theatre, forum play, and the spect-actor are defined in Chapter 2.
- Greenwashing – 'the dissemination of false or deceptive information regarding an organisation's environmental strategies, goals, motivations, and actions' (Becker-Olsen & Potucek, 2013, p. 1318).

| Key sustainability-related outcomes |
|---|
| Embodying sustainability values |
| Valuing sustainability/self-awareness and normative competencies |
| Supporting fairness |

DOI: 10.4324/9781003496359-37

| Embracing complexity in sustainability |
| --- |
| Systems thinking |
| Critical thinking |
| Problem framing/integrated problem-solving competence |
| **Envisioning sustainable futures** |
| Futures literacy/anticipatory competence |
| Adaptability |
| Exploratory thinking |
| **Acting for sustainability** |
| Political agency |
| Collective action/strategic/collaboration competence |
| Individual initiative |

# Context of application

This workshop was delivered to around 20 faculty members belonging to a single department at a university in The Netherlands. They included a diverse group of PhD students, lecturers, as well as assistant and associate professors. The workshop ran for 1.5 hours and was facilitated by two people. It was part of a departmental team building event that included reflections on research, vision, and impact for the group as a whole. The workshop was designed to showcase novel and different approaches to classroom engagement, and in the process, supported educational capacity building.

The workshop was formatted to invite educators in the field of communication science to experience the use of hands-on, theatre-based approaches in the classroom and equip them with some tools to use creativity and drama in educational practice. The key focus was on demonstrating how forum play can be applied to 'greenwashing' (a concept that is utilised frequently in one of the courses). The participative format of the workshop aimed to showcase to educators, in an experiential manner, the possibility of engaging the affective dimension in a classroom, creating opportunities for students to practice action and agency, promoting critical thinking and imaginative solutions-focused ideation while sharing power through the creation of a safe space.

# Step-by-step guidance

1. Pre-organisation: pre-organise groups, placing five to eight people within each group. Ensure there are spaces where groups can work on their instructions and rehearse their performances without disturbing each other. Ensure there is a sufficiently large common area where preliminary activities and the final performances can be held.

2. Active Introduction: start with some warm-up theatre activities that can put the participants at ease and create a physically and conversationally engaged atmosphere. These activities can include walking around the common area in different ways, such as walking on their toes, then walking on their heels, walking with hands up and to the side, etc. The facilitator should begin and demonstrate each movement, moving along with the group so that participants do not feel awkward. Another activity could be on *micro dialogues* where participants describe to each other, in pairs, what 'irritates' about teaching and their summer or winter vacation (in the second case, not one word should be true – it can be based entirely on fantasy). The purpose of this is just to elicit a few laughs and make the atmosphere comfortable. If time permits, participants can do a round of relaying their micro dialogues in brief to the entire group. Lastly, participants can practice *push not to win* (MacDonald & Rachel, 2000), where participants form two equal rows facing each other and place their hands, after requesting permission, on the shoulders of the person in front of them. Then they gently push against each other, but the purpose is not to win or push the other person down. It is a gentle exercise of supporting each other while creating light pressure. This is an apt starter to the minor tension forum play can sometimes generate.

3. Explain context and utility: explain why drama can and should be used in classrooms, see Chapter 2 of this book (see Lehtonen et al., 2020; Österlind, 2018). Explain the specific relevance of drama practice to the subject matter being explored (in this case, it was corporate communication). Here, you could compare the inquiry processes in theatre and science to substantiate the insights that theatre can bring to structured learning (see Ødegaard, 2023).

4. Agenda: set the agenda for the next hour so participants know what to expect. Discuss what forum play is and how it came into being, and the steps that will follow: working within their pre-assigned groups, preparing and practising a play as per the theme provided, enacting their performance voluntarily, one at a time, and repeating the performance to enable audience input and participation. Each play will be performed twice, and spectators will become 'spectactors'. There will be time carved out for reflection. Finally, support educators in relating the technique to their subject matter and discuss strategies and opportunities for applying the method to their teaching.

5. Forum play situation: introduce the theme for the forum play. In this case, it was greenwashing (see Becker-Olsen & Potucek, 2013 for more information). The situation provided should be distinct and the instructions indicative but not prescriptive. During this workshop, the following situation was described with the accompanying instructions:

There is a press conference being held by the representatives of a company that participates in greenwashing. The scene includes the CEO of the company, its head of Corporate Social Responsibility, 1 or 2 journalists (one pro, one anti), and activists.

Instructions:

- ■ Develop a scene of 2–3 minutes with dialogue, movement, and action – as you like.
- ■ The characters must include an oppressor and a protagonist (victim), as well as other negotiators and bystanders. The role play should let the audience explore the issue.
- ■ Escalate the problem slowly. End badly with a conflict at its peak.
- ■ The scene does not have to be perfect – the task is to show very clearly what the specific problem is, in the context of greenwashing – and it must escalate into a conflicted ending.
- ■ Do not care about solutions at all but focus on showing the conflict very clearly.
- ■ Everyone should have a role. Your position in the drama does not have to reflect your own opinion.
- ■ Each group can take their own corner to prepare. Preparation time is 15 minutes.

6. Preparation: after introducing the theme and the instructions for the activity, respond to queries, if any, and then allow the groups to prepare. As the groups prepare, walk around and respond to questions if any. Make a mental note of which groups seem to have developed rich narratives and followed the instructions closely. Remind the groups at 5- and 10-minute marks of the time they have remaining for preparation. You may decide the time frameworks based on the time you allocate for the entire activity.

7. Performance: create the space for performance by setting up a stage-like arena (it does not have to be a raised surface) and arranging chairs in a manner where performances can be easily viewed by the remaining members of the group (if possible, in a semi-circle). When all groups are ready, ask everyone to settle in and explain, in further detail, the guidelines for each performance:

- ■ Each group plays the scene until the conflict peaks. The facilitator checks in with the audience at the end of the performance to ensure the problem is being understood and the actors are being recognised in their roles, primarily the oppressor and the oppressed. Can the audience identify areas or characters (among the oppressed) where interventions are possible to transform the scenario being presented through a solutions-focused lens? (There is space here for a brief one-minute reflection, either individual or as a paired discussion.)
- ■ The same group then re-enacts the scene. Any member of the audience can intervene at any point of the performance by shouting STOP, then stepping in to replace an oppressed character. The audience member can bring in new dialogue, movement, and other tools to modify the situation, and therefore, the ending, through possibly unexpected but realistic and believable new arguments or actions. Other actors are accordingly expected to improvise their dialogues and actions in an extemporaneous manner.

■ The participants should use realistic approaches, remain respectful, and abstain from any real or pantomimed violence. The key is to stay fluid throughout the process; the performance is about rehearsing for real change and trying to find openings for solutions by understanding and playing with varied perspectives.

Once the guidelines are clear, one of the groups may volunteer to perform. If no group volunteers, you can select a group based on your observations of their preparations. Follow the steps above for each group. The re-enactment and intervention process by a 'spectactor' can be repeated a couple of times by each group, depending on the time allocated to the activity. If no audience member volunteers to step in (this is rare), you can either encourage someone in the audience to jump in, or ask for suggestions from the audience at the end of the performance on what the oppressed character might try to do.

8. Reflections: at the end of all of the performances, or as many performances as possible, create a safe, reflective space. This is especially important for exploring how educators experienced the process as participants, and also for demonstrating that a discussion is key at the end of a forum play. The reflection could begin with simple questions on how this activity made the educators feel, and whether they experienced any lightbulb moments or had any thoughts about the purpose, application, and impact of the activity. It is good to touch upon the purpose and utility of forum play, for example, in re-thinking pre-set ideas, encouraging creativity, enabling empowerment, bringing unexpected solutions to the fore, and in shaking up the frame or the narrative as we know it. Consider also, different ways in which this activity can be integrated into the subject matter, and the kinds of educational material that would optimally lend itself to this form of learning. Finally, remind educators that the success of this activity depends on creating a safe and supportive environment and enabling fluid and interpretative spaces.

## Framing or pre-work

Pre-reading about forum play may be helpful (see Chapters 13–16), as well as icebreakers if you are a beginner to these techniques (see Chapters 4–7). Confidence often comes second to practice, so bravery in integrating some aspects of forum play into your own classroom is recommended. This enables you to respond competently to practical questions and solve any hiccups or hurdles that may present themselves.

## When to use and when not to use

Offering this 'training of trainers' is appropriate and effective when the participants are open, engaged, and interested in exploring new teaching and learning practices.

This particular workshop was an invited one. Participating in and adapting to such an activity requires stepping out of one's comfort zone, so it is important to identify which group or community is open to such an experience. Start with those educators who are already open to using the power of storytelling, creativity, and engaged activities in the classroom and limit the number of participants to 25 to enable effective time management and to support active participation.

## Reflections from the field

Training the trainers can be more daunting than simply experimenting with a new activity in one's own classroom. After using forum play, I found students were quite enthused. Student evaluations indicated they felt creativity was essential in dealing with the sustainability transition, in considering various circumstances that impact different lives, and in communicating. They found it hopeful, empowering, and easier to deal with emotions in an interactive manner. They felt emboldened to step out of their comfort zone, actively participate, and grasp the multitude of approaches that might be possible in dealing with difficult situations. Movement was reported as a key enabling factor. If you are the first to use forum play in the classroom, you might want to report student observations and reactions to help colleagues understand the impact of such an activity.

During the workshop, the activity resulted in an initially cautious but open acceptance. I witnessed a shift from relatively unprepared, uncertain faces to engaged, active participants who showcased moments of brilliance while taking the narrative into their own hands as 'spectactors'. There were some hiccups – for instance, one colleague interrupted the play during its first run. However, for the most part, colleagues engaged whilst also bringing their maturity, vast teaching experience, and subject knowledge to their performances. Moving forward, the colleagues who felt comfortable and enthused by this new approach adopted it into their own teaching.

One colleague used the scene and formatting from the workshop with minor modifications for integration into the main course that was offered in the program for undergraduate students. This attempt was met with success. Another colleague consulted with me to integrate the activity as a stakeholder engagement exercise in a research proposal for a grant application. On my part, I appreciated the empowerment and confidence offered through drama, the realisation that I could build on my own understanding of using drama in the classroom by teaching it to others, and the liberating experience of using one's entire body-mind apparatus, whether in the role of a participant, or an instructor.

## Things to consider

It is important to nurture an open and supportive environment while training mature individuals. Consider their concerns and uncertainties but support them in pushing their comfort zone. At the end of the training, some colleagues said they would be afraid to push too much with their students. I could understand their concerns and responded positively, offering support, if required, to develop the activities. You could also offer to provide support as an experienced co-facilitator. However, it is important to note that an educator should attempt performance-based techniques only if they feel comfortable in doing so. Sometimes this comfort level may be a result of practice with other colleagues and of some trial and error in their own classroom. Reading literature that supports and outlines the use of this practice can also be helpful. From a practical perspective, open space, ample natural or artificial light, the ability and permission to move around tables and chairs and use them as props, a blank whiteboard, spare writing material, technical equipment to project the presentation, and instructions for the first part of the training are likely to be needed and so should be arranged beforehand.

## Learning extensions

This workshop can help train educators and offer possibilities for integration of drama-based approaches into the teaching and learning unit of a faculty. A drama-based module can be developed where different techniques and approaches are documented and made available to teachers. Regular training sessions, problem-solving round tables, and sharing of experiences can be organised. Success stories and subject-specific ideas can be shared to distribute ideas and enable other teachers to gain confidence. The integration of forum play into a large undergraduate course, where I taught also helped the course coordinator structure the format for this activity, showed us that subject matter can be leveraged to activate the play and enhance learning goals. For example, in the field of corporate communication, crisis communication, issue management, stakeholder engagement, and topics within Corporate Social Responsibility can form the theoretical base for developing original arguments while presenting forum play. Similarly, conceptual understanding from the course material and nuanced understanding of the dynamics between different social groups and institutions can support the practical interventions that a 'spect-actor' brings to their intervention.

## References

Becker-Olsen, K., & Potucek, S. (2013). Greenwashing. In S. O. Idowu, N. Capaldi, L. Zu, & A. D. Gupta (Eds.), *Encyclopedia of corporate social responsibility* (pp. 1318–1323). Springer. https://doi.org/10.1007/978-3-642-28036-8_104.

Lehtonen, A., Österlind, E., & Viirret, T. L. (2020). Drama in education for sustainability: Becoming connected through embodiment. *International Journal of Education & the Arts, 21*(19). https://doi.org/10.26209/ijea21n19.

MacDonald, S., & Rachel, D. (2000). Boal's Arsenal of Games. Retrieved from https://organizingforpower.files.wordpress.com/2009/03/games-theater-of-oppressed.pdf

Ødegaard, M. (2023). Using drama in science education and for sustainability issues. In D. McGregor & D. Anderson (Eds.), *Learning science through drama: Exploring international perspectives* (pp. 69–86). Springer International Publishing.

Österlind, E. (2018). Drama in higher education for sustainability: Work-based learning through fiction? *Higher Education, Skills and Work-Based Learning, 8*(3), 337–352.

Rittel, H. W. J., & Webber, M. M. (1973). Dilemmas in a general theory of planning. *Policy Sciences, 4*(2), 155–169. https://doi.org/10.1007/bf01405730

## Chapter 31

# Future developments to embrace a 'pedagogy of passion'

Tony Wall, Sarah Jayne Williams, Eva Österlind, Laura Dixon, and Dave Soehren

## Pedagogies of passion

What brought us together for this book was a shared curiosity about channelling our collective inquiry around a passion for pedagogy – an applied drama and performance approach which is rich, complex and which excites us, as much as it excites our students. As you reach the end of this book, the importance of the 'pedagogies of passion' idea feels as relevant now as was over a decade ago when it was penned (Shrivastava, 2010). Back then, it was described as 'a holistic pedagogy that integrates physical and emotional or spiritual learning with traditional cognitive (intellectual) learning about sustainable management' (p. 443). But the idea also seems relevant to the people who engage with passionate pedagogical work, like applied drama and performance, representing something deeper and stronger in the higher education facilitator's own identity and interests. It represents the facilitator's passion for change, and that is why it is important to those who embrace applied drama and performance work or even small elements of it.

During the project associated with this book, facilitators (higher education teachers) across disciplines and topic areas, including those with and without any experience of applied drama and performance, explored their experiences in implementing

DOI: 10.4324/9781003496359-38

**267**

the ideas and tools presented in this book. These facilitators identified a range of aspects that are still lingering areas of inquiry which will take themselves into their own futures of using such high impact practices in higher education. We share them here to suggest possible ways of handling those aspects to enable the deeper transformational work of high impact pedagogies. These futures consider:

■ How to manage your energy in undertaking highly interactive pedagogical work?

■ How to enrich the characters that participants bring to life in applied drama and performance work, especially if students (the participants) are new to the field?

■ How to reach across systems which impact sustainability, to expand learning in new and systemic directions?

■ How to scale up highly interactive forms of pedagogy in large groups and classes?

■ How to utilise and embrace digital pedagogies in the context of applied drama and performance work?

## Managing your energy

Applied drama and performance work can become emotionally exhausting, especially for facilitators with a more introverted personality. This can be carefully managed in ways which are already familiar to higher education teachers who use interactive methods, as well as experienced applied drama and performance practitioners. Ways of managing your energy include:

■ **Entering a 'performance role'.** This approach involves the facilitator taking on a specific persona or character that aligns with their teaching objectives, creating a psychological separation between their personal identities and professional roles. Such a strategy could aid in managing the emotional complexities of teaching by providing a buffer against stress and personalisation of conflicts with students. Additionally, this detachment facilitates a smoother transition out of the professional role at the end of the teaching session, minimising emotional carryover into personal life. Experience, from the project related to this book, suggests that practice over time helps facilitators *shift* into roles quickly (immediately) once familiar and also helps find one's own way to bring those roles to *life*.

■ **Entering 'facilitator mode'.** This is another, slightly different approach. A classic quality of an actor is a high level of presence, but a 'facilitator mode' does not suggest that the facilitator enters a role, as in being someone else. Instead, the facilitator is advised to be highly *present as oneself*, in the teaching situation. Although, in line with the former approach, it may be useful to enter a 'teaching mode' or 'facilitator persona'. This serves to combine a high level of personal presence 'here and now' with a professional approach. A high level of presence is not the same as being a very active teacher, trying to do the work 'for the students' or or to 'earn their own salary', which are not an uncommon views on what a good teacher is supposed to do. The facilitator mode implies doing the hard work when preparing for interactive teaching events and be willing to withdraw, observe and let participants be active and explore the pre-planned learning situation as it unfolds. Of course, the facilitator is always in charge, ready to inform, guide, and take the process further.

■ **Spacing out interventions.** Incorporating space between interventions involves deliberate planning to alternate between periods of direct facilitator engagement and intervals where students independently explore and assimilate new information. Specifically, you should look for a rhythm or flow that suits you, your students, and the current activity. Just like the facilitator, the participants need to shift between more playful or intense activities that ask for a lot of (cognitive) attention and more distanced, verbal reflections. This mitigates the risk of facilitator (and participant) overload by preventing the exhaustion that can come from continuous active monitoring and interaction but also promotes a learning environment conducive to developing student autonomy and self-directed learning skills. By strategically planning these periods of 'intervention' and then 'retreat', facilitators can effectively manage their energy, allowing opportunities to recharge and reflect on the educational journey's progress.

■ **Building a team of facilitators to share the activity.** Collaborating with colleagues to share the workload and responsibilities enhances the educational process by pooling diverse strengths and ideas. This collective approach also manages the risk of burnout, fosters a supportive environment, and enriches the learning experience for students through varied perspectives, personas, and methodologies. The exchange of teaching strategies among team members can lead to more engaging sessions and a revitalisation of teaching practices. Whilst it might take time to develop a capacity across colleagues, it can also build a team cohesion and spirit alongside a joyful experimentation and creativity within the teaching team.

# Enriching participant characterisations

As can be seen throughout this book, many approaches invite participants to take on a role. Sometimes, students (or staff) might find this challenging, perhaps because of limited experience of how a role might be lived out (e.g. what a person within a role might say or do) or because the role is just so distant from their own experience in life. Or perhaps it is because they are unable to enact the role in front of others (e.g. because of anxiety), or because of cultural expectations limiting how someone may act in front of others (e.g. relating to public display of gendered roles or challenges in educational spaces). This might result in participants resisting involvement in the process or characters fixating in a position, both of which limit the possible explorations that can follow. Here, the aspiration is to provide alternative ways to accommodate different participants so they can benefit from the experience. Ways of enriching participants' characters in applied drama and performance include:

- **Choice of role.** Enabling some level of choice in the characters or roles that participants want to play is a key aspect that can support enriched engagement. Enable participants to choose roles where they feel there is some sort of affiliation or some level of confidence in knowing how the role plays out in real life. Most importantly, encourage the participant to choose a role they want to explore, and never impose a specific role on someone who isn't willing to try it out. If this happens with the flow of events, provide the opportunity to re-design the role. An alternative is to allow students to prepare for a role by creating opportunities for dialogue or 'interviews' in pairs to give some deeper richness to a role (e.g. participants could interview each other as the designated role, with questions like 'Do you thrive at work? Do you have a hobby?').

- **Provide or create character descriptors.** Some approaches to applied drama and performance can involve the participants either becoming familiar with roles or personas through either creating a detailed profile of a role/person (if there is time) or reading about a role/person before their participation is required (using role cards, like in a 'murder mystery'). You can decide how detailed these profiles should be, and include, for example, the preferences of these people and how they typically react to certain 'hot topics', to phrases, or to other roles. It is useful here to indicate where, when, and to what extent the role descriptions might compromise or flex their opinions to give permission to being flexible in the character.

- **Private 'rehearsal' space to explore ideas before presenting to others.** If the tools you are implementing involve some element of presenting something to a whole group, it can be helpful to allocate some time to participants to rehearse what they would like to in a more private space. This should not be too long as to build expectations of 'perfection', but long enough so they can rehearse together to refine their performance at least once.

- **Facilitators pause the activity to invite the student (or staff member) to try out different responses that may be possible.** If you, as the facilitator of the experience, find roles become fixed or too rigid and it is not creating movement in the experience, you can feel free to pause the process. The pause provides an opportunity to invite alternative possibilities of what might happen in the scenario. For example, you can ask to hear the characters' thoughts or suggestions about what to say next. You can then return to the process and invite the participants to respond slightly differently to see what happens. It is then important to draw attention to how the alternative perspective impacts the process and the outcomes. When paused, focus on 'the topic' not 'the enactment' (normally everyone is in role without an audience). In the context of sustainability learning, a core principle is to explore, to try other perspectives, and to pay attention to own responses. As the facilitator and participants may well be new to these formats, it is recommended to put aside assessments related to performing and instead focus on meaning and learning.

■ **Positive reinforcement.** The power of positive reinforcement cannot be underestimated, and can be delivered through a subtle smile or nod by the facilitator to show positive achievement. Or it might be stepping out of role in the process to give full attention to the 'message' that is being communicated. But it is also useful to give positive reinforcement by more subtle encouragement like saying 'stay with it' to progress explorations. As above, it is important to avoid anything that draws attention to how well something was done (i.e. its technical qualities).

# Reaching across sustainability systems to expand learning

In exploring solutions to complex or difficult sustainability issues, students can sometimes focus their thinking on the immediate, known context or role. This can limit creative thinking about what needs to change or creative solutions which cross current boundaries or systems. Within these contexts, there are a number of ways to open up thinking:

■ Facilitators can pause the activity to invite the student (or staff member) to try out different perspectives, systems, or roles. Here, gently pausing the activity can invite these new perspectives or systems, but it might need some additional learning or vocabulary to enable the new insights or perspectives.

■ Facilitators might add additional learning or vocabulary around the wider environmental factors which impact the sustainability of the solutions/actions: this might include introducing particular Sustainable Development Goals (SDGs) which might impact (or stop) the implementation of their creative solutions in the future.

■ Facilitators might add learning or vocabulary about systems and systemic thinking in relation to enabling and constraining conditions: here, working with 'synthesis reports' of the IPCC (Intergovernmental Panel on Climate Change, see https://www.ipcc.ch/), you can consider key facts beyond the SDGs and introduce wider conditions which might impact numerous SDGs.

# Scaling-up: small to large group impacts

Often, applied drama and performance practices are seen as working only in small groups, but examples in this book demonstrate how they can be expressed in the context of larger groups, too (see Chapters 21 and 29). A key principle here is thinking about pedagogy as an 'event', which has been developed by very large-scale universities in Australia and the US. This idea rests on an understanding of pedagogy as non-linear. Instead of being understood as a linear transferral of knowledge, pedagogy should be recognised as pedagogy should be recognised as an 'ecosystem' that is a dynamic (sometimes chaotic) experience that unfolds in specific moments of teaching and learning (Bryant, 2024). Advocates of ecosystem thinking in learning highlight its potential to broaden students' horizons by encouraging innovation and collaboration through a 'crowd' approach (Ardner, 2006).

Since Surowiecki (2005) outlined the 'wisdom of crowds', it is clear that the aggregation of knowledge and experiences found within groups often results in decisions that are better than could have been made by any single member of the group alone. Although social pressure may have an impact on outcomes, in general, crowds perform to a higher level and more consistently than individuals working alone (Simoiu et al., 2019). By leveraging the benefits of the crowd, ecosystem thinking moves away from traditional linear educational models, driven by either the fear of failure or the pursuit of rewards, towards a more dynamic understanding of learning influenced by the collective insights and experiences of the group (Ardner, 2006). It promotes a learning environment where the intersections of various life experiences and professional backgrounds amongst students and staff contribute to a richer, more collaborative educational journey. To benefit from the power of applied drama and performance in large-scale educational contexts, the following points are vital:

- ■ Understand the wider ecosystem: recognise that the application of performance and drama in a large-scale teaching and learning context does not happen in a vacuum but occurs within a broader ecosystem. In particular, the learning experience should take account of the fact that students and staff not only bring different experiences to the learning environment, but that they also operate within a wider institutional context, with specific learning outcomes which students and staff are expected to meet (Bryant, 2024).
- ■ Responsive design: develop adaptable teaching strategies that respond to the dynamic ecosystem. Be open to adjusting content, methods, and goals based on emerging needs and opportunities, but avoid reducing complexity – it can be the complexity itself that provides students with the best learning outcomes (Gough, 2013).
- ■ Embrace emergent learning: encourage students to explore unexpected pathways, engage with real-world challenges and learn from unplanned interactions within the ecosystem (Ardner, 2006).

- Co-create content: collaborate with students to engage in reciprocal learning where everyone contributes and benefits (Huber et al., 2023).
- Leverage digital tools: explore online platforms, social media, and virtual spaces to foster connections between students in large-scale groups. Use technology for documentation, reflection, and sharing of applied performance and drama projects (Allen et al., 2021; Petrović & Pale, 2021).

# New frontiers of digital learning

The final area which occupied the reflections of our project relates to the ways in which we engage in high impact teaching using applied drama and performance in digital spaces. This project started when the global situation was filled with precarity from the 2020 pandemic. Whilst we still progressed during the pandemic, our initial practice sharing involved applied drama and performance online through standard online conferencing facilities such as MS Teams and Zoom (i.e. not specialised space of technology). We observed many of the activities working well with clear instructions and the extensive use of breakout rooms, but we did not delve into the emerging practices of Artificial Intelligence (AI), which is ripe for interactional work typical for the drama and performance work discussed in this book. Our reflections on developing this work in digital spaces include:

- High impact applied drama and performance work for sustainability can be conducted using standard teleconferencing facilities: the use of breakout rooms is essential to creating more intimate digital spaces where rehearsal and dialogue can happen. Other tools can be adopted too, such as digital 'whiteboards' to capture ideas and dialogue.
- Digital tools in teleconferencing facilities can enrich and enable rapid feedback during applied drama and performance experiences. Digital tools such as polling can rapidly collect reflections or get opinions from those engaging in the process (other examples include Jamboard, Slido, and Kahoot! – it is worth exploring each of these and to keep up to date, as they can become outdated very quickly).
- Interactive digital tools, facilitated by AI, provide rehearsal opportunities. There are many platforms that can be utilised, the most famous of which is currently ChatGPT (but others include Claude, Google Bard, Bing AI, YouChat, etc.). For example, ChatGPT can help students create characters and profiles, create storylines, create scripts, create ideas for performances, each of which gives ideas as to how to enrich character and story. At the same time, ChatGPT (and other similar Large Language Models) can become and enact a role or character. This potential means students can talk with the technology, creating new opportunities for real time rehearsal or enactment of a conversation 'as if' the technology is indeed the character with which to engage. And it also

becomes very easy for students to make slight tweaks in a character profile and/or storyline, to very quickly test how slight differences in interactions or conversations may progress differently and conclude with alternative outcomes. This area is rapidly developing, and so some of the conversational activities between two people – presented within this book – may well become available through person-to-(virtual)-person platforms, in a way which is highly scalable (without a facilitator needing to be present in the moment).

A general aim – and challenge – for all education is to build bridges or facilitate connections between the individual student and the learning content. This is especially the case in the so-called theoretical education present in many academic disciplines. If this fails, the impact of education, in terms of applying new practices or changing behaviour, is likely to decrease. Another 'eternal' challenge is student motivation. It can be raised by extrinsic means, but intrinsic motivation is far more effective and lasting. In higher education, the teaching pattern, driven by contextual factors (like group size, lecture halls, etc.) and (norms connected to) expectations from academic teachers as well as students, is mainly based on lectures, individual reading and written exams. This pattern underestimates the intrinsic power of human interaction, shared experiences, and joint reflection. Playfulness and creativity have a huge potential for learning, generating energy and motivation, and providing bridges for knowledge integration. It is time to welcome explorative, high impact forms of teaching and learning, like applied drama and performance, into The Academy.

## Further reading

Hermes, J., & Rimanoczy, I. (2018). Deep learning for a sustainability mindset. *The International Journal of Management Education, 16*(3), 460–467. https://doi.org/10.1016/j.ijme.2018.08.001

Principles for Responsible Management Education. (2023). *i5 Playbook – Transforming Business Education with 5 Impactful Methods.* Online publication (open access): https://i5.unprme.org/

## References

Ardner, R. (2006). Match your innovation strategy to your innovation ecosystem. *Harvard Business Review, 84*(4), 98.

Allen, B., McGough, A. S., & Devlin, M. (2021). Toward a framework for teaching artificial intelligence to a higher education audience. *ACM Transactions on Computing Education, 22*(2), 1–29. https://dl.acm.org/doi/10.1145/3485062.

Bryant, P. (2024). Learning design ecosystems thinking: Defying the linear imperative and designing for higher education at-scale. *Journal of Work-Applied Management.* https://doi.org/10.1108/jwam-11-2023-0123.

Gough, N. (2013). Towards deconstructive nonalignment: A complexivist view of curriculum, teaching and learning. *South African Journal of Higher Education, 27*(5), 1213–1233. https://www.journals.ac.za/sajhe/article/view/3606.

Huber, E., Lê, N. C., Nguyen, H. T., & Wall, T. (2023). Co-design for connected learning at scale: A cross-cultural review of guidance. *Higher Education, Skills and Work-Based Learning.* https://doi.org/10.1108/HESWBL-05-2023-0106

Petrović, J., & Pale, P. (2021). Achieving scalability and interactivity in a communication skills course for undergraduate engineering students. *IEEE Transactions on Education,* 1–10. https://doi.org/10.1109/te.2021.3067098

Shrivastava, P. (2010). Pedagogy of passion for sustainability. *Academy of Management Learning & Education, 9*(3), 443–455. https://doi.org/10.5465/amle.9.3.zqr443.

Simoiu, C., Sumanth, C., Mysore, A., & Goel, S. (2019). Studying the "wisdom of crowds" at scale. *Proceedings of the AAAI Conference on Human Computation and Crowdsourcing, 7,* 171–179.

Surowiecki, J. (2005). *The wisdom of crowds.* Anchor.

## Chapter 32

# Merging academic content and explorative teaching formats

Eva Österlind

## How to make space for applied drama in the academic course curriculum?

Introducing highly interactive forms of teaching like applied drama or performance in academic courses can be challenging due to the firm traditions of academic teaching. Higher education courses, not least in humanities and social sciences, are normally quite dense with a heavy load of course literature or mandatory reading, often combined with only a few lessons or learning opportunities other than lectures and individual reading. But new, more varied teaching formats are often requested by students.

Developing teaching formats which widen the idea of how academic teaching can be delivered and thus be more inclusive towards students with varying backgrounds is often recognised as teaching skills advancement and adds to your educational portfolio. Such initiatives are usually appreciated, at least by some parts of a university, and recognised in faculties' and departments' continuing efforts to improve teaching and learning. Taking this into account, try things out and elaborate your teaching in a transparent way, announce it as development work, keep a log of what you want to achieve, what you did, how it was received by the students, and maybe even publish your findings in a journal.

DOI: 10.4324/9781003496359-39

If you are keen to try out some new elements in your teaching, but cannot see any possibilities within the formal schedule, offer a voluntary workshop to students – present it as a joint exploration. This means you will have to spend time on planning and facilitating the extra-curricular event, maybe even without being 'paid' for it. Of course, this is not sustainable in the long run, but it can be worth doing once or twice to get it embedded into the curriculum later on. If you want to try this strategy, make sure that you pay attention to how to evaluate this input in a trustworthy manner. Students' evaluations, if they are positive, will probably be one of the reasons to add something new to the syllabus. A workshop or new teaching format may also have an impact on students' results in exams, but that might be more difficult to know for sure.

The key to successfully introduce an element of applied drama or performance in any academic subject will be to merge the drama work with the course content, either in terms of general theories, models, or perspectives, or by addressing a specific aspect or problem. In applied drama, the purpose can be anything from scanning the students' pre-understanding of a topic to examine what they have learned towards the end of a course, clarifying something complicated, addressing dilemmas, or building a bridge between theory and personal experiences.

Below, we share advice about the merging process, as inspiration for how to integrate elements of explorative learning, like applied drama, into your academic teaching.

## Pinpointing a purpose

Before you start, it is recommended to have a clear idea about what you want to address or change in your teaching practice, what you want to achieve, and consider what you believe applied drama or performance may add. In other words, you should be ready to answer the question 'Why are we doing this?'. *Identify a problem* or something you want to *improve*. If you just want to try something new or add some fun, that is good enough, as long as you know the purpose.

Applied drama and performance can be utilised to *introduce a new topic*, a subject-specific content. In this case, the interactive teaching can be based on fairly open questions to initiate students' thinking about the topic. It will also give you a hint about the students' previous knowledge, possible misunderstandings or lack of basic knowledge. If the latter becomes evident, it should be fully accepted (i.e. simply noticed) and taken as an excellent starting point to identify knowledge gaps – together with the students. If students feel accepted and invited, it may contribute to increased motivation for learning.

Interactive practices can also be useful to explore *theoretical perspectives*. At a more general level, it may be suitable to find the essence of varying methodological approaches, and then compare them based on a deeper understanding. This could be done by close reading of relevant literature to inform group discussions, to be presented in embodied still images followed by joint reflection. Another example could be to take a close look into research ethics, by role playing based on experienced or plausible, ethically problematic situations.

Applied drama can also be used to unpack *theoretical concepts*. One example is to go deeper into a certain aspect of socio-cultural theory, like the concept of 'habitus' (Bourdieu, 1990) and literally explore what it means and how it is manifested in everyday situations, by activities like embodied interactions on social status (Johnstone, 1981, Chapter 4) or forum play (Österlind, 2008, 2011, Chapter 15). Another example concerns the concept of *nature-based solutions* (Chapter 8). Please note that this can be applied also in natural sciences and technology. To surprise or challenge the students by introducing unfamiliar learning activities, e.g. inviting them to use their senses and imagination and share their experiences and thoughts with each other, may contribute to learning in all disciplines.

Finally, applied drama can also be very useful to *improve the learning environment* and generate a positive classroom climate. This is often recognised in education for young children but deserves attention in higher education too. For instance, to dare to ask questions is essential for learning, not only for the individual student but for the whole class. An open atmosphere, where prestige and competition are downplayed and joint knowledge seeking and understanding are encouraged, is a priority. An open atmosphere and a sense of community may strengthen students' engagement and motivation to learn. A positive classroom climate often appears as a side-effect of applying drama for content-specific learning (see Chapters 2 and 4–7 for icebreakers).

# Creating support for applied drama and performance in the course curriculum

Hopefully, you have already gained inspiration from the chapters in this book, and if you just want to try something 'quick and easy', it may not need a lot of preparation. But if you want to do something more substantial, like a workshop or two, you must consider how these activities can be relevant and tied to the course content and the syllabus. Strategies mentioned in this book include:

- Asking for advice from experienced colleagues or experts in applied drama if available.
- Presenting some elements of drama or performance to colleagues, who want to find out more about new ways of teaching (e.g. Chapter 30).
- Including relevant research articles and creating an interplay between research and applied drama/performance activities (e.g. Chapter 12).
- Connecting the applied drama work to assessment either directly, by including individual reflection as part of a written examination, or indirectly as preparation for presentations and other forms of examination (e.g. Chapter 8).
- Evaluating new elements of teaching systematically from the students' point of view, but also from your own perspective, and present the outcome to relevant staff in your academic context (e.g. Chapter 13).

## Course content as point of departure

The course content is the most obvious point of departure when planning for applied drama. Look for something that can be understood as *relations*, an interaction between entities. In most cases, this will appear between humans, but it can also be other kinds of relations. When there is interaction, there are potential obstacles and maybe even dilemmas. Think about what is problematic, or what can be problematised, to make an exploration through drama worthwhile.

For example, if you want to work on a concept like 'empathy', search for tensions, meeting points, and interactive situations where it can be explored. It might not be where the drama work starts, you may need to create a context, a fictive situation with role characters, and gradually build up some internal tensions or external challenges to increase the participants' motivation to become involved in the explorative situation. For a totally different area, like mathematics, again, look for relational aspects or dimensions, e.g. it could be possible to prepare and experience an enacted, embodied sequence of events, that afterwards can be described and written as an equation.

If the explorative interaction takes place *before* the theory or concept is presented, the students will have an embodied experience and pre-understanding. Thus, when the concept is then introduced, its ability to capture and condense practice becomes evident, and the theoretical understanding increases. To achieve this, the facilitator needs to direct the gaze by pointing out the interface between the fictive, embodied activity and the theoretical concept. Another crucial aspect of learning is to allocate time and pay attention to joint reflections, as the reflective phase is when most of the learning occurs.

Sometimes it can be hard to find any relational aspects related to specific content, so you can create contexts where the relational aspect can be developed. You can, for instance, establish two (or more) teams of researchers who work on different hypotheses within the same area. Here, let the teams prepare an application for a research grant and try to convince the funder at 'a funding meeting'. Or, work in a historical context, asking students to try and solve a specific problem, only using the knowledge and instruments that was available to them during that period of time. These are only attempts to generate ideas in various disciplines and should be adapted and developed by experts in their respective fields.

## Explorative interaction for sustainability

This book is an outcome of a project called *Explorative Inter-Action in Higher Education for Sustainability*. Based on a call for higher education to contribute to transformation by educating for sustainability, the project investigated how applied drama and performance may encourage transformational learning and how such approaches could be merged with academic subjects and applied by university teachers across academic fields.

The project convened international workshops involving higher education teachers from applied drama and theatre, applied ecology, business, creative practice, economics, engineering, education, health and society, management, media and communication, science education, political science, and sustainability science. Organised by book contributors Daw, Fries, Hallgren, Österlind, and Wall, participants came from universities across Denmark, Finland, Latvia, the Netherlands, Norway, Turkey, the UK, and Sweden. The first workshop in Sweden shared practices and then invited participants to plan, carry out, and evaluate some of the teaching formats they had experienced back in their own institutions. The second workshop created a pool of data, shared teaching experiences, and discussed learning – and collaboratively developed conference contributions, outlines of research articles, and this book proposal, based on cases from all universities. A final workshop undertook comparative analysis, co-writing, and praxis development. Overall, the project generated tentative answers to the questions of the project (outlined in Chapter 1):

- If applied drama may contribute to developing Green Competences among students in higher education – how can it be adopted by university teachers with no previous drama experience? All chapters give concrete, detailed answers to this question – half of the chapters are written by those with no prior experience, and half are written for those with no experience, by and also for academics in the fields of applied drama and performance.
- Which forms of applied drama are more accessible, more likely to be tried out by teachers in fields like science, technology, business and other disciplines? Based on the participants' reports, role play and forum play draw the most attention and thus appear to be more graspable for beginners in applied drama. Icebreakers also gained a lot of interest and were widely applied, and some performative interventions were carried out. More complex, extended drama processes were only applied by persons who already had substantial experience in applied drama or performance.
- How is such interactive teaching received by the students? The interventions were often highly appreciated by the students. So far, this is only tentative but in line with previous studies (e.g. Österlind, 2020). A systematic analysis of lesson plans, students' evaluations, and other materials is needed to draw more solid conclusions. For a critical discussion of students' learning and the outcome of single drama workshops, see Österlind (2022).
- What do the students learn, and how can the possible impact of applied drama in teaching for sustainability be evaluated in a reasonable and credible way, over time? Long-term follow-up studies are extremely valuable in order to examine lasting impact, but they are unfortunately quite rare (see Österlind 2013). Lehtonen et al. (2020) provide a small case study indicating lasting impact one year later. This project and its success in applying new teaching formats across many disciplines is a substantial step towards increased knowledge

about the potential and practice of applied drama and performance in higher education for sustainability.

Overall, the answers are ripe for ongoing research and practice development. This book is a powerful platform to stimulate international practices across fields. Our hope – as editors and contributors to this book – is that you embrace the spirit of the original project above and create your own change projects in and out of higher education. To repeat our call in Chapter 1, if there was ever a time we needed transformational education, that time is now.

# References

Bourdieu, P. (1990). Structures, *habitus*, practices. In P. Bourdieu (Ed.), *The Logic of Practice* (pp. 52–65). Polity Press.

Johnstone, K. (1981). Impro: *Improvisation and the theatre*. Routledge, Chapman & Hall.

Lehtonen, A., Österlind, E., & Viirret, T.L. (2020). Drama in education for sustainability: Becoming connected through embodiment. *International Journal of Education & the Arts, 21*(19). https://doi.org/10.26209/ijea21n19.

Österlind, E. (2008). Acting out of habits: Can Theatre of the Oppressed promote change? Boal's theatre methods in relation to Bourdieu's concept of Habitus. *Research in Drama Education, 13*(1), 71–82.

Österlind, E. (2011). Forum Play – a Swedish mixture for consciousness and change. In S. Schonmann (Ed.), *Key concepts in theatre/drama education* (pp. 247–251). SENSE Publishers.

Österlind, E. (2013). Evaluation of theatre for social change – what counts and what is being counted? *Applied Theatre Research, 1*(1), 91–106.

Österlind, E. (2020). "I can be the beginning of what I want to see in the world": outcomes of a drama workshop on sustainability in teacher education. In V. Brinia & J. Paulo Davim (Eds.), *Designing an innovative pedagogy for sustainable development in higher education* (pp. 49–68). Taylor & Francis.

Österlind, E. (2022). Drama workshops as single events in higher education – what can we learn? In M. McAvoy & P. O'Connor (Eds.), *The Routledge companion to drama in education* (pp. 324–337). Taylor & Francis.

Printed in the United States
by Baker & Taylor Publisher Services